**Houghton
Mifflin
Harcourt**

STUDENT EDITION

Inside the
TEXT

Reading Strategies
with Informational Text

Lawrence Gable

Dr. Ron Klemp

Dr. Bill McBride

PHOTO CREDITS

Cover

(bg) *grunge texture* © happykanppy/Shutterstock; *blue texture* © MegaShabanov/Shutterstock; (bl) *volunteering* © iStock/Getty Images; (br) *basketball game* ©Monkey Business Images/Shutterstock; (bc) *students in science class* © age footstock

Text

14 *police officers* Photodisc/Getty Images; 14 *political rally* © Digital Vision/Getty Images; 14 *skyline* © Dennis MacDonald/Alamy; 14 *political party symbols* © JupiterImages/Comstock Images/Alamy

Inside the Text

Table of Contents

Unit 1: Human Rights and History

Unit 2: Science and Environment

Unit 3: Global Issues

Unit 4: Sports, Arts, and Self-Expression

Human Rights and History

Name _____ Date _____

ANTICIPATION GUIDE

Directions: Before you read the article "Questions Linger About Tasers," read the statements below. If you agree with a statement, put a checkmark on the line next to it. If you disagree, put an X on the line.

_____ **1.** Tasers do not present any long-term dangers.

_____ **2.** Police departments around the country use Tasers today instead of nightsticks and pepper spray.

_____ **3.** There should be rules around when to use Tasers.

Once you have responded to the statements above, write in the section below why you agree or disagree with each statement.

1. _____

_____

2. _____

_____

3. _____

_____

In the box below, draw a picture of what you think this article is about.

Unit 1: Human Rights and History

WORDSTORM

Directions: It's good to know more than just the dictionary definition of a word. Completing a wordstorm lets you write down information to help you understand what a word means, how it's related to other words, and how to use it in different ways.

What is the word?

controversy

The sentence from the text in which the word is used:

"The Taser has become a weapon of controversy in police departments."

What are some other words or phrases that mean the same thing?

_____

What are three things people might do during a controversy?

1. _____ 2. _____ 3. _____

Name three people other than teachers who would likely use this word.

1. _____ 2. _____ 3. _____

Draw a picture below that reminds you of the word *controversy*.

TIME MY READ #1

Directions: With a partner, see how many words you can read correctly in 45 seconds. As you read, your partner will put an X through any word read incorrectly on his or her copy. When you are finished, trade your books or papers, and let your partner read while you keep score. Count the total number of words you read correctly. Write this score at the bottom of your page.

long-term organizations electricity current powerful Taser healthy control	8
appeal departments reduce barbs weapon safety injuries victim	16
paralysis suspects unarmed medications impact research nervous diseases	24
long-term organizations electricity current powerful Taser healthy control	32
appeal departments reduce barbs weapon safety injuries victim	40
paralysis suspects unarmed medications impact research nervous diseases	48
long-term organizations electricity current powerful Taser healthy control	56
appeal departments reduce barbs weapon safety injuries victim	64
paralysis suspects unarmed medications impact research nervous diseases	72
long-term organizations electricity current powerful Taser healthy control	80

Number of words read correctly _____

ECHO READING

Directions: When you read, you should make breaks, and sometimes pauses, between groups of words. As your teacher reads each phrase, repeat aloud what is read and put a slash or line after that phrase. Then read the whole sentence aloud as a class. Do the first paragraph together as a class, and then do the second one on your own. The first sentence has been marked for you.

Tasers are becoming / a popular weapon / in police departments. / In some situations, these electro-stun weapons are safer than other weapons. They have contributed to some deaths, however, and nobody really knows if there are other long-term dangers. Now several human rights organizations are asking police to stop using them until further research is done.

A Taser looks like a gun. Instead of bullets, it shoots 50,000 volts of electricity. The current comes from batteries, and a nitrogen cartridge supplies power for the shot. When an officer pulls the trigger, the Taser shoots two barbs that are like small fishhooks. They are attached to the end of copper wires, and they can hit a person 21 feet away.

What's Happening

IN THE USA?

BY LAWRENCE GABLE
© 2014 What's Happening Publications

SUBJECT: HUMAN RIGHTS and HISTORY

Questions Linger About Tasers

1 The Taser has become a weapon of controversy in police departments. Sometimes these electro-stun weapons are safe, but they have contributed to some deaths. In addition, nobody really knows if there are other long-term dangers. Several human rights organizations have asked police to stop using tasers until they know more.

2 A Taser looks like a gun. Instead of bullets, it shoots a 50,000-volt charge of electricity. The Taser shoots two little hooks at the end of copper wires. They can hit a person 21 feet away. The effect is strongest when the hooks enter the victim's skin. The shock also can pass through two inches of clothing.

3 The shock is short, but powerful. It causes pain and paralysis for five seconds, and it usually knocks the victim to the ground. In those few seconds officers usually can gain control of the person.

4 Taser is not the first weapon to shoot an electric current. The first stun guns shot darts, and later models shot hooks. They were hard to handle, so few police departments used them. The Taser gun is ten times more powerful than the old stun guns.

5 The Taser's appeal has been its safety. It can reduce injuries to officers and suspects. An officer does not need to use a nightstick or pepper spray, and does not need to struggle with a suspect.

6 It took a few years to learn how police departments are using Tasers. Reports showed that police use them most often on people who are unarmed. Police have shocked people who are already in handcuffs. They also have shocked children, the elderly, and pregnant women.

7 Questions continue about the effects of electric current on people. A short, weak current probably will not harm a healthy person. For people with weak hearts, though, a strong shock can cause a heart attack. It also can affect the hearts of people taking medications. Nobody knows yet what the effects are on people who have diseases like Parkinson's or multiple sclerosis. Tasers may harm pregnant women and children too.

8 Some police officers at schools also carry Tasers. Doctors say that the current is more intense in a small body. The voltage could cause damage in developing nerves, muscles and brains.

9 It is still not clear when it is appropriate to use a Taser. Some police around the country already have limited their use. After several deaths in Las Vegas, the department stopped using them on people in handcuffs. It also discouraged multiple shocks. Some police chiefs stopped using Tasers until they knew more about their safety.

10 The organization Amnesty International has asked police to limit the use of Tasers. It states that Tasers have been involved in hundreds of deaths, and have been the direct cause of 60 of them. It also asked police to stop using them on children and the elderly unless they threaten to harm themselves or others.

11 Most people agree that Tasers can help police. As with any weapon, there is some risk of physical injury to the victim. When researchers learn more about those risks, police will know better when it is appropriate to use Tasers.

GET A CONTEXT CLUE

Directions: Below are sentences from "Questions Linger About Tasers". First, read the sentence. Then, look back in the article and reread the paragraph in which the sentence is found. Circle the best answer to each question.

"In addition, nobody really knows if the Taser causes *long-term* dangers."

1. The word *long-term* means

    A. instant
    B. lasting
    C. bad
    D. alongside

"The *effect* is strongest when the hooks enter the victim's skin."

2. An *effect* is

    A. an outcome or result
    B. a collision
    C. a warning
    D. a loud noise

"It can reduce injuries to officers and *suspects*."

3. The word *suspects* means

    A. soldiers
    B. doctors
    C. people thought to be criminals
    D. people who fight criminals

"The Taser's *appeal* has been its safety."

4. The word *appeal* has to do with

    A. attraction
    B. hazard
    C. a court decision
    D. a lack of decision

"It can also affect the hearts of people taking *medications*."

5. The word *medications* means

    A. exercises
    B. explosions
    C. substances used to treat illnesses
    D. doctors and nurses

"Doctors say that the *current* is more intense in a small body."

6. The word *current* is related to

    A. electricity
    B. law
    C. warfare
    D. gravity

WORD CHOICE

Directions: The sentences below contain blanks for missing words. Three answer choices are listed after each blank. Read the sentence past the blank and choose the correct word. Write it in the blank.

Tasers® are becoming a popular weapon in police departments. In some situations these electro-stun _____ (*voltage, weapons, safety*) are safer than others. They have _____ (*excitement, found, contributed*) to some deaths, however, and nobody _____ (*really, never, wonders*) knows if there are other long-term _____ (*shock, organizations, dangers*). Now several human rights organizations are _____ (*asking, want, wish*) police to stop using them until _____ (*further, often, never*) research is done.

A Taser looks _____ (*like, some, just*) a gun. Instead of bullets, it _____ (*holds, fires, shoots*) 50,000 volts of electricity. The current _____ (*comes, start, will*) from batteries, and a nitrogen cartridge _____ (*give, supplies, send*) power for the shot. When an officer _____ (*pull, pulls, pulling*) the trigger, the Taser shoots two _____ (*barbs, barb, barbed*) that are like small fishhooks. They _____ (*are, is, be*) attached to the end of copper _____ (*wires, wired, wiry*), and they can hit a person 21 feet away.

LOOK WHO'S TALKING

Directions: Below are sentences that relate to "Questions Linger About Tasers." Look back in the article and reread the paragraph in which you find the reference. Circle the best answer to each question.

1. In the last sentence of paragraph 1, the word *they* refers to

   A. human rights organizations
   B. Tasers
   C. weapons
   D. effects

2. In the fourth sentence of paragraph 2, the word *they* refers to

   A. the bullets
   B. the charge
   C. the hooks
   D. the victims

3. In the third sentence of paragraph 4, the word *they* refers to

   A. the Taser
   B. earlier stun guns
   C. the darts
   D. the departments

4. In the fourth sentence of paragraph 7, the word *it* refers to

   A. the heart
   B. the person
   C. the people
   D. the current

5. In the fourth sentence of paragraph 9, the word *it* refers to

   A. the department
   B. the Taser
   C. the shocks
   D. the time to use the Taser

6. In the second sentence of paragraph 10, the word *It* refers to

   A. Amnesty International
   B. Tasers
   C. the organization
   D. police department

NOTE MAKING

Directions: Read the boldfaced key words on the left side of the chart below. Then add notes that answer the question in parentheses under the key word.

Human rights organizations (What are they?)	
Tasers (How do they work?)	
Police (Why do they use Tasers?)	
Effects on people (What are they?)	
Restrictions on use (What kind of restrictions exist?)	

IS THAT A FACT?

Directions: Read the definitions of a fact and an inference below. Then read the paragraph that follows. At the bottom of the page, write an F on the blank if the sentence is a fact. Write an I if the sentence is an inference. Use the following definitions:

Fact—a statement that can be proven true from the article.

Inference—a guess as to what MIGHT be true, based on what you have read and what you already know about the subject.

> Tasers are a popular weapon in police departments. Sometimes these electro-stun weapons are safe, but they have contributed to some deaths. In addition nobody really knows if there are any other long-term dangers. Now several human rights organizations are asking police to stop using Tasers until they know more. The Taser's appeal has been its safety. It can reduce injuries to officers and suspects. An officer no longer needs to use a nightstick or pepper spray and does not need to struggle with a suspect.

_____ **1.** Police like to use Tasers because they can be more effective than nightsticks or pepper spray.

_____ **2.** Some human rights organizations are against the use of Tasers by police officers.

_____ **3.** We don't know enough about how the Taser really works on people.

_____ **4.** Most human rights groups are against the use of Tasers.

_____ **5.** The use of the Taser can sometimes result in a fatality.

_____ **6.** It is not known how the Taser affects a person over time.

MAKE A SPACE

Directions: Below are sentences that are missing punctuation and capitalization. First draw slash marks (/) between the words. Then rewrite each sentence in the space below it, filling in the missing punctuation and capitalization.

Example:

tasers / are / becoming / a / popular / weapon / in / police / departments

Tasers are becoming a popular weapon in police departments.

1. theshockisshortbutpowerful

_____

_____

2. ithastakenafewyearsforthepolicetolearnhowtousetasers

_____

_____

_____

3. somepoliceofficersatschoolscarrytasers

_____

_____

4. doctorssaythatthecurrentismoreintenseinasmallbody

_____

_____

TIME MY READ #2

Directions: With a partner, see how many words you can read correctly in 45 seconds. As you read, your partner will put an X through any word read incorrectly on his or her copy. When you are finished, trade your books or papers, and let your partner read while you keep score. Count the total number of words you read correctly. Write this score at the bottom of your page.

long-term organizations electricity current powerful Taser healthy control	8
appeal departments reduce barbs weapon safety injuries victim	16
paralysis suspects unarmed medications impact research nervous diseases	24
long-term organizations electricity current powerful Taser healthy control	32
appeal departments reduce barbs weapon safety injuries victim	40
paralysis suspects unarmed medications impact research nervous diseases	48
long-term organizations electricity current powerful Taser healthy control	56
appeal departments reduce barbs weapon safety injuries victim	64
paralysis suspects unarmed medications impact research nervous diseases	72
long-term organizations electricity current powerful Taser healthy control	80

Number of words read correctly _____

Is the score higher than it was in Time My Read #1? _____

WORD PARTS

Directions: The Latin word *medicus* means "physician" or "doctor." Read the definitions below. Then draw a picture that shows the word's meaning.

1. **medicine**—(noun) something one takes to treat an illness or injury

2. **medic**—(noun) a doctor or student learning to be a doctor, often working in a war zone

3. **medical**—(adjective) having to do with one's health, a hospital, or a doctor; for example, a medical emergency

4. **medicinal**—(adjective) something relating to medicine, or having a bad taste

medicine	medic	medical	medicinal

Directions: The Latin root *poli* means "city." Each of the following words has the root *poli* in it: *politics, metropolitan, police, politician*. Write the word on the blank that describes each picture.

_____ _____ _____ _____

Unit 1: Human Rights and History

WRITING FRAME

Directions: Use your knowledge and information from the article to complete the writing frame below.

A Taser looks like a gun and shoots _____ volts

_____. The shock comes from two

_____ at the end of _____.

The reason why police officers like the Taser is _____

_____. They feel that they can be more effective than

nightsticks or pepper spray in _____ who commit

_____. Reports claim that police use Tasers on people who

are _____. This is why human rights organizations

think that _____. There have been questions

raised about how the Taser affects _____.

Amnesty International, a human rights organization, is asking that

_____. They feel that the Taser

should not be used until _____

_____.

At least when we learn more about the Taser, it can be used

_____.

TASER WORD PUZZLE

Directions: Complete the crossword puzzle.

Word List

METROPOLIS

APPEAL

MEDICINAL

POLICE

MEDIC

POLITICIAN

CONTROVERSY

SUSPECTS

EFFECT

LONG-TERM

Across

2. someone elected to work for government
4. a disagreement about something
6. people thought to be guilty
9. an outcome or result
10. something with a bad taste

Down

1. a city
3. lasting a long period of time
5. an attraction
7. someone who enforces the law
8. a doctor working in a war zone

REACTION GUIDE

Directions: Now that you have read and studied information about "Questions Linger About Tasers," reread the statements below, which you responded to before reading the article. Then think about how the author might respond to these statements. If you think the author would agree, put a checkmark on the line before the number. If you think the author would disagree, put an X on the line. Then, below the statement, copy the words, phrases, or sentences from the article that provide evidence of the views stated by the author. Also note if there is no evidence to support the statement.

_____ **1.** Tasers do not present any long-term dangers.

Evidence: _____

_____

_____

_____ **2.** Police departments around the country use Tasers today instead of nightsticks and pepper spray.

Evidence: _____

_____

_____

_____ **3.** There should be rules around when to use Tasers.

Evidence: _____

_____

_____

TAKE A STAND

Directions: People often have differing feelings or opinions about an issue. When they discuss or argue their opposing views, they are taking part in a debate. A good persuasive argument is based on a claim that is supported by

Facts—statements that can be proven to be true

Statistics—numerical data gotten through research

Examples—instances that support an opinion

You and a partner are going to debate two of your other classmates. The topic you are going to debate is the following:

Police should be able to use any force needed to stop a suspect.

Decide with the other pair who will agree and who will disagree with this statement. Then answer these questions in order to win your debate.

1. What are your two strongest points to persuade the other side? (You can do Internet research to include facts, statistics, and examples.)

   A. _____

   B. _____

2. What might the other side say to argue against point A?

   _____

3. What might the other side say to argue against point B?

   _____

4. What will you say to prove the other side's arguments are wrong?

   _____

ASSESSMENT

Comprehension: Answer the questions about the following passage.

Tasers are becoming a popular weapon in police departments. In some situations these electro-stun weapons are safer than others. They have contributed to some deaths, however, and nobody really knows if there are long-term dangers. Now several human rights organizations are asking police to stop using them until further research is done.

A Taser looks like a gun. Instead of bullets, it shoots 50,000 volts of electricity. The current comes from batteries, and a nitrogen cartridge supplies power for the shot. When an officer pulls the trigger, the Taser shoots two barbs that are like small fishhooks. They are attached to the end of copper wires, and they can hit a person 21 feet away.

1. What are two ways that Tasers are safer than guns?

_____

_____

2. What questions still linger about Tasers?

_____

_____

3. What was the author's purpose for writing about the Taser?

_____

_____

Fluency: The words in the two sentences below are all connected. The sentences are also missing punctuation and capitalization. Draw slash marks (/) between the words. Then rewrite each sentence by filling in the punctuation and capitalization.

1. theshockisshortbutpowerful

_____

2. mostpeopleagreethattaserscanhelppolice

_____

_____

Fluency: Read the three sentences below. Imagine where you would pause within each sentence as you read it aloud. Draw a slash (/) mark between the phrases where you would pause. The first slash is done.

3. The Taser / is not the first weapon to shoot an electric current.

4. It is not clear when it is appropriate to use a Taser.

5. The Taser shoots two little hooks at the end of copper wires.

Vocabulary: Based on what you have learned in this lesson, match the following words with their definitions. Write the letter of the definition on the blank in front of the word it defines.

1. _____ effect

A. a doctor working in a war zone

2. _____ medicinal

B. something with a bad taste

3. _____ police

C. a city

4. _____ controversy

D. people thought to be guilty

5. _____ long-term

E. a disagreement about something

6. _____ politician

F. an outcome or result

7. _____ medic

G. someone who enforces the law

8. _____ suspects

H. someone elected to work for government

9. _____ metropolis

I. an attraction

10. _____ appeal

J. lasting a long period of time

Name _____ Date _____

ANTICIPATION GUIDE

Directions: Before you read the article "The Beautiful Game Faces Ugliness," read the statements below. If you agree with a statement, put a checkmark on the line next to it. If you disagree, put an X on the line.

_____ **1.** The world of sports is one area where there is no racism.

_____ **2.** Soccer is an international game where all are welcome.

_____ **3.** If a team's fans express racist comments, the team should be penalized.

Once you have responded to the statements above, write in the section below why you agree or disagree with each statement.

1. _____

_____

2. _____

_____

3. _____

_____

In the box below, draw a picture of what you think this article is about.

PREDICTING ABCs

Directions: The article you are going to read is about racism in soccer. See how many boxes you can fill in below with words relating to soccer. For example, put the word *goal* in the G–I box. Put at least one word in every box, and then try to write a word for every letter.

A–C	D–F	G–I
J–L	**M–O**	**P–R**
S–T	**U–V**	**W–Z**

LANGUAGE MINI-LESSON

The subject of a sentence is <u>whom</u> or <u>what</u> the sentence is about. If the subject is just <u>one thing</u>, or **singular**, the verb of the sentence must agree, or be **singular** too. If the subject of a sentence is <u>more than one thing</u>, or **plural**, the verb must agree, or be **plural** also.

Here are the singular and plural forms of the verb to be.

Singular (one):

I **am**
You (one person) **are**
He, She, It i**s**
One person or thing **is**

Plural (more than one):

We **are**
You (two or more people) **are**
They **are**
More than one person, thing **are**

Directions: Circle the correct form of the verb *to be* below.

1. Soccer teams [*is, are*] changing around the world.

2. A player on the German team [*is, are*] not necessarily from Germany.

3. Unfortunately some fans [*is, are*] racists.

4. They [*is, are*] yelling racist remarks at some players.

5. No one knows how a team [*is, are*] going to react.

6. In some games the players [*is, are*] walking off the field.

7. Black players, in particular, [*is, are*] facing racism during games.

8. Soccer's governing body (FIFA) [*is, are*] also reacting to racism.

9. Some racist fans [*is, are*] banned from their teams' stadiums.

10. Each fan [*is, are*] getting the message that racism [*is, are*] not allowed.

ECHO READING

Directions: When you read, you should make breaks, and sometimes pauses, between groups of words. As your teacher reads each phrase, repeat aloud what is read and put a slash or line after that phrase. Then read the whole sentence aloud as a class. Do the first paragraph together as a class, and then do the second one on your own. The first sentence has been marked for you.

Soccer / and its various organizations / have been trying / to deal with racists. / In the past the referees have stopped games temporarily until fans get under control. An organization that represents soccer players worldwide now wants more. It believes that referees should be able to end games if fans are racially abusive.

The international soccer organization FIFA is also responding to racism. It urges leagues to penalize teams that cannot control their fans. One idea is to take points away from teams in the league standings. In February FIFA announced penalties against the national teams of Bulgaria and Hungary. In 2012 fans of both teams were abusive during international games. As a result, FIFA is forcing each country to play one international game in March in an empty stadium. FIFA also threatened to expel the two countries from the World Cup.

What's Happening

IN THE WORLD?

BY LAWRENCE GABLE
© 2014 What's Happening Publications

SUBJECT: HUMAN RIGHTS and HISTORY

The Beautiful Game Faces Ugliness

1 occer is the world's most popular sport. The great Brazilian star Pelé once called it "the beautiful game." That does not mean that soccer has no problems though. Racism has been an old, ugly problem, but recent responses to it are completely new.

2 Today there are many foreign-born players playing on teams around the world. Clubs everywhere are offering contracts to stars from other countries. Those players get to play in the best leagues and earn a lot of money.

3 A racist incident during a game in Italy in January 2013 led to an unusual, powerful response. The famous club AC Milan was playing an exhibition game against a team called Pro Patria. Early in the game some fans directed monkey chants at three of Milan's Black players. A short time later they also chanted racial slurs at another Black player, Kevin-Prince Boateng.

4 Mr. Boateng's response was swift. First he picked up the ball and kicked it toward the fans. Then he began walking off the field. Several players from both teams embraced him. Then both teams followed him off the field. Quickly officials called off the match. It was the first time that a soccer team had ended a game because of racism.

5 The responses to Mr. Boateng's actions have been supportive. AC Milan's director expressed pride in his players' decision to leave the field. The coach hopes that Mr. Boateng and his teammates have set an example for players everywhere. The owner of the club maintained that his team would leave the field in the future.

6 Racism in soccer has been too common across Europe in the last 20 years. Black players in particular have felt frustrated and angry. Mr. Boateng insists that he will walk off fields again, if he must. In addition, he argues that the authorities in soccer and in government must fight racism.

7 Soccer and its various organizations have been trying to deal with racists. In the past the referees have stopped games temporarily until fans get under control. An organization that represents soccer players worldwide now wants more. It believes that referees should be able to end games if fans are racially abusive.

8 The international soccer organization FIFA is also responding to racism. It urges leagues to penalize teams that cannot control their fans. One idea is to take points away from teams in the league standings. In February 2013 FIFA announced penalties against the national teams of Bulgaria and Hungary. In 2012 fans of both teams were abusive during international games. As a result, FIFA forced each country to play one international game in March 2013 in an empty stadium. FIFA also considered expelling the two countries from the 2014 World Cup.

9 Racist fans are also receiving punishment. Some teams have banned certain fans from their stadiums. Police and prosecutors took legal action against Pro Patria's fans. They charged about a dozen of them with inciting racial hatred.

10 Kevin-Prince Boateng risked getting a suspension or fine for leaving the game. However, he decided it was time to stand up for himself and other minorities. His decision did not remove the hatred from the hearts of racists. However, they are starting to get the message that their ugly behavior has no place in public.

QUICK READ/DRAW AND WRITE

Directions: First Reading—As you do your first reading of the article, your teacher will time you for one minute. When time is called, write the number of the paragraph where you stopped.   **Paragraph # _____**

In the box below, draw a picture summarizing what you read.

Second Reading—As you do your second reading of the article, your teacher will time you for one minute. When time is called, write the number of the paragraph where you stopped.   **Paragraph # _____**

Directions: Now continue reading the rest of the article. Below, write five important words that will help you remember the information from the article.

_____   _____   _____

_____   _____

Unit 1: Human Rights and History

CLOSE READING ANNOTATION

Third Reading—As you reread each paragraph in the article closely, answer the questions by annotating the text. Each numbered question corresponds to a paragraph in the article where the answer can be found. Write your brief answers in the space below each question.

1. Why do you think the author uses the reference to soccer as "the beautiful game"?

_____

2. What might be some advantages for teams that contract foreign players?

_____

3. What is the author's purpose for writing paragraph 3?

_____

4. What do you think about Mr. Boateng's responses?

_____

5. How did AC Milan's director and coach respond?

_____

6. Why do you think the author says that these racist incidents are not new?

_____

7. How has the sport been dealing with racial incidents?

_____

8. What specific things is FIFA doing regarding these incidents?

_____

9. How does FIFA propose to punish the fans that commit racist acts?

_____

10. Why do you think the author chose the phrase "the hatred from the hearts"?

_____

GRAMMAR GAMES

Directions: Reread the two paragraphs below. Words have been left out from each sentence. Think about the information from the article you have read and fill in words that make sense. The part of speech of each missing word is provided.

Soccer is the world's most popular _____, and the great
(1. noun)

Brazilian star Pelé once called _____ "the beautiful game."
(2. pronoun)

That does not mean that soccer is _____ problems though.
(3. preposition)

Racism has _____ a constant, ugly problem, but recent
(4. verb)

responses to it are _____ new.
(5. adverb)

Today there are many foreign-born _____ playing on
(6. plural noun)

teams _____ the world. Clubs everywhere are _____
(7. preposition)   (8. verb)

contracts to stars from other countries. _____ players
(9. pronoun)

get to play on teams in some of the _____ leagues. They
(10. adjective)

_____ a lot of money _____ international recognition.
(11. verb)   (12. conjunction)

Unit 1: Human Rights and History

CLOSE READING STRUCTURE

Directions: Understanding the structure of a text is important for two reasons. First, understanding the structure of a selection can help you remember the main idea and important details. Second, most academic writing you will encounter uses text structures to organize ideas.

1. Writers often include a statement in the **introduction** that catches the reader's attention. Then, the writer tells what the article will be about. On the space provided, copy the last sentence of the introduction to the article.

_____

_____

2. On the space below, copy the sentence that best states what the author's **claim, main idea,** or **thesis** is for this article.

_____

_____

3. On the space below, copy the sentence that shows where the author introduces the other side's opinions, or **opposing claims**, about the statement "Soccer is a beautiful game."

_____

_____

4. Near the end of an article, the writer often restates the main idea and summarizes the evidence. This is called the **conclusion**. On the space below, write the sentence that best shows where the conclusion **begins**.

_____

_____

IS THAT A FACT?

Directions: Read the definitions of a fact and an inference below. Then read the paragraph that follows. At the bottom of the page, write an F on the blank if the sentence is a fact. Write an I if the sentence is an inference. Use the following definitions:

Fact—a statement that can be proven to be true from the paragraph.

Inference—a guess as to what MIGHT be true, based on what you have read and what you already know about the subject.

Racism in soccer has been too common across Europe in the last 20 years. Black players in particular have felt frustrated and angry. Mr. Boateng insists that he will walk off fields again, if he must. In addition, he argues that the authorities in soccer and in government must fight racism. Soccer and its various organizations have been trying to deal with racists. In the past the referees have stopped games temporarily until fans get under control. An organization that represents soccer players worldwide now wants more. It believes that referees should be able to end games if fans are racially abusive.

_____ **1.** There is racism that occurs in the sport of soccer.

_____ **2.** Mr. Boateng took action and didn't care about the consequences.

_____ **3.** Some soccer organizations recognize problems with racism in the sport.

_____ **4.** Soccer players were not satisfied with how the sport was dealing with the issue.

_____ **5.** Currently referees cannot decide to end games on their own.

_____ **6.** The issue of racism in soccer is still a problem.

SUMMARIZING ABCs

Directions: Now that you've read the article on racism in soccer, see how many words you can write about soccer in the boxes below.

A–C	D–F	G–I
J–L	**M–O**	**P–R**
S–T	**U–V**	**W–Z**

REACTION GUIDE

Directions: Now that you have read and studied information about "The Beautiful Game Faces Ugliness," reread the statements below, which you responded to before reading the article. Then think about how the author might respond to these statements. If you think the author would agree, put a checkmark on the line before the number. If you think the author would disagree, put an X on the line. Then below the statement, copy the words, phrases, or statements from the article that provide **evidence** of the views stated by the author. Also note if there is no evidence to support the statement.

_____ **1.** The world of sports is one area where there is no racism.

Evidence: _____

_____

_____

_____ **2.** Soccer is an international game where all are welcome.

Evidence: _____

_____

_____

_____ **3.** If a team's fans express racist comments, the team should be penalized.

Evidence: _____

_____

_____

SENTENCE TRANSITIONS

An informational essay answers questions and provides information. Writers use transitional phrases to link ideas. Some transitional words and phrases include *to show, to prove, because, to explain, to verify, due to, instead of, furthermore, as a result of,* and *in order to*.

Directions: Complete the following sentences using the phrases given.

Example: Fans are becoming more interested in good sportsmanship. Fans are becoming more interested in good sportsmanship *due to recent FIFA penalties*.

1. The international soccer organization has acted *as a result of*

_____

2. Mr. Boateng decided to take his action on the field *in order to*

_____

3. Several players from both teams embraced Mr. Boateng *to show*

_____

4. FIFA forced teams to play in an empty stadium *to prove*

_____

5. Referees may be able to end a game in progress *due to*

_____

PICKING UP PUNCTUATION

There are many reasons you **capitalize** letters in words and abbreviations. Here are 15 rules to remember. Capitalize the following:

1. The first word in every sentence: **T**he debate over gun control is not new.

2. People's names and initials: **M**ichael **B**loomberg

3. Titles and abbreviations of titles used before names: **S**en. **G**iffords

4. Official titles, such as those of royalty or government offices: **M**ayor **B**loomberg

5. Words showing family relationships: **A**unt Sally

6. The names of sacred days, religious texts, and gods: **B**ible or **K**oran

7. The names of nationalities, races, languages, and ethnic groups: **A**merican

8. Important words in a title or name of something: **T**he **S**tar **S**pangled **B**anner

9. Names of places, roads, towns, and special land forms: **N**ew **Y**ork **C**ity or **A**rizona

10. Names of special buildings, bridges, and landmarks: **G**olden **G**ate **B**ridge

11. Names of specific planes, ships, cars, and spacecraft: **T**itanic or **F**ord **M**ustang

12. Names of organizations or companies: **U**nited **S**tates **S**occer **A**ssociation or **G**oogle

13. Names of special events and awards: **B**oston **M**arathon or the **O**scars

14. Names of months, days, and holidays: **J**une or **L**abor **D**ay

15. The brand name of a product: **K**rackle potato chips

Directions: Circle the letters that should be capitalized in the paragraph below.

in february FIFA announced penalties against the national teams of bulgaria and hungary. in october 2013 bulgarian fans abused a black player on denmark's national team. in 2012 hungarian fans chanted anti-semitic chants during an exhibition game against israel. fifa is forcing both countries to play one world cup qualifying game in march without spectators. racist fans are also receiving punishment.

ANALYZING A PROMPT

Directions: Read the writing prompt in the box below. Then follow the directions to learn how to analyze and answer it.

> You are a member of a soccer club that is concerned about the rise in racial incidents on the field and in the stands at soccer matches. You have been asked to write an editorial essay for FIFA. Review what has occurred in the past, and recommend future actions that should be taken. Think about why these events are occurring. Use information from the article to support your position.

1. A writing prompt begins with some background information known as the **set up.** Underline the sentences that set up this assignment.

2. Use the following **R.A.F.T.** technique to finish analyzing the prompt.

Role: What are you supposed to be to answer it? A student? A politician?

Write what you are here: _____

Audience: To whom are you writing? A friend? A particular group?

Write who it is here: _____

Format: Check to see what type of writing you are doing. Is it an essay, a letter, a speech, a story, a description, an editorial, or a report?

Write what it is here: _____

Task: Another sentence in the prompt will tell you what you must do, or your task. Question words such as **why, how,** or **what** may tell you the task.

If the question word is **why**, you will *give the reasons* that something is done.

If the question word is **how**, you will *explain the way* that something is done.

If the question word is **what**, you will *identify the thing* that is done.

Below, copy the sentence or question below that describes your task.

_____

_____

ANALYZING ARGUMENTATIVE TEXTS

1. Argumentative articles are written to change someone's opinion. Below, name three groups below that might be interested in reading this article besides students and teachers.

   a. _____ **b.** _____ **c.** _____

2. What main point or **precise claim** is the author making?

   _____

   _____

3. Give two reasons that provide **evidence** to support the author's **claim.**

   a. _____

   b. _____

4. **Domain-specific vocabulary** consists of words used in a specific subject, such as math, science, or social studies. Reread the article and list six domain-specific words used with this subject. After you select the words, write their definitions on the lines provided.

   a. _____ : _____

   b. _____ : _____

   c. _____ : _____

   d. _____ : _____

   e. _____ : _____

   f. _____ : _____

ASSESSMENT

1. Underline the sentences that support the inference that the other people on the field supported Mr. Boateng's reaction to racism.

"Mr. Boateng's response was swift. First he picked up the ball and kicked it toward the fans. Then he began walking off the field. Several players from both teams embraced him. Then both teams followed him off the field. Quickly officials called off the match. It was the first time a soccer team had ended a match because of racism."

2. Support the claim that organizations are finally trying to stop or limit racist actions in soccer. Look back through the article. Then on the space below, cite three pieces of evidence from the article to support this claim.

a. _____

b. _____

c. _____

3. The reader can infer that Mr. Boateng is committed to fighting racism in soccer in the future. Circle the letters of the two pairs of sentences that support this inference.

a. Mr. Boateng's response was swift. First he picked up the ball and kicked it toward the fans.

b. Kevin-Prince Boateng risked getting a suspension or fine for leaving the game. However, he decided it was time for him to stand up for himself and other minorities.

c. Mr. Boateng insists he will walk off the field again, if he must. In addition, he argues that the authorities in soccer and in government must fight racism.

d. The coach hopes that Mr. Boateng and his teammates have set an example for players everywhere. The owner of the club maintained that his team would leave the field in the future.

4. What idea is not fully supported by the article?

a. Racist actions have also occurred at soccer matches in the United States.

b. Racism in soccer has existed for some time.

c. Soccer's international ruling organization is trying to stop racist events.

d. One reason for racist actions is because some players on a team come from other countries.

5. A student has made a plan for research. Read the plan and the directions that follow.

Research Report Plan

Topic: racism in soccer

Audience: our high school soccer team

Research Question: Where in the world have the most racist acts in soccer taken place and why have so many occurred there?

The student needs to find a credible, or trustworthy, source with relevant, or recent, information. Circle the letter of the source below that would **most likely** have credible and relevant information.

a. www.worldcupbrazilevents.com—See how Brazil prepared the city of Rio de Janeiro for the 2014 World Cup matches, including its preparation for demonstrations and racially charged events.

b. www.soccerspersonalhistory.com—This site provides over 100 personal letters describing both the good and bad side of soccer—from seeing one of the best shots to dealing with some of its worst racist fans.

c. www.endingworldracism.com—Racist events occur daily in our world. They occur in government, in sports, in the arts and in society in general. The End World Racism site explores how to stop racism.

d. www.soccerforall.com—The world's most popular sport draws fans of all races from around the globe. This website reports on the behaviors of fans and team members that have drawn criticism for racist actions or behavior.

Name _____ Date _____

ANTICIPATION GUIDE

Directions: Before you read the article "The Court Rules on the Second Amendment," read the statements below. If you agree with a statement, put a checkmark on the line next to it. If you disagree, put an X on the line.

_____ **1.** Handguns cause a huge amount of crime in cities.

_____ **2.** People need guns to protect their country.

_____ **3.** Every adult American should be allowed to own a handgun.

Once you have responded to the statements above, write in the section below why you agree or disagree with each statement.

1. _____

_____

_____

2. _____

_____

_____

3. _____

_____

_____

In the box below, draw a picture of what you think this article is about.

PREDICTING ABCs

Directions: The article you are going to read is about banning handguns. See how many boxes you can fill in below with words relating to this topic. For example, put the word *law* in the J–L box. Put at least one word in every box, and then try to write a word for every letter.

A–C	D–F	G–I
J–L	M–O	P–R
S–T	U–V	W–Z

TIME MY READ #1

Directions: With a partner, see how many words you can read correctly in 45 seconds. As you read, your partner will put an X through any word read incorrectly on his or her copy. When you are finished, trade your books or papers, and let your partner read while you keep score. Count the total number of words you read correctly. Write this score at the bottom of your page.

amendment supreme regulated firearms actually militias guarantee security 8

individuals citizen registered illegal rulings ensure interference handgun 16

restrictions experts debate specify permits dispute unconstitutional arms 24

amendment supreme regulated firearms actually militias guarantee security 32

individuals citizen registered illegal rulings ensure interference handgun 40

restrictions experts debate specify permits dispute unconstitutional arms 48

amendment supreme regulated firearms actually militias guarantee security 56

individuals citizen registered illegal rulings ensure interference handgun 64

restrictions experts debate specify permits dispute unconstitutional arms 72

amendment supreme regulated firearms actually militias guarantee security 80

Number of words read correctly _____

ECHO READING

Directions: When you read, you should make breaks, and sometimes pauses, between groups of words. As your teacher reads each phrase, repeat aloud what is read and put a slash or line after that phrase. Then read the whole sentence aloud as a class. Do the first paragraph together as a class, and then do the second one on your own. The first sentence has been marked for you.

The Second Amendment / to the Constitution / guarantees the right / to bear arms. / However, it has never been clear what the amendment actually means. In March 2008 the U.S. Supreme Court heard a case about the Second Amendment for the first time since 1939.

The case from 1939 was called *United States v. Miller*. In it the court ruled that sawed-off shotguns were illegal because they played no role in maintaining a militia. It ruled that the Second Amendment does not guarantee the right to keep such a weapon, but it did not discuss individual versus collective rights.

Others also expressed their opinions about the case. In January, eleven cities sent a document to the Supreme Court. They argued that large cities suffer more violence from firearms than other places do and that they should be able to place reasonable restrictions on weapons.

BY LAWRENCE GABLE
© 2014 What's Happening Publications

SUBJECT: HUMAN RIGHTS and HISTORY

The Court Rules on the Second Amendment

1 The Second Amendment to the Constitution guarantees the right to bear arms. However, it never has been clear what the amendment actually means. In March 2008 the U.S. Supreme Court heard its first case about the Second Amendment since 1939.

2 The Second Amendment has only 27 words. It reads: "A well regulated Militia, being necessary to the security of a free State, the right of the people to keep and bear Arms, shall not be infringed." Some people say it gives individuals the right to own firearms. Others say it gives a collective right for states to arm citizens and form militias like the National Guard.

3 In the case from 1939 the Court ruled that sawed-off shotguns were illegal. It said that the Second Amendment does not guarantee the right to keep such weapons, because militias do not use them. The Court did not discuss individual rights.

4 Nine federal appeals courts also made rulings after that. Each time they supported a collective right to bear arms, not an individual right. However, in 2007 a court ruled in favor of an individual's right to keep a handgun.

5 That case involved a security guard in Washington, D.C. He carried a handgun at work, and he wanted to have it at home too. The city refused his request, so he took his case to a federal court. It ruled that D.C.'s law on handguns violates the Second Amendment.

6 Washington, D.C., passed its law in 1976. Because of the high numbers of crimes, it required handgun owners to register them with the city. It also stopped registering any more handguns. The law did allow individuals to keep rifles and shotguns either under a trigger lock or disassembled.

7 The District of Columbia appealed the federal court's 2007 decision. That sent the case called *District of Columbia v. Heller* before the Supreme Court. Lawyers for Mr. Heller argued that the Second Amendment allows individuals to protect themselves in their own homes.

8 Lawyers for the District of Columbia argued that the amendment refers to the security of a state. In their view, the amendment gives states the right to form militias for the defense of the state. The state may arm its citizens, but there is no right for individuals to keep arms.

9 Others also expressed their opinions to the Supreme Court. Eleven cities argued that large cities suffer more violence from firearms than other places do, so they should be able to place reasonable restrictions on weapons. Hundreds of members of Congress asked the Court to allow citizens to keep handguns in their homes for self-defense.

10 Most of the debate about bearing arms centers around handguns. Cities argue that criminals can hide them too easily. If they take them onto buses and into schools and offices at work, public safety is at risk. People like Mr. Heller argued that handguns are handy, so individuals can defend themselves easily at home. Both sides accepted the need for governments to regulate military-style firearms.

11 In June 2008 the Supreme Court ruled 5–4 in favor of Mr. Heller. It found D.C.'s law unconstitutional, but that did not end the debate. The District of Columbia is neither a state nor a city. Therefore, it is unclear whether the ruling applies to the fifty states and cities around the U.S. In the future their public safety laws about guns might also end up up before the Supreme Court.

GET A CONTEXT CLUE

Directions: Below are sentences from "The Court Rules on the Second Amendment." First, read the sentence. Then, look back in the article and reread the paragraph in which the sentence is found. Circle the best answer to each question.

"The Second Amendment to the Constitution guarantees the right to *bear* arms."

1.) The word *bear* means

    A. to cover
    B. to be naked
    C. to carry
    D. to steal

"Nine federal appeals *courts* also made rulings after that."

2.) The word *courts* refers to

    A. where a king lives
    B. where countries do business
    C. where people play basketball
    D. where judges decide conflicts

"Each time they supported a *collective* right to bear arms, not an individual right."

3.) The word *collective* means

    A. for one person
    B. to hold in your arms
    C. for a group of people
    D. to share weapons

"It ruled that D.C.'s law on handguns *violates* the Second Amendment."

4.) The word *violates* means

    A. to break the rules or laws
    B. to clear up
    C. to support
    D. to include

"It also stopped *registering* them with the city."

5.) The word *registering* means

    A. allowing
    B. signing up or documenting
    C. fining
    D. using or practicing

"Most of the *debate* about bearing arms centers around handguns."

6.) The word *debate* means

    A. a trial before a judge
    B. a law
    C. a belief about something
    D. an argument between two sides

WORD MAP

Directions: Follow the directions to map the word in the box below.

restriction

List two more words that mean the same.

ban

List two more examples of restrictions.

List two more words that mean the opposite.

allowance

Draw a picture below to help you remember the meaning.

Write a definition IN YOUR OWN WORDS.

LOOK WHO'S TALKING

Directions: Below are sentences that relate to "The Court Rules on the Second Amendment." Look back in the article and reread the paragraph in which you find the reference. Circle the best answer to each question.

1. In the last sentence of paragraph 2, the word *it* refers to

   A. the amendment
   B. the Supreme Court
   C. the Constitution
   D. the militia

2. In the second sentence of paragraph 3, the word *It* refers to

   A. the Second Amendment
   B. the Supreme Court
   C. the militias
   D. the individual's rights

3.) In the second sentence of paragraph 5, the word *he* refers to

   A. the federal court
   B. the city
   C. the amendment
   D. the security guard

4. In the second sentence of paragraph 8, the word *their* refers to

   A. the lawyers
   B. the state
   C. the citizens
   D. the city

5. In the second sentence of paragraph 9, the word *they* refers to

   A. the lawyers
   B. the cities
   C. the Congress
   D. the Supreme Court

6. In the second sentence of paragraph 10, the word *them* refers to

   A. the government
   B. the city
   C. the handguns
   D. the citizens

HOW'S IT ORGANIZED?

This article is organized in **chronological order**, or in the time order that things happened.

Directions: Answer these questions in the spaces at the bottom.

1. When was the previous case about the Second Amendment heard by the Supreme Court?

2. What does the Second Amendment say?

3. What was the ruling, or decision, of the 1939 Court case?

4. Since 1939, how have nine federal appeals courts ruled?

5. How did a court rule differently in 2007?

6. What law was passed in Washington, D.C., in 1976 that the federal court decided against in 2007?

7. Where did the case go when Washington, D.C., appealed the decision?

8. What did the Supreme Court decide?

Answers:

1.	
2.	
3.	
4.	
5.	
6.	
7.	
8.	

*On a separate sheet of paper write a summary of what your notes say about the problems with the Second Amendment.

IS THAT A FACT?

Directions: Read the definitions of a fact and an inference below. Then read the paragraph that follows. At the bottom of the page, write an F on the blank if the sentence is a fact. Write an I if the sentence is an inference. Use the following definitions:

Fact—a statement that can be proven true from the paragraph.

Inference—a guess as to what MIGHT be true, based on what you have read and what you already know about the subject.

> Most of the debate about bearing arms centers around handguns. Cities argue that criminals can hide them too easily. If they take them into schools, buses, or offices, public safety is at risk. People like Mr. Heller argued that handguns are handy so individuals can easily defend themselves at home. Both sides accepted the need for government to regulate military-style firearms.

_____ **1.** Handguns are the major issue with this amendment.

_____ **2.** You are likely to experience a crime involving a handgun.

_____ **3.** Registering handguns is a matter of public safety.

_____ **4.** Many people enjoy owning a handgun.

_____ **5.** People agree that military-style guns need to be regulated.

_____ **6.** The Second Amendment is about a safety issue.

MAKE A SPACE

Directions: Below are sentences that are missing punctuation and capitalization. First draw slash marks (/) between the words. Then rewrite each sentence in the space below it, filling in the missing punctuation and capitalization.

Example:

However / it / has / never / been / clear / what / the / amendment / means

However, it has never been clear what the amendment means.

1. overtheyearsninefederalappealscourtsalsohavemaderulings

_____

_____

2. thecourtrefusedhisrequestsohiscasewenttotrial

_____

_____

3. injanuaryelevencitiessentadocumenttothesupremecourt·

_____

_____

4. citiesarguethatcriminalscanhidethemtooeasily

_____

_____

TIME MY READ #2

Directions: With a partner, see how many words you can read correctly in 45 seconds. As you read, your partner will put an X through any word read incorrectly on his or her copy. When you are finished, trade your books or papers, and let your partner read while you keep score. Count the total number of words you read correctly. Write this score at the bottom of your page.

amendment supreme regulated firearms actually militias guarantee security	8
individuals citizen registered illegal rulings ensure interference handgun	16
restrictions experts debate specify permits dispute unconstitutional arms	24
amendment supreme regulated firearms actually militias guarantee security	32
individuals citizen registered illegal rulings ensure interference handgun	40
restrictions experts debate specify permits dispute unconstitutional arms	48
amendment supreme regulated firearms actually militias guarantee security	56
individuals citizen registered illegal rulings ensure interference handgun	64
restrictions experts debate specify permits dispute unconstitutional arms	72
amendment supreme regulated firearms actually militias guarantee security	80

Number of words read correctly _____

Is the score higher than it was in Time My Read #1?_____

WORD PARTS

Directions: A **base word** is a word that can stand alone. A **prefix** is a word part added to the beginning of a base word. For example, in the word **improper**, **proper** is the base word and **im-** is the prefix, the word part added at the beginning. The prefixes **im-, ir-, il-,** and **in-** all mean "not." *Improper* means "not proper or not correct." Write a definition for the words below on the line. Do not use the base word in the definition. If you don't know the base word, such as *proper* in *improper,* look it up in a dictionary or ask a partner.

1. illegal— _____

2. impossible— _____

3. irregular— _____

4. inaccurate— _____

5. immature— _____

6. irresponsible— _____

7. inadequate— _____

8. illogical— _____

9. immeasurable— _____

10. incorrect— _____

11. illiterate— _____

12. indefensible— _____

13. impartial— _____

14. irrational— _____

15. inexpensive— _____

SUMMARIZING ABCs

Directions: Now that you've read the article on the debate over handguns, see how many words you can write about handguns in the boxes below.

A–C	D–F	G–I
J–L	**M–O**	**P–R**
S–T	**U–V**	**W–Z**

Unit 1: Human Rights and History

SENTENCE SUMMARIES

Directions: Below are four key words or phrases from the article "The Court Rules on the Second Amendment." Your job is to summarize, or restate, what you've learned in this article by using these four words or phrases in two sentences. Then, as a challenge, try to use all four words or phrases in one sentence to summarize the article.

Key Words or Phrases

court(s)   Second Amendment

handgun(s)   Washington, D.C.

Sentence Summaries:

1. _____

_____

2. _____

_____

Challenge Summary: (all four words or phrases in one sentence!)

1. _____

_____

REACTION GUIDE

Directions: Now that you have read and studied information about "The Court Rules on the Second Amendment," reread the statements below, which you responded to before reading the article. Then think about how the author might respond to these statements. If you think the author would agree, put a checkmark on the line before the number. If you think the author would disagree, put an X on the line. Then below the statement, copy the words, phrases, or sentences from the article that provide evidence of the views stated by the author. Also note if there is no evidence to support the statement.

_____ **1.** Handguns cause a huge amount of crime in cities.

Evidence: _____

_____

_____

_____ **2.** People need guns to protect their country.

Evidence: _____

_____

_____

_____ **3.** Every adult American should be allowed to own a handgun.

Evidence: _____

_____

_____

TAKE A STAND

Directions: People often have differing feelings or opinions about an issue. When they discuss or argue their opposing views, they are taking part in a debate. A good persuasive argument is based on a claim that is supported by

Facts—statements that can be proven to be true

Statistics—numerical data gotten through research

Examples—instances that support an opinion

You and a partner are going to debate two of your other classmates. The topic you are going to debate is the following:

Every adult American should be allowed to own a handgun.

Decide with the other pair who will agree and who will disagree with this statement. Then answer these questions in order to win your debate.

1. What are your two strongest points to persuade the other side? (You can do Internet research to include facts, statistics, and examples.)

    A. _____

    B. _____

2. What might the other side say to argue against point A?

    _____

    _____

3. What might the other side say to argue against point B?

    _____

    _____

4. What will you say to prove the other side's arguments are wrong?

    _____

    _____

    _____

ASSESSMENT

Comprehension: Answer the questions about the following passage.

The Second Amendment to the Constitution guarantees the right to bear arms. However, it has never been clear what the amendment actually means. In March 2008 the U. S. Supreme Court heard a case about the Second Amendment for the first time since 1939. The case from 1939 was called *United States v. Miller.* It ruled that the Second Amendment does not guarantee the right to keep a weapon such as a sawed-off shotgun, but it did not discuss individual versus collective rights.

1. What is the difference between individual and collective rights?

_____

_____

2. Why do many people think the Second Amendment allows handguns?

_____

_____

3. What was the author's purpose for writing about the Second Amendment?

_____

_____

Fluency: The words in the two sentences below are all connected. The sentences are also missing punctuation and capitalization. Draw slash marks (/) between the words. Then rewrite each sentence by filling in the punctuation and capitalization.

1. ithasneverbeenclearwhatthesecondamendmentmeans

_____

2. thesecondamendmentdidnotdiscussindividualversuscollectiverights

_____

_____

Fluency: Read the three sentences below. Imagine where you would pause within each sentence as you read it aloud. Draw a slash (/) mark between the phrases where you would pause. The first slash is done.

3. Over the years / nine federal appeals courts also have made rulings.

4. In March 2008 the U. S. Supreme Court heard a case about the Second Amendment for the first time since 1939.

5. As a matter of public safety, it passed a law that required handgun owners to register them with the city.

Vocabulary: Based on what you have learned in this lesson, match the following words with their definitions. Write the letter of the definition on the blank in front of the word it defines.

1. _____ bear   **A.** not enough

2. _____ immature   **B.** cheap

3. _____ collective   **C.** an argument between two sides

4. _____ inadequate   **D.** to break the rules or laws

5. _____ illiterate   **E.** childish, not grown up

6. _____ debate   **F.** where judges and juries decide conflicts

7. _____ inexpensive   **G.** not done correctly; not normal

8. _____ violate   **H.** carry or hold

9. _____ court   **I.** a group of people

10. _____ irregular   **J.** unable to read

Name _____ Date _____

ANTICIPATION GUIDE

Directions: Before you read the article "Freedom of Speech Gets a Test," read the statements below. If you agree with a statement, put a checkmark on the line next to it. If you disagree, put an X on the line.

_____ **1.** Cities do not have the right to control what people can say.

_____ **2.** Under the First Amendment, people should have the right to share their religious beliefs anywhere.

_____ **3.** Monuments that are religious should also be considered historical.

Once you have responded to the statements above, write in the section below why you agree or disagree with each statement.

1. _____

_____

2. _____

_____

3. _____

_____

In the box below, draw a picture of what you think this article is about.

```
┌─────────────────────────────────────────────┐
│                                             │
│                                             │
│                                             │
│                                             │
│                                             │
│                                             │
│                                             │
└─────────────────────────────────────────────┘
```

WORDSTORM

Directions: It's good to know more than just the dictionary definition of a word. Completing a wordstorm lets you write down information to help you understand what a word means, how it's related to other words, and how to use it in different ways.

What is the word?

monument

Here is the sentence from the text in which the word is used:

"When the group wanted to put a monument in a park, the city refused."

What are some other words or phrases that mean the same thing?

1. _____ 2. _____ 3. _____

Name three people other than teachers who would likely use this word.

1. _____ 2. _____ 3. _____

Draw a picture below that reminds you of the word *monument*.

LANGUAGE MINI-LESSON

Remember that any word that represents a person, place, or thing is called a noun. A **common noun** represents any general thing, such as *singer, museum,* or *state*. A **proper noun** represents a particular person, place, or thing, such as *Elvis Presley*, *Smithsonian,* or *Texas*.

Nouns can represent persons, places, or things, but they can also represent ideas or beliefs. Nouns that represent ideas such as *independence*, *sadness*, or *pride* can't be touched, so they are called **abstract nouns**.

Sometimes a noun refers to a <u>group</u> of people or things, such as *team, audience,* or *family*. These are called **collective nouns**.

Finally there are nouns made up of one or more separate words, such as *airplane, mother-in-law,* or *City Hall*. These are called **compound nouns.**

Directions: In the chart below, put a check in each box that describes what kind of noun the word in the left-hand column is. Remember the noun in the left-hand column may be called two or more things.

Noun	Common	Proper	Abstract	Collective	Compound
church					
Moses					
group					
courthouse					
freedom					
Supreme Court					
monument					
religion					
grounds					
runner-up					

ECHO READING

Directions: When you read, you should make breaks, and sometimes pauses, between groups of words. As your teacher reads each phrase, repeat aloud what is read and put a slash or line after that phrase. Then read the whole sentence aloud as a class. Do the first paragraph together as a class, and then do the second one on your own. The first sentence has been marked for you.

> Pleasant Grove / used "government speech" / as its defense. / Government can say whatever it wants without having to give anyone else an opportunity to respond. The city says that the Ten Commandments monument has become the city's message, and that it is not required to accept monuments with other messages.
>
> The case went to several courts. Summum lost its first case, but it won in 2007. That court ruled that a city park must allow speakers with different opinions and monuments with different messages. The city then appealed to the Supreme Court.

What's Happening

IN THE USA?

BY LAWRENCE GABLE
© 2014 What's Happening Publications

SUBJECT: HUMAN RIGHTS and HISTORY

1   In November 2008 an interesting case went to the Supreme Court. On one side was a small religious group in Utah. On the other side stood Pleasant Grove City, Utah. When the group wanted to put a monument in a park, the city refused. After going to lower courts, the case finally reached the highest court in the U.S.

2   The Church of Summum started in Utah in 1975. It believes that Moses received two versions of God's law. According to Summum, the original version contained Seven Principles of Creation. It claims that Moses said that his people were not yet ready for them. Instead God gave Moses the Ten Commandments.

3   In 2003 the founder of Summum contacted Pleasant Grove City. He wanted to place a monument with the Seven Principles in Pioneer Park. The small park already displays things like a millstone, a water well, and a September 11 memorial. It also has large stone tablets with the Ten Commandments.

4   The city refused the Summum monument. It claimed that the things in Pioneer Park have local historical value. Even the tablets of the Ten Commandments had been a donation from a local organization in 1971.

5   The church took Pleasant Grove City to court. It felt that the city was violating its First Amendment right to freedom of speech. The First Amendment to the Constitution states that the U.S. cannot establish a religion or limit the freedom of speech. Although Summum was raising a free-speech issue, religion was clearly part of the problem. The church compared its monument to the park's monument with the Ten Commandments.

6   The Church of Summum made several arguments. It argued that the First Amendment protects all speech. It said that a park that gives space to the Ten Commandments also must give space to other religious messages. The church also argued that the First Amendment protects its monument as free speech, just as it protects people who make speeches or hand out leaflets. Finally, it argued that the city park must make room either for all opinions, or for none.

7   Pleasant Grove City used "government speech" as its defense. Government can say whatever it wants without having to give anyone else an opportunity to respond. The city said that the Ten Commandments monument had become the city's message, and that it was not required to accept monuments with other messages.

8   The case went to several courts. Summum lost its first case, but it won in 2007. That court ruled that a city park must allow speakers with different opinions and monuments with different messages. The city then appealed to the Supreme Court.

9   The Supreme Court already had made rulings in similar cases. In 2005 it ruled against the display of the Ten Commandments in two courthouses in Kentucky. It said that they represented religion. However, it allowed Texas to keep them on the grounds at the state capitol. It said that they were among other monuments that are historical and moral, but not religious.

10   In February 2009 the Supreme Court ruled in favor of Pleasant Grove City. The justices all agreed that a city must protect an individual's right to free, private speech in a public park. Such speech is always temporary. However, they ruled that government speech allows a city to place a permanent monument in a park as an expression of the city's values and ideas. The First Amendment, though, does not require a city to display any such permanent expressions from its citizens.

FREEDOM OF SPEECH GETS A TEST

QUICK READ/DRAW AND WRITE

Directions: First Reading—As you do your first reading of the article, your teacher will time you for one minute. When time is called, write the number of the paragraph where you stopped. **Paragraph #** _____

In the box below, draw a picture summarizing what you read.

Second Reading—As you do your second reading of the article, your teacher will time you for one minute. When time is called, write the number of the paragraph where you stopped. **Paragraph #** _____

Directions: Now continue reading the rest of the article. Below, write five important words that will help you remember the information from the article.

_____ _____ _____ _____

CLOSE READING ANNOTATION

Third Reading—As you reread each paragraph in the article closely, answer the questions by annotating the text. Each numbered question corresponds to a paragraph in the article where the answer can be found. Write your brief answers in the space below each question.

1. What conflict is set up in the first paragraph?

_____

2. What is the author's purpose in writing the second paragraph?

_____

3. Why might the Church of Summum believe it has the right to put a monument in the park?

_____

4. What does the phrase *historical value* have to do with the Church of Summum's monument?

_____

5. Why did the Church of Summum use the First Amendment as part of its argument?

_____

6. What is the importance of the phrase *for all opinions, or for none*?

_____

7. What is meant by the phrase *government speech*?

_____

8. What is the author's purpose for writing paragraph 8?

_____

9. Why did the Supreme Court make different decisions in Kentucky and Texas?

_____

10. What does the author mean by saying that "such speech is always temporary"?

_____

GRAMMAR GAMES

Directions: Reread the two paragraphs below. Words have been left out from the sentences. Think about the information from the article you have read and fill in words that make sense. The part of speech of each missing word is provided.

In November 2008 an interesting case _____ to the
                                        (1. verb)

Supreme Court. On one side was a small religious group in Utah. On the

other _____ _____ Pleasant Grove City, Utah. When
       (2. noun)   (3. verb)

the group asked for _____ to put a monument in a city park,
                      (4. noun)

the city refused. After going to lower courts, _____ dispute
                                                  (5. article)

finally reached the highest court in the United States.

The Church of Summum started _____ Utah in 1975. Its
                               (6. preposition)

headquarters are in Salt Lake City. It _____ that Moses
                                         (7. verb)

received two _____ of God's law on Mount Sinai. According to
              (8. plural noun)

Summum, the original version contained Seven Principles of Creation.

Summum _____ that Moses rejected them _____
        (9. verb)   (10. conjunction)

his people were not yet ready for them.

HOW'S IT ORGANIZED?

This article presents two sides of a controversial issue.

Directions: Answer these questions in the spaces at the bottom.

1. What made the case so challenging?

2. Why did the Church of Summum feel justified about building its monument?

3. What made the city refuse to allow the monument's placement?

4. What was the argument regarding the First Amendment?

5. What was the argument that Pleasant Grove City used?

6. What were the rulings of the Supreme Court in previous cases?

7. What was noted by the Supreme Court justices in their decision?

Answers:

1.	
2.	
3.	
4.	
5.	
6.	
7.	

The main idea of a selection reflects what the article is about. Put an X on the space next to the sentence that best states the main idea, and write a reason for that choice below.

_____ **1.** People have a right to free speech.

_____ **2.** The issue of free speech guaranteed by the First Amendment becomes complicated when the issue is about religion.

_____ **3.** The rights of cities are different from the rights of individuals.

Explain why your choice is the best main or central idea.

_____

_____

IS THAT A FACT?

Directions: Read the definitions of a fact and an inference below. Then read the paragraph that follows. At the bottom of the page, write an F on the blank if the sentence is a fact. Write an I if the sentence is an inference. Use the following definitions:

Fact—a statement that can be proven true from the paragraph.

Inference—a guess as to what MIGHT be true, based on what you have read and what you already know about the subject.

> The church took Pleasant Grove City to court. It felt that the city was violating its First Amendment right to freedom of speech. The First Amendment to the Constitution states that the U.S. cannot establish a religion or limit the freedom of speech. The Supreme Court already has made rulings in similar cases. In 2005 it ruled against the display of the Ten Commandments in two courthouses in Kentucky. It said that they represented religion. However, it allowed Texas to keep them on the grounds at the state capitol. It said that they were among other monuments that are historical and moral, but not religious..

_____ **1.** The U.S. government doesn't establish religions.

_____ **2.** A monument can be legal or illegal depending on how a court interprets its purpose.

_____ **3.** The Supreme Court ruled against a display in 2005.

_____ **4.** Religious people may go to extreme measures to put their religion on display.

_____ **5.** A monument can have religious content but still be historical.

_____ **6.** This Supreme Court had ruled on cases similar to this one.

TIC-TAC-TOE SUMMARIZING

When you **summarize** in writing, you present all the key points the author is trying to make.

Directions: Write four sentences to summarize the article "Freedom of Speech Gets a Test." To help you, there are nine words or phrases in the Tic-Tac-Toe graphic organizer below. To write a sentence, you must use three words or phrases in a row. The row can be horizontal (—), vertical (I), or diagonal (/).

First Amendment	government speech	historical
Supreme Court	Constitution	monument
freedom of speech	violation	display

1. _____

_____

2. _____

_____

3. _____

_____

4. _____

_____

REACTION GUIDE

Directions: Now that you have read and studied information about "Freedom of Speech Gets a Test," reread the statements below, which you responded to before reading the article. Then think about how the author might respond to these statements. If you think the author would agree, put a checkmark on the line before the number. If you think the author would disagree, put an X on the line. Then below the statement, copy the words, phrases, or sentences from the article that provide evidence of the views stated by the author. Also note if there is no evidence to support the statement.

_____ **1.** Cities do not have the right to control what people can say.

Evidence: _____

_____

_____

_____ **2.** Under the First Amendment, people should have the right to share their religious beliefs anywhere.

Evidence: _____

_____

_____

_____ **3.** Monuments that are religious should also be considered historical.

Evidence: _____

_____

_____

TAKE A STAND

Directions: People often have differing feelings or opinions about an issue. When they discuss or argue their opposing views, they are taking part in a debate. A good persuasive argument is based on a claim that is supported by

Facts—statements that can be proven to be true

Statistics—numerical data gotten through research

Examples—instances that support an opinion

You and a partner are going to debate two of your other classmates. The topic you are going to debate is the following:

Under the First Amendment, people should have the right to share their religious beliefs anywhere.

Decide with the other pair who will agree and who will disagree with this statement. Then answer these questions in order to win your debate.

1. What are your two strongest points to persuade the other side? (You can do Internet research to include facts, statistics, and examples.)

   A. _____

   B. _____

2. What might the other side say to argue against point A?

   _____

   _____

3. What might the other side say to argue against point B?

   _____

   _____

4. What will you say to prove the other side's arguments are wrong?

   _____

   _____

WHAT'S THE COMBINATION?

Writing is more interesting when the writer joins, or combines, short sentences. Follow the directions below to learn different ways to combine two sentences.

What to do: If two sentences have the same subject, or are about the same thing, you can join them by using the word *which* to add information from one sentence into the other. *Grammar Note*: Be sure to put commas (,) around a clause that begins with *which*.

Example: The game *was exciting*. It went into overtime.

New Sentence: The game, *which was exciting*, went into overtime.

Directions: Combine these sentences using the method above.

1. A religious group wanted to put up a monument. The group was in Utah.

   _____

2. The church believed that there were two versions of God's law. It was the Church of Summum.

   _____

3. The church was located in Pleasant Grove City. It wanted to put the monument in a park.

   _____

4. The case was filed in the Supreme Court by the church. The Supreme Court was in Washington, D.C.

   _____

5. The city council said there were already monuments there. The council refused the church's request.

   _____

6. The city said it could say what it wants. It used *government speech* as its defense.

   _____

ANALYZING A PROMPT

Directions: Read the writing prompt in the box below. Then follow the directions to learn how to analyze and answer it.

> You are an aide to a member on the city council, and a religious group has requested permission to place a monument in a local park. The park already has monuments that have historical and religious messages. You will write an essay to the city council that informs its members about the issues so that they can cast their votes on the request. Use information from the article to explain what issues the members should consider.

1. A writing prompt begins with some background information known as the **set up.** Underline the sentences that set up this assignment.

2. Use the following **R.A.F.T.** technique to finish analyzing the prompt.

Role: What are you supposed to be to answer it? A student? A politician?

Write what you are here: _____

Audience: To whom are you writing? A friend? A particular group?

Write who it is here: _____

Format: Check to see what type of writing you are doing. Is it an essay, a letter, a speech, a story, a description, an editorial, or a report?

Write what it is here: _____

Task: Another sentence in the prompt will tell you what you must do, or your "task."

If the question word is **why**, you will *give the reasons* that something is done.

If the question word is **how**, you will *explain the way* that something is done.

If the question word is **what**, you will *identify the thing* that is done.

Below, copy the sentence or question that describes your task.

_____

_____

WHAT'S YOUR POINT?

When writing an essay it is important to have a strong claim. A **claim,** or **thesis statement** states the main point the writer wants to get across. Once the thesis is introduced, the body of the essay should support that thesis with key points that provide evidence.

The information presented in the article, "Freedom of Speech Gets a Test," is about the Supreme Court's decision on what exactly is free speech in our country. The article explains how different courts have given different judgments about when someone's freedom to say what he or she believes has been violated.

Directions: Which of these sentences provides the best **claim** for an essay on this topic? Circle the letter of your choice.

  a. Freedom of Speech in the Constitution must be defined on a case-by-case basis by our courts.

  b. A church should have the right to place a monument in a city park.

  c. Our city governments must be the final deciders of what goes in a city park.

In the space below, explain what is weak or wrong about the other two statements.

1. _____

_____

_____

2. _____

_____

_____

ASSESSMENT

1. This question has two parts. First, answer Part A. Then, answer Part B.

Part A: Underline the sentence that best states the author's main purpose in "Freedom of Speech Gets a Test."

a. The author wants Americans to understand that the First Amendment allows all people to speak what they believe.

b. The author wants Americans to understand that freedom of speech is something our country must continually redefine in many court cases.

c. The author wants Americans to understand that all religious beliefs should be respected in our country.

d. The author wants Americans to understand that people love their monuments.

Part B: Circle the letter of the pair of sentences below that support your answer to part A.

a. The justices all agreed that a city must protect an individual's right to free, private speech in a public park. Such speech is always temporary.

b. In 2003 the founder of Summum contacted Pleasant Grove City. He wanted to place a monument with the Seven Principles in Pioneer Park.

c. The Church of Summum made several arguments. It argued that the First Amendment protects all speech.

d. The city refused the Summum monument. It claimed that things in Pioneer Park have local historical value.

2. The U.S. Constitution says the government cannot establish a religion or limit freedom of speech. Underline the sentences that prove that the Supreme Court has had different interpretations of the First Amendment.

"The Supreme Court had made similar rulings in similar cases. In 2005 it ruled against the display of the Ten Commandments in two courthouses in Kentucky. It said they represented religion. However, it allowed Texas to keep them on the grounds of the state capitol. It said that they were among other monuments that are historical and moral, but not religious."

3. Support the claim that the Church of Summum had the right to put a monument in a city park. Look back through the article. Then on the space below, cite evidence by listing facts from the article to support this claim.

_____

_____

_____

4. A student is writing an editorial for a local newspaper to argue that putting up a religious monument in a city park is against the First Amendment. Read the paragraphs from the draft of the student's letter and complete the task that follows.

The First Amendment says that our government shall not establish a state religion or limit our freedom of speech. Where do we draw the line, however, when a local church wants to put up a religious monument in our city park? Everyone likes monuments in parks. Cities erect monuments in parks to note great historical events that affected the people who live in the area. Historical monuments help us understand our shared history and what people did who came before us. A religious monument does not represent everyone's beliefs, though. I am very religious, don't get me wrong. If we let one religious group "speak freely" in a public park, then our government has supported one religion over others.

Below, copy the two sentences that do not support the underlined sentence and should be removed from the second paragraph.

a. _____

_____

_____

b. _____

_____

_____

Name _____ Date _____

ANTICIPATION GUIDE

Directions: Before you read the article "The Law Gets Tough with Paparazzi," read the statements below. If you agree with a statement, put a checkmark on the line next to it. If you disagree, put an X on the line.

_____ **1.** Celebrities should not get special treatment.

_____ **2.** It is okay to take pictures of a celebrity's family.

_____ **3.** Photographers should respect everyone's privacy.

Once you have responded to the statements above, write in the section below why you agree or disagree with each statement.

1. _____

_____

2. _____

_____

3. _____

_____

In the box below, draw a picture of what you think this article is about.

WORDSTORM

Directions: It's good to know more than just the dictionary definition of a word. Completing a wordstorm lets you write down information to help you understand what a word means, how it's related to other words, and how to use it in different ways.

What is the word?

privacy

Here is the sentence from the text in which the word is used:

"Often they are just a bother, but sometimes they invade the celebrity's privacy."

What are some other words or phrases that mean the same thing?

_____

What are three reasons why people's privacy needs to be respected?

1. _____ 2. _____ 3. _____

Name three people other than teachers who would likely use this word.

1. _____ 2. _____ 3. _____

Draw a picture below that reminds you of the word *privacy*.

TIME MY READ #1

Directions: With a partner, see how many words you can read correctly in 45 seconds. As you read, your partner will put an X through any word read incorrectly on his or her copy. When you are finished, trade your books or papers, and let your partner read while you keep score. Count the total number of words you read correctly.

privacy celebrity invasion trespass physically property photographs amendment	8
strict equipment strengthens exposure audio expectation protects crime	16
released criticized distance experts decoys unguarded figures tougher	24
privacy celebrity invasion trespass physically property photographs amendment	32
strict equipment strengthens exposure audio expectation protects crime	40
released criticized distance experts decoys unguarded figures tougher	48
privacy celebrity invasion trespass physically property photographs amendment	56
strict equipment strengthens exposure audio expectation protects crime	64
released criticized distance experts decoys unguarded figures tougher	72
privacy celebrity invasion trespass physically property photographs amendment	80

Number of words read correctly _____

ECHO READING

Directions: When you read, you should make breaks, and sometimes pauses, between groups of words. As your teacher reads each phrase, repeat aloud what is read and put a slash or line after that phrase. Then read the whole sentence aloud as a class. Do the first paragraph together as a class, and then do the second one on your own. The first sentence has been marked for you.

Paparazzi can get / hundreds of thousands of dollars / for a single photograph. / Photos of celebrities are big business. This makes them willing to invade someone's privacy. Paparazzi have trespassed at homes and at schools, and at private events like funerals and weddings.

Celebrities fight paparazzi in a number of ways. They use false names and secret entrances at hotels. They hire security guards and hire extra cars as decoys. Recently some stars have released their own photos of their families at weddings and funerals so that they bring down the value of the paparazzo's pictures. Finally, some have taken the paparazzi to court.

What's Happening

IN CALIFORNIA ?

BY LAWRENCE GABLE
© 2014 *What's Happening Publications*

SUBJECT: HUMAN RIGHTS and HISTORY

The Law Gets Tough with Paparazzi

1   Some photographers try to get photos of celebrities in private or unguarded moments. Often they are just a bother, but sometimes they invade the celebrity's privacy. In 2010 California strengthened a law that protects people from these photographers called "paparazzi."

2   In 1999 California created the first law in the U.S. to control paparazzi. There was great public outcry against them then, because they had played a role in the car crash that killed England's Princess Diana. Her brother criticized the press when he spoke at her funeral, which more than two billion people watched on television.

3   The law protects celebrities against invasion of privacy. That could be a trespass, when the photographer physically enters the celebrity's property. It could also be the use of audio or video equipment from a distance. The State updated the law again in 2006. That made paparazzi responsible for altercations that they cause.

4   An amendment in 2010 strengthened the law. It makes it a crime to take and sell unauthorized photos of celebrities in "personal or familial activity." It also makes it a crime for newspapers, magazines and TV shows to buy those photos. They are responsible for a paparazzi's misbehavior too. Finally, it increases the penalty for breaking the law to $50,000.

5   Photos of celebrities are big business. A photographer can get hundreds of thousands of dollars for a single photo. That makes them willing to invade someone's privacy. Paparazzi have trespassed at homes and schools, and at private events like funerals and weddings. They also have used their vehicles to block celebrities' vehicles and to chase them at high speeds.

6   Celebrities fight paparazzi in a number of ways. They use false names and secret entrances at hotels. They hire security guards. Often they hire extra cars as decoys. Some stars have released their own photos of children or weddings so that the photos from paparazzi lose their value. Finally, of course, some have taken paparazzi to court.

7   Privacy laws cover people differently. Ordinary citizens have the right to be free from public exposure. However, the law is different for "public figures" like movie stars, athletes and politicians. It allows public exposure, but still gives them a "reasonable expectation of privacy."

8   No other state has a law quite like this. Experts think that someday a court will decide whether the law is too strict. For now, though, public figures are glad that the law that protects their privacy is tougher than ever.

GET A CONTEXT CLUE

Directions: Below are sentences from "The Law Gets Tough with Paparazzi." First, read the sentence. Then, look back in the article and reread the paragraph in which the sentence is found. Circle the best answer to each question.

"Some photographers try to get photos of celebrities in private or *unguarded* moments."

1. The word *unguarded* means

   A. in prison
   B. careful
   C. unprotected
   D. watchful

"There was great public *outcry* against them then, because they had played a role in the car crash that killed England's Princess Diana."

2. An *outcry* means

   A. loud disapproval
   B. gossip
   C. warning
   D. joking

"The State *updated* the law again in 2006."

3. The word *updated* means

   A. stopped for a time
   B. judged
   C. disapproved
   D. made more current

"Now a new *amendment* strengthens the law."

4. The word *amendment* means

   A. a change in the law
   B. a decision that changes the law
   C. a question about the law
   D. a position on a law

"Often they hire extra cars as *decoys*."

5. The word *decoys* means

   A. leaders
   B. followers
   C. fakes or imitations
   D. friends or acquaintances

"*Experts* think that someday courts will decide whether the law is too strict."

6. The word *experts* means

   A. college professors or teachers
   B. parents
   C. senators
   D. people who know a subject well

WORD CHOICE

Directions: The sentences below contain blanks for missing words. Three answer choices are listed after each blank. Read the sentence past the blank and choose the correct word. Write it in the blank.

Some photographers try to get pictures of celebrities in private or unguarded moments. In 1999 California _____ (*creating, creation, created*) the first law in the U.S. to _____ (*control, controlled, controlling*) paparazzi. At that time there _____ (*were, was, wasn't*) a great public outcry against them because they _____ (*has, have, had*) played a role in the car crash in Paris that had killed Princess Diana of England. The law _____ (*protecting, protection, protects*) a celebrity against invasion of privacy. What might be considered a trespass is when a photographer _____ (*enters, entering, enter*) the _____ (*celebrities, celebrities's, celebrity's*) property without his or her permission. A new amendment _____ (*makes, making, make*) it a crime to sell unauthorized pictures of famous people in private or family settings. Public figures and famous people are now happy that the law is tougher than ever and that it _____ (*protects, protected, protecting*) their right to privacy.

LOOK WHO'S TALKING

Directions: Below are sentences that relate to "The Law Gets Tough with Paparazzi." Look back in the article and reread the paragraph in which you find the reference. Circle the best answer to each question.

1. **In the second sentence of paragraph 2, the word *them* best refers to**

   A. the stars
   B. celebrities
   C. the photographers
   D. the public

2. **In the third sentence of paragraph 3, the word *It* refers to**

   A. the photographers
   B. the trespassing
   C. the use of audio
   D. the invasion of privacy

3. **In the last sentence of paragraph 4, the word *it* refers to**

   A. the amendment
   B. the use of photographs
   C. the use of audio
   D. the crime

4. **In the last sentence of paragraph 5, the word *they* refers to**

   A. the paparazzi
   B. the security guards
   C. the people
   D. the celebrities

5. **In the last sentence of paragraph 7, the word *them* refers to**

   A. the lawmakers
   B. the paparazzi
   C. the public figures
   D. the citizens

6. **The word *this* in the first sentence of the final paragraph refers to**

   A. the problem
   B. the law
   C. the use of photographs
   D. the court

NOTE MAKING

Directions: Read the boldfaced key words on the left side of the chart below. Then add notes that answer the question in parentheses under the key word.

Paparazzi (What are paparazzi?)	
Dangerous (Why are paparazzi dangerous?)	
Invasion of privacy (When do paparazzi invade celebrities' privacy?)	
Celebrities fight back (How are celebrities fighting back?)	
Privacy laws cover (Which people are covered by privacy laws?)	

*On a separate sheet of paper, write a summary of what your notes say about the issues with the paparazzi.

IS THAT A FACT?

Directions: Read the definitions of a fact and an inference below. Then read the paragraph that follows. At the bottom of the page, write an F on the blank if the sentence is a fact. Write an I if the sentence is an inference. Use the following definitions:

Fact—a statement that can be proven true from the paragraph.

Inference—a guess as to what MIGHT be true, based on what you have read and what you already know about the subject.

Privacy laws cover people differently. Ordinary citizens have the right to be free from public exposure. However, the law is different for public figures like movie stars, athletes and politicians. It allows public exposure, but still gives them a reasonable expectation of privacy. No other state has a law quite like this. Experts think that someday a court will decide whether the law is too strict. For now, though, public figures are glad that the law that protects their privacy is tougher than ever.

_____ **1.** Public figures expect to be photographed when in public.

_____ **2.** By law, celebrities have a reasonable expectation of privacy.

_____ **3.** The law might eventually be changed.

_____ **4.** California, as a state, tries to take care of its celebrities.

_____ **5.** Paparazzi have taken advantage of movie stars, athletes, and politicians.

_____ **6.** Ordinary people don't need to worry about paparazzi invading their privacy.

MAKE A SPACE

Directions: Below are sentences that are missing punctuation and capitalization. First draw slash marks (/) between the words. Then rewrite each sentence in the space below it, filling in the missing punctuation and capitalization.

> Example:
>
> some / paparazzi / try / to / get / celebrities / in / uncomfortable / situations
>
> Some paparazzi try to get celebrities in uncomfortable situations.

1. sometimestheyareonlyabotherbutsometimestheyinvadepeoplesprivacy

_____

_____

2. celebritiesmayfightpaparazziinanumberofways

_____

_____

3. ordinarycitizenshavearighttobefreefrompublicexposure

_____

_____

4. itmakesitacrimefortvnewspapersandmagazinestobuythephotographs

_____

_____

TIME MY READ #2

Directions: With a partner, see how many words you can read correctly in 45 seconds. As you read, your partner will put an X through any word read incorrectly on his or her copy. When you are finished, trade your books or papers, and let your partner read while you keep score. Count the total number of words you read correctly. Write this score at the bottom of your page.

privacy celebrity invasion trespass physically property photographs amendment	8
strict equipment strengthens exposure audio expectation protects crime	16
released criticized distance experts decoys unguarded figures tougher	24
privacy celebrity invasion trespass physically property photographs amendment	32
strict equipment strengthens exposure audio expectation protects crime	40
released criticized distance experts decoys unguarded figures tougher	48
privacy celebrity invasion trespass physically property photographs amendment	56
strict equipment strengthens exposure audio expectation protects crime	64
released criticized distance experts decoys unguarded figures tougher	72
privacy celebrity invasion trespass physically property photographs amendment	80

Number of words read correctly _____

Is the score higher than it was in Time My Read #1? _____

WORD PARTS

Directions: A base word is a word that can stand alone. A **prefix** is a word part added to the beginning of a base word. In the word **retry**, **try** is the base word and **re-** is the prefix. The prefix **re-** means "again." *Retry* means "to attempt to do something again." (Sometimes the **re-** at the beginning of a word is NOT a prefix. For example, in the word *repeat*, you do not "peat" again.) Write ten words that begin with the prefix **re-** on the lines below. Then share your words with the class.

1. _____ 2. _____

3. _____ 4. _____

5. _____ 6. _____

7. _____ 8. _____

9. _____ 10. _____

Directions: A **suffix** is added to the end of a word to change its part of speech. The suffix **-able** means "can be" or "made to be." In the following sentence, see how the **verb** *depend*, which means "to trust," becomes an **adjective** that describes the postal carrier.

Our postal carrier is very *dependable*, delivering the mail every day.

Think of ten verbs you can turn into adjectives by adding the suffix **-able**. Write them on the blanks below and share them with the class.

1. _____ 2. _____

3. _____ 4. _____

5. _____ 6. _____

7. _____ 8. _____

9. _____ 10. _____

PAPARAZZI WORD PUZZLE

Directions: Complete the crossword puzzle.

Word List

RETURNABLE   AMENDMENT   OUTCRY   RECLOSE   UNGUARDED

UPDATED   PRIVACY   EXPERTS   UNDERSTANDABLE   DECOY

Across	Down
1. to shut again	**2.** people who know a subject well
5. a change	**3.** the right to be left alone
7. loud disapproval	**4.** made more current
9. to be able to make some sense of something	**6.** not protected
10. able to be given back	**8.** a fake or imitation

WRITING FRAME

Directions: Use your knowledge and information from the article to complete the writing frame below.

Some photographers, or "paparazzi," try to get photos of celebrities in private or unguarded moments. Sometimes they appear at _____. California created the first law to _____. The law was created because there had been public outcry about _____. The new law protects celebrities against _____. Paparazzi might invade a celebrity's privacy by _____ or _____. The amendment to the law in 2010 makes it a crime to _____. Privacy laws cover people differently. For example, ordinary citizens have _____. The law is different for public figures such as _____, _____, and _____. The law allows public exposure, but still gives them a _____.

REACTION GUIDE

Directions: Now that you have read and studied information about "The Law Gets Tough with Paparazzi," reread the statements below, which you responded to before reading the article. Then think about how the author might respond to these statements. If you think the author would agree, put a checkmark on the line before the number. If you think the author would disagree, put an X on the line. Then below the statement, copy the words, phrases, or sentences from the article that provide evidence of the views stated by the author. Also note if there is no evidence to support the statement.

_____ **1.** Celebrities should not get special treatment.

Evidence: _____

_____

_____

_____ **2.** It is okay to take pictures of a celebrity's family.

Evidence: _____

_____

_____

_____ **3.** Photographers should respect everyone's privacy.

Evidence: _____

_____

_____

TAKE A STAND

Directions: People often have differing feelings or opinions about an issue. When they discuss or argue their opposing views, they are taking part in a debate. A good persuasive argument is based on a claim that is supported by

Facts—statements that can be proven to be true

Statistics—numerical data gotten through research

Examples—instances that support an opinion

You and a partner are going to debate two classmates. The topic you are going to debate is the following:

Photographers should respect everyone's privacy.

Decide with the other pair who will agree and who will disagree with this statement. Then answer these questions in order to win your debate.

1. What are your two strongest points to persuade the other side? (You can do Internet research to include facts, statistics, and examples.)

   A. _____

   B. _____

2. What might the other side say to argue against point A?

   _____

   _____

3. What might the other side say to argue against point B?

   _____

   _____

4. What will you say to prove the other side's arguments are wrong?

   _____

   _____

ASSESSMENT

Comprehension: Answer the questions about the following passage.

The law protects celebrities against invasion of privacy. That could be a trespass, when the photographer physically enters the celebrity's property. It could also be the use of audio or video equipment from a distance. The state updated the law again in 2006. That made paparazzi responsible for altercations that they cause when they get too close. Fighting or accidents sometimes happen. Now a new amendment strengthens the law, making it a crime to sell unauthorized photos of celebrities in a personal or familial activity.

1. How did the state update the law to make it stronger?

_____

_____

2. What kinds of altercations do paparazzi cause?

_____

_____

3. What was the author's purpose for writing about the paparazzi?

_____

_____

Fluency: The words in the two sentences below are all connected. The sentences are also missing punctuation and capitalization. Draw slash marks (/) between the words. Then rewrite each sentence by filling in the punctuation and capitalization.

1. thelawprotectscelebritiesagainstinvasionofprivacy

_____

2. italsomakesitacrimefornewspapersandmagazinestobuythepictures

_____

_____

Fluency: Read the three sentences below. Imagine where you would pause within each sentence as you read it aloud. Draw a slash (/) mark between the phrases where you would pause. The first slash is done.

3. Finally / it increases the penalty to $50,000 for breaking the law.

4. A photographer can get hundreds of thousands of dollars for a single photo.

5. However, the law is different for public figures, like movie stars, athletes, and politicians.

Vocabulary: Based on what you have learned in this lesson, match the following words with their definitions. Write the letter of the definition on the blank in front of the word it defines.

1. _____ unguarded	**A.** to shut again
2. _____ reclose	**B.** loud disapproval
3. _____ understandable	**C.** a fake or imitation
4. _____ amendment	**D.** not protected
5. _____ outcry	**E.** change or improvement to a law
6. _____ decoy	**F.** able to make sense of
7. _____ experts	**G.** people who know a subject well
8. _____ returnable	**H.** made more current
9. _____ privacy	**I.** able to be given back
10. _____ updated	**J.** the right to be left alone

Unit 1: Human Rights and History

Name _____ Date _____

ANTICIPATION GUIDE

Directions: Before you read the article "The International Slavery Museum Opens in England," read the statements below. If you agree with a statement, put a checkmark on the line next to it. If you disagree, put an X on the line.

_____ **1.** The United States was the primary country to capture slaves.

_____ **2.** Slaves were able to survive better on plantations than in their own countries.

_____ **3.** Although international law bans slavery, there are still slaves in some countries in the world.

Once you have responded to the statements above, write in the section below why you agree or disagree with each statement.

1. _____

_____

2. _____

_____

3. _____

_____

In the box below, draw a picture of what you think this article is about.

WORDSTORM

Directions: It's good to know more than just the dictionary definition of a word. Completing a wordstorm lets you write down information to help you understand what a word means, how it's related to other words, and how to use it in different ways.

What is the word?

slavery

Here is the sentence from the text in which the word is used:

"Britain is proud that it abolished slavery earlier than other nations."

What are some other words or phrases that mean the same thing?

_____

What are three things you know about slavery?

1. _____ 2. _____ 3. _____

Name three people other than teachers who would likely use this word.

1. _____ 2. _____ 3. _____

Draw a picture below that reminds you of the word *slavery*.

LANGUAGE MINI-LESSON

The subject of a sentence is whom or what the sentence is about. If the subject is just one thing, or **singular,** the verb of the sentence must agree, or be **singular,** too. If the subject of a sentence is more than one thing, or **plural,** the verb must agree, or be **plural,** also.

For example: The *musician* (singular subject) *plays* (singular verb) the music. The *musicians* (plural subject) *play* (plural verb) the music.

Sometimes a verb is made up of two words. A multiple-word verb is called a **verb phrase**. In a verb phrase, it is sometimes the first word, or helping verb, and sometimes the main verb, that must agree with the subject.

For example: The *musician* (singular subject) *has* (singular helping verb) *played* this music. Or: The *musicians* (plural subject) *have* (plural helping verb) *played* this music

Directions: Circle the correct form of the verb below

1. The International Slavery Museum [*has, have*] opened in Liverpool.

2. Europeans and Americans [*was, were*] shipping millions of slaves a year before the abolition of slavery.

3. The Portuguese [*was, were*] the first to capture slaves in Africa.

4. The slaves [*was, were*] sold as cheap labor on plantations.

5. The port of Liverpool [*was, were*] especially active in the slave trade.

6. Captains would [*crowd, crowds*] many slaves on their ships.

7. Slaves would [*live, lives*] about seven years on a plantation.

8. A famous slave revolt [*is, are*] the one on the ship *La Amistad*.

9. International law [*bans, ban*] slavery today, but it still exists.

10. Women and children still [*suffers, suffer*] under horrible working conditions.

ECHO READING

Directions: When you read, you should make breaks, and sometimes pauses, between groups of words. As your teacher reads each phrase, repeat aloud what is read and put a slash or line after that phrase. Then read the whole sentence aloud as a class. Do the first paragraph together as a class, and then do the second one on your own. The first sentence has been marked for you.

Slave traders and merchants / traded among Africa, / the Americas, / and Europe. Sometimes they simply kidnapped Africans, but they also traded cloth, guns, and beads for slaves. Then they shipped the slaves to the Americas and sold them as cheap labor on plantations. When the ships returned to Europe with sugar, cotton, coffee, and tobacco, merchants sold them and grew wealthy.

Slaves often resisted their situation. One uprising in Haiti led to its becoming an independent country. In one famous revolt in 1839, slaves took control of the ship *La Amistad*. They killed the captain, but they faced murder charges in the U.S. However, a court ruled in their favor and they returned home

What's Happening
IN THE WORLD?

BY LAWRENCE GABLE
© 2014 *What's Happening Publications*

SUBJECT: HUMAN RIGHTS and HISTORY

The International Slavery Museum Opens in England

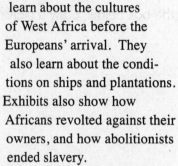

1 For four hundred years Europeans and Americans bought and sold Africans as slaves. They shipped 12 million slaves across the Atlantic. Britain abolished slavery in 1807, so 2007 was the 200th anniversary. As part of the bicentennial events, the International Slavery Museum opened in Liverpool.

2 Portugal and Spain were the first European nations to take Africans as slaves. Britain's first significant slave trading came in 1562. A naval commander captured 300 Africans and shipped them to the Caribbean. He sold them and returned to England with 10,000 pounds of exotic goods. Soon other European nations were trading slaves too.

3 Slave traders and merchants traded among Africa, the Americas and Europe. Sometimes they simply kidnapped Africans, but they also traded cloth, guns and beads for slaves. Then they shipped the slaves to the Americas and sold them as cheap labor on plantations. When the ships returned to Europe with sugar, cotton, coffee and tobacco, merchants sold them and grew wealthy.

4 The port of Liverpool was especially active in the slave trade. The first slave ship left there in 1699. By 1800 the port controlled 80 percent of the British slave trade. By the time Britain abolished slavery, ships from Liverpool had taken 1.5 million Africans to the Americas.

5 Conditions were horrible on those ships. Some were so crowded that slaves had to lie on top of each other during the six-week voyage. Twenty percent of the slaves died on the ships. On plantations they survived an average of only seven years.

6 Liverpool is the home of the world's first International Slavery Museum. There visitors can learn about the cultures of West Africa before the Europeans' arrival. They also learn about the conditions on ships and plantations. Exhibits also show how Africans revolted against their owners, and how abolitionists ended slavery.

7 Slaves often resisted their situation. One uprising in Haiti led to its becoming an independent country. In one famous revolt in 1839, slaves took control of their ship, *La Amistad*. They killed the captain, but then faced murder charges in the U.S. However, a court ruled in their favor and they returned home. In the summer of 2007 a reconstruction of that ship was in Liverpool for the museum's opening. It sailed for another year along the triangular route of old slave ships.

8 The abolition movement in Britain began with the Quakers in 1727. Abolitionists presented the government with their first demand to end slavery in 1783. Abolition finally came in 1807, but Britain waited another 26 years to ban slavery in its colonies.

9 The museum also teaches about slavery today. International law bans slavery, but about 20 million men, women and children still suffer under some form of it. Employers threaten them and strip them of their freedoms. These people work for little or no pay in dehumanizing conditions, just as slaves did in the past.

10 The International Slavery Museum opened on August 23, which is Slavery Remembrance Day around the world. Britain is proud that it abolished slavery earlier than other nations. However, the museum also expresses its sorrow for participating in the awful business of slavery.

QUICK READ/DRAW AND WRITE

Directions: First Reading—As you do your first reading of the article, your teacher will time you for one minute. When time is called, write the number of the paragraph where you stopped. **Paragraph # _____**

In the box below, draw a picture summarizing what you read.

Second Reading—As you do your second reading of the article, your teacher will time you for one minute. When time is called, write the number of the paragraph where you stopped. **Paragraph # _____**

Directions: Now continue reading the rest of the article. Below, write five important words that will help you remember the information from the article.

_____ _____ _____

_____ _____

CLOSE READING ANNOTATION

Third Reading—As you reread each paragraph in the article closely, answer the questions by annotating the text. Each numbered question corresponds to a paragraph in the article where the answer can be found. Write your brief answers in the space below each question.

1. What does the word *bicentennial* mean?

_____

2. Reread paragraph 2. Then explain what caused an increase in slavery.

_____

3. How do you think traders regarded the worth of slaves?

_____

4. Why did Liverpool become so involved in slave trading?

_____

5. Why do you think the survival rate of slaves on plantations was so low?

_____

6. Why do you think Liverpool wanted to build a museum to slavery?

_____

7. What is the significance of the ship *La Amistad*?

_____

8. What is the meaning of *abolitionist* in this context?

_____

9. What are some problems with slavery in the world today?

_____

10. What is the author's purpose for writing paragraph 10?

_____

GRAMMAR GAMES

Directions: Reread the two paragraphs from the article below. Words have been left out from the sentences. Think about the information from the article you have read and fill in words that make sense. The part of speech of each missing word is provided.

The Portuguese were probably the first Europeans to _____
_____(1. verb)

Africans and enslave them. Spain also was an early _____ of
_____(2. noun)

slaves. Britain's first significant slave trading came _____ 1562.
_____(3. preposition)

A naval commander captured 300 Africans and _____ them to the
_____(4. verb)

Caribbean. He sold _____ and returned to England with 10,000
_____(5. pronoun)

pounds of exotic goods. _____ other powerful nations like France,
_____(6. adverb)

Sweden, Denmark, and Holland were trading _____ too.
_____(7. plural noun)

Slave traders and merchants traded among _____ points:
_____(8. adjective)

Africa, the Americas, and Europe. Sometimes _____ simply
_____(9. pronoun)

kidnapped Africans, but they also _____ cloth, guns, and beads
_____(10. verb)

to Africa and traded them _____ slaves. Then they shipped
_____(11. preposition)

the _____ to the Americas and _____ them as cheap
_____(12. plural noun) _____(13. verb)

labor on plantations.

CLOSE READING STRUCTURE

Directions: Understanding the structure of a text is important for two reasons. First, understanding the structure of a selection can help you remember the main idea and important details. Second, most academic writing you will encounter uses text structures to organize ideas.

1. Writers often include a statement in the **introduction** that catches the reader's attention. Then, the writer tells what the article will be about. On the space provided, copy the last sentence of the introduction to the article.

_____

_____

2. On the space below, copy the sentence that best states what the author's **claim, main idea,** or **thesis** is for this article.

_____

_____

3. On the space below, copy a sentence that shows where the author uses **chronological**, or time order, to present the history of slavery.

_____

_____

4. Near the end of an article, the writer often restates the main idea and summarizes the evidence. This is called the **conclusion.** On the space below, write the sentence that best shows where the conclusion to the article begins.

_____

_____

IS THAT A FACT?

Directions: Read the definitions of a fact and an inference below. Then read the paragraph that follows. At the bottom of the page, write an F on the blank if the sentence is a fact. Write an I if the sentence is an inference. Use the following definitions:

Fact—a statement that can be proven true from the paragraph.

Inference—a guess as to what MIGHT be true, based on what you have read and what you already know about the subject.

Now Liverpool has opened the world's first International Slavery Museum. Visitors can learn about the cultures of West Africa before the Europeans' arrival. They also learn about the conditions on the ships and plantations. Exhibits show how Africans revolted against their owners and how abolitionists ended slavery. The new museum teaches about slavery today, too. International law bans slavery, but about 20 million men, women, and children still suffer under some form of it. These people work for little pay in dehumanizing conditions.

_____ **1.** Liverpool wanted to apologize about slavery.

_____ **2.** Most of the slaves taken to Liverpool were captured and sent from West Africa.

_____ **3.** The purpose of the museum is to teach people about slavery.

_____ **4.** Slaves often revolted against slavery.

_____ **5.** There are places where slavery still exists.

_____ **6.** International law has little effect on controlling slavery.

TIC-TAC-TOE SUMMARIZING

When you **summarize** in writing, you present all the key points the author is trying to make.

Directions: Write four sentences to summarize the article about the International Slavery Museum. To help you, there are nine words or phrases in the Tic-Tac-Toe graphic organizer below. To write a sentence, you must use three words or phrases in a row. The row can be horizontal (—), vertical (I), or diagonal (/).

Britain	slave trade	museum
Liverpool	merchants	ships
slaves	abolitionists	government

1. _____

_____

2. _____

_____

3. _____

_____

4. _____

_____

REACTION GUIDE

Directions: Now that you have read and studied information about "The International Slavery Museum Opens in England," reread the statements below, which you responded to before reading the article. Then think about how the author might respond to these statements. If you think the author would agree, put a checkmark on the line before the number. If you think the author would disagree, put an X on the line. Then below the statement, copy the words, phrases, or sentences from the article that provide **evidence** of the views stated by the author. Also note if there is no evidence to support the statement.

_____ **1.** The United States was the primary country to capture slaves.

Evidence: _____

_____

_____

_____ **2.** Slaves were able to survive better on plantations than in their own countries.

Evidence: _____

_____

_____

_____ **3.** Although international law bans slavery, there are still slaves in some countries of the world.

Evidence: _____

_____

_____

TAKE A STAND

Directions: People often have differing feelings or opinions about an issue. When they discuss or argue their opposing views, they are taking part in a debate. A good persuasive argument is based on a claim that is supported by

Facts—statements that can be proven to be true

Statistics—numerical data gotten through research

Examples—instances that support an opinion

You and a partner are going to debate two of your other classmates. The topic you are going to debate is the following:

America was responsible for the rise of slavery in the nineteenth century.

Decide with the other pair who will agree and who will disagree with this statement. Then answer these questions in order to win your debate.

1. What are your two strongest points to persuade the other side? (You can do Internet research to include facts, statistics, and examples.)

    A. _____

    B. _____

2. What might the other side say to argue against point A?

_____

_____

3. What might the other side say to argue against point B?

_____

_____

4. What will you say to prove the other side's arguments are wrong?

_____

_____

WHAT'S THE COMBINATION?

Writing is more interesting when the writer joins, or combines, short sentences. Follow the directions below to learn different ways to combine two sentences.

What to do: You can join two sentences using the words *who* or *which*. The subject, or person doing the action, must be the same for both sentences. In the example below, both subjects are David.

Example: David *loves* to *travel*. David went to Mexico. **New Sentence:** David, *who loves to travel,* went to Mexico.

Grammar Note: If the words you insert are **nonessential** to the main idea of the sentence, put commas (,) around the words. *Nonessential* means that without these words, the main idea of the sentence is the still the same. In the example sentence above, the main idea is that David went to Mexico, and it is the same with or without the added words. If the words you insert are **essential,** or necessary for understanding the sentence, do not put commas around the words.

Example: Students are in Mrs. Garcia's math class. They do not have to take the exam. **New Sentence:** Students who are in Mrs. Garcia's math class do not have to take the exam.

In this example sentence, the information added to the sentence is necessary for understanding the main idea.

Directions: Combine these sentences using the method above and write them in the space provided.

1. England was one of the largest slave traders. It abolished slavery in 1807

   _____

2. The naval commander captured three hundred Africans. The commander returned to England

   _____

3. Slaves were shipped to America. They were sold as cheap labor to plantations

   _____

4. Over 1.5 million slaves were shipped from Liverpool. They were sent to America

   _____

5. People come to the museum. They learn about the cultures of West Africa

   _____

ANALYZING A PROMPT

Directions: Read the writing prompt in the box below. Then follow the directions to learn how to analyze and answer it.

> You are a representative from the International Slavery Museum in England who speaks to groups touring the museum. You have been asked to make a speech explaining the purpose of the museum. Your speech will inform listeners about how and why slavery in some countries today is much like slavery two hundred years ago.

1. A writing prompt begins with some background information known as the **set up.** Underline the sentences that set up this assignment.

2. Use the following **R.A.F.T.** technique to finish analyzing the prompt.

Role: What are you supposed to be to answer it? A student? A politician?

Write what you are here: _____

Audience: To whom are you writing? A friend? A particular group?

Write who it is here: _____

Format: Check to see what type of writing you are doing. Is it an essay, a letter, a speech, a story, a description, an editorial, or a report?

Write what it is here: _____

Task: Another sentence in the prompt will tell you what you must do, or your "task." Question words like **why, how,** or **what** may tell the task.

If the question word is **why,** you will *give the reasons* that something is done.

If the question word is **how,** you will *explain the way* that something is done.

If the question word is **what,** you will *identify the thing* that is done.

Below, copy the sentence or question that describes your task.

_____

_____

ANALYZING INFORMATIONAL TEXT

1. **Informational** articles are written to provide data or descriptions that explain something. Below, name three groups that might be interested in reading this article besides students and teachers.

   a. _____ b. _____ c. _____

2. What main point is the author making in this article?

   _____

   _____

3. Give two of the most important facts you learned in this article.

   a. _____

   b. _____

4. **Domain-specific vocabulary** consists of words used in a specific subject, such as math, science, or social studies. Reread the article and list six domain-specific words used with this subject. After you select the words, write their definitions on the lines provided.

   a. _____ : _____

   b. _____ : _____

   c. _____ : _____

   d. _____ : _____

   e. _____ : _____

   f. _____ : _____

ASSESSMENT

1. Based on the article, support the claim that Liverpool was the right international city to open a slavery museum. Look back through the article. Then, on the space below, cite three pieces of evidence from the article to support this claim.

a. _____

_____

b. _____

_____

c. _____

_____

2. Circle the letters of the conclusions below that are best supported by evidence from the article.

a. Slavery in the Americas was dependent upon European countries.

b. Once slaves made it to the Americas, they lived long lives.

c. Some people in Liverpool became wealthy from trading slaves.

d. Many slaves were treated well once they reached America.

e. There are different forms of slavery alive today.

3. Circle the letter of the paragraph in which the author indicates that the city of Liverpool still feels regret about its part in the slave trade.

a. paragraph 4

b. paragraph 6

c. paragraph 9

d. paragraph 10

4. Circle the letter of the statement below which **best** shows that many of the slaves in the Americas came through the port of Liverpool.

    a. The port of Liverpool was especially active in the slave trade.

    b. Liverpool is the home of the world's first international slavery museum.

    c. The International Slavery Museum opened on August 23, which is Slavery Remembrance Day around the world.

    d. By 1800 the port controlled 80 percent of the British slave trade.

5. A student is writing a script for a short movie about the extent of Europe's involvement in the slave trade to America. Read the paragraphs from the draft of the student's script and complete the task that follows.

The plantations of the southern United States needed cheap labor, and it was the Europeans who realized they could make money by supplying this demand. By shipping and selling slaves, they could buy products in America to take back to Europe and sell for a profit. People in Europe probably didn't care where the stuff they were buying came from.

Many countries took part in the slave trade. Spain and Portugal were the first two to capture slaves and sell them in America. Britain became involved in 1562 when a British naval commander captured 300 Africans. He sold them in the Caribbean and returned to England with 10,000 pounds of goods to sell. I bet at this point many British sailors wished they had gotten into the slave trade. Eventually Liverpool, England controlled almost all of the slave trade from England.

Copy the two sentences below that do not provide specific evidence to support the underlined sentence.

a. _____

_____

_____

b. _____

_____

_____

Name _____ Date _____

ANTICIPATION GUIDE

Directions: Before you read the article "New Jersey Abolishes the Death Penalty," read the statements below. If you agree with a statement, put a checkmark on the line next to it. If you disagree, put an X on the line.

_____ **1.** Putting criminals to death keeps others from murdering.

_____ **2.** Sometimes innocent people in jail are put to death.

_____ **3.** The death penalty is a fair punishment.

Once you have responded to the statements above, write in the section below why you agree or disagree with each statement.

1. _____

_____

2. _____

_____

3. _____

_____

In the box below, draw a picture of what you think this article is about.

PREDICTING ABCs

Directions: The article you are going to read is about the death penalty. See how many boxes you can fill in below with words relating to this topic. For example, put the word *prison* in the P–R box. Try to put at least one word in every box, and then try to write a word for every letter.

A–C	D–F	G–I
J–L	**M–O**	**P–R**
S–T	**U–V**	**W–Z**

TIME MY READ #1

Directions: With a partner, see how many words you can read correctly in 45 seconds. As you read, your partner will put an X through any word read incorrectly on his or her copy. When you are finished, trade your books or papers, and let your partner read while you keep score. Count the total number of words you read correctly. Write this score at the bottom of your page.

penalty execution abolition legislators sentence expensive approve states	8
preferred opinions commission chemicals national appeals chambers court	16
witnesses legislature innocent parole whether prison housing unusual	24
penalty execution abolition legislators sentence expensive approve states	32
preferred opinions commission chemicals national appeals chambers court	40
witnesses legislature innocent parole whether prison housing unusual	48
penalty execution abolition legislators sentence expensive approve states	56
preferred opinions commission chemicals national appeals chambers court	64
witnesses legislature innocent parole whether prison housing unusual	72
penalty execution abolition legislators sentence expensive approve states	80

Number of words read correctly _____

ECHO READING

Directions: When you read, you should make breaks, and sometimes pauses, between groups of words. As your teacher reads each phrase, repeat aloud what is read and put a slash or line after that phrase. Then read the whole sentence aloud as a class. Do the first paragraph together as a class, and then do the second one on your own. The first sentence has been marked for you.

The commissioners looked / into a number / of questions. / One question was whether the death penalty lowers murder rates. It was impossible for them to find a clear answer. On the one hand, national rates have fallen since 1976 when the U. S. Supreme Court allowed the death penalty. On the other hand, in 2005 murder rates were higher in states that have the death penalty. Experts say that many things affect murder rates, including employment rates and gun laws.

The commission also studied costs. It found that the death penalty was a much more expensive sentence than life in prison. In 2006 the state spent $84,474 housing each person on death row. However, among other prisoners it spent only $32,400 per prisoner.

What's Happening

IN THE USA?

BY LAWRENCE GABLE
© 2014 *What's Happening Publications*

SUBJECT: *HUMAN RIGHTS and HISTORY*

1 Each state in the U.S. can decide whether it has the death penalty. New Jersey had it, but had not executed anyone since 1963. In December 2007 its legislature voted to abolish the death penalty. It became the first state in forty years to do that.

2 In 2006 New Jersey formed a Death Penalty Study Commission. The commission's 13 members studied the effects of the death penalty in their state. Then in November 2006 they recommended the abolition of the death penalty.

3 The commissioners looked into a number of questions. One was whether the death penalty lowers murder rates. It was impossible for them to find a clear answer. On the one hand, national rates had fallen since 1976 when the U.S. Supreme Court allowed the death penalty. On the other hand, in 2005 murder rates were higher in states that have the death penalty. Experts also say that many things affect murder rates, including employment rates and gun laws.

4 The commission also studied costs. It found that the death penalty was a more expensive sentence than life in prison. In 2006 the state spent $84,474 housing each person on death row. However, among other prisoners it spent only $32,400 per prisoner. The state also spent millions fighting the many legal appeals that came after a death sentence.

5 New Jersey's commission investigated whether the death penalty serves the victims' families. Because the punishment is extreme, the courts take extra time with the cases. The legal appeals delay the execution. Commissioners felt that this extends the families' suffering.

NEW JERSEY ABOLISHES THE DEATH PENALTY

6 Finally, it looked at the risk of executing an innocent person. Sometimes crime labs or witnesses make mistakes. Even worse, sometimes police lie or lawyers hide information. Years after a trial DNA tests sometimes prove someone's innocence. Since 1973, 154 innocent people on death rows in the U.S. had gone free. The commission recommended sentences of life in prison.

7 Americans' opinions about the death penalty change. A poll in 2006 showed that change. When they had the choice, people preferred a life sentence without parole (48 percent) to the death penalty (47 percent).

8 Most states execute prisoners by lethal injection. The method uses three chemicals and takes only a few minutes. However, some executioners have injected the chemicals incorrectly, so the deaths have been long and painful. After one such case in Florida in 2006 the governor suspended executions.

9 A case before the U.S. Supreme Court in 2008 caused states to delay their executions. Two prisoners in Kentucky felt that lethal injection violates U.S. law, which bans "cruel and unusual" punishment." The case was important because Americans do not approve of old methods like electric chairs, gas chambers and firing squads. The Court, however, ruled in favor of lethal injections.

10 Some states have stopped executions, but not abolished them. Those decisions came from courts or governors. New Jersey's decision was different because it came from legislators. It became the 14th state to abolish the death penalty, and since then four more states have chosen to live without it too.

GET A CONTEXT CLUE

Directions: Below are sentences from "New Jersey Abolishes the Death Penalty." First, read the sentence. Then, look back in the article and reread the paragraph in which the sentence is found. Circle the best answer to each question.

"In 2006 New Jersey formed a Death Penalty Study *Commission*."

1. The word *commission* means

   A. test
   B. group
   C. session
   D. idea

"The legal appeals *delay* the execution."

2. The word *delay* means

   A. to consider
   B. to forbid or restrict
   C. to quicken
   D. to put off for another time

"Most states execute prisoners by *lethal* injection."

3. The word *lethal* means

   A. causing death
   B. preserving life
   C. painful
   D. expensive

"Finally, it looked at the *risk* of executing an innocent person."

4. The word *risk* means

   A. a danger
   B. a reason
   C. a method or technique
   D. a fairness

"A *poll* in 2006 showed that change."

5. The word *poll* means

   A. a discussion
   B. a new law
   C. a survey
   D. a newspaper

"The Court, however, ruled *in favor of* lethal injections."

6. The phrase *in favor of* means

   A. in support of
   B. in reaction to
   C. about
   D. against

WORD MAP

Directions: Follow the directions to map the word in the box below.

> ### abolish

List two more words that mean the same.

end

List two more examples of something to abolish.

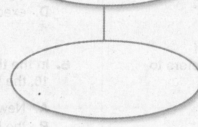
teaching religion in school

List two more words that mean the opposite.

uphold

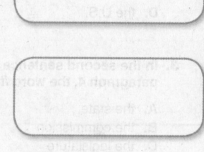

Draw a picture below to help you remember the meaning.

Write a definition IN YOUR OWN WORDS.

LOOK WHO'S TALKING

Directions: Below are sentences that relate to "New Jersey Abolishes the Death Penalty." Look back in the article and reread the paragraph in which you find the reference. Circle the best answer to each question.

1. **In the last sentence of paragraph 1, the word *it* best refers to**

   A. the death penalty
   B. the U.S.
   C. New Jersey
   D. the legislature

2. **In the second sentence of paragraph 2, the word *their* refers to**

   A. the commission
   B. the legislature
   C. the state of New Jersey
   D. the U.S.

3. **In the second sentence of paragraph 4, the word *it* refers to**

   A. the state
   B. the commission
   C. the legislature
   D. the U.S.

4. **In the second sentence of paragraph 8, the word *method* refers to**

   A. the lethal injection
   B. the chemicals
   C. the means of injecting
   D. life sentence without parole

5. **In the first sentence of paragraph 10, the word *them* refers to**

   A. states
   B. injections
   C. legislators
   D. executions

6. **In the third sentence of paragraph 10, the word *it* refers to**

   A. New Jersey
   B. the legislature
   C. the prisons
   D. the decision

HOW'S IT ORGANIZED?

This article is organized by comparison and contrast. This means some things are *compared,* which is to show how they are like one another, and some are *contrasted,* which is to show how they are different from one another.

Directions: Answer these questions in the spaces at the bottom.

1. How did the actions of New Jersey in 2007 contrast with those of all other states for forty years?

2. What are two things about the death penalty that the commission compared?

3. How do the costs of the death penalty and life in prison compare?

4. In 2006, how did Americans' opinions about the death penalty compare with their opinions about life in prison?

5. How did the Supreme Court ruling about lethal injections contrast with the feelings of two prisoners in Kentucky?

6. How did New Jersey's decision contrast with the way other states have halted executions?

Answers:

1.	
2.	
3.	
4.	
5.	
6.	

IS THAT A FACT?

Directions: Read the definitions of a fact and an inference below. Then read the paragraph that follows. At the bottom of the page, write an F on the blank if the sentence is a fact. Write an I if the sentence is an inference. Use the following definitions:

Fact—a statement that can be proven true from the paragraph

Inference—a guess as to what MIGHT be true, based on what you have read and what you already know about the subject

> Americans' opinions about the death penalty are changing. A poll in 2006 showed that change. When they had the choice, people preferred a life sentence without parole (48 percent) to the death penalty (47 percent). Most states execute prisoners by lethal injection. This method uses three chemicals and takes only a few minutes. However, some executioners have injected the chemicals incorrectly, so the deaths were long and painful.

_____ **1.** Americans are divided in their opinions about the death penalty.

_____ **2.** The way prisoners are executed has had some problems.

_____ **3.** The use of chemicals for executions is efficient most of the time.

_____ **4.** Most states use the method of lethal injection.

_____ **5.** Most states no longer use the electric chair for executions.

Name _____ Date _____

MAKE A SPACE

Directions: Below are sentences that are missing punctuation and capitalization. First draw slash marks (/) between the words. Then rewrite each sentence in the space below it, filling in the missing punctuation and capitalization.

Example:

americans / opinions / are / changing / about / the / death / penalty

Americans' opinions are changing about the death penalty.

1. moststatesexecuteprisonersbylethalinjection

   _____

   _____

2. becausethepunishmentisextremecourtstakemoretimewiththecase

   _____

   _____

3. americansdonotapproveoftheoldmethodslikeelectricchairsorgaschambers

   _____

   _____

4. murderrateswerehigherinstatesthathadthedeathpenalty

   _____

   _____

TIME MY READ #2

Directions: With a partner, see how many words you can read correctly in 45 seconds. As you read, your partner will put an X through any word read incorrectly on his or her copy. When you are finished, trade your books or papers, and let your partner read while you keep score. Count the total number of words you read correctly. Write this score at the bottom of your page.

penalty execution abolition legislators sentence expensive approve states	8
preferred opinions commission chemicals national appeals chambers court	16
witnesses legislature innocent parole whether prison housing unusual	24
penalty execution abolition legislators sentence expensive approve states	32
preferred opinions commission chemicals national appeals chambers court	40
witnesses legislature innocent parole whether prison housing unusual	48
penalty execution abolition legislators sentence expensive approve states	56
preferred opinions commission chemicals national appeals chambers court	64
witnesses legislature innocent parole whether prison housing unusual	72
penalty execution abolition legislators sentence expensive approve states	80

Number of words read correctly _____

Is the score higher than it was in Time My Read #1? _____

WORD PARTS

Directions: A suffix can be added to the end of a base word to change the way a word is used. Suffixes do this in many ways. The suffix *-ing* is most often used to form part of a **compound verb** showing action. For example, in the sentence "Juan is flying to Mexico today," *-ing* changes the verb *fly* to *flying*, which is part of the compound verb *is flying*.

The suffix *-ing* can also be added to the end of a **verb** to make a **noun**, or thing. For example, by adding *-ing* to the **verb** *build*, you get the noun *building*. Sometimes a word ending in *-ing* acts like an **adjective** by describing something. For example, "My mother is at her *sewing* machine." The word *sewing* tells us what kind of machine.

The following sentences are from the article on the death penalty. Write a definition of the words ending in *-ing* on the line below the sentence. You can look in a dictionary, check the Internet, or ask a partner if you don't know.

1. "Experts also say that many things affect murder rates, **including** employment rates and gun laws."

    Definition: _____

2. "In 2006 the state spent $84,474 **housing** each person on death row."

    Definition: _____

3. "Commissioners felt that this extends the families' **suffering**."

    Definition: _____

4. "Finally, it looked at the risk of **executing** an innocent person."

    Definition: _____

5. "The case was important because Americans do not approve of old methods like electric chairs, gas chambers, and **firing** squads."

    Definition: _____

SUMMARIZING ABCs

Directions: Now that you've read the article about the death penalty, see how many words you about the topic you can write in the boxes below.

A–C	D–F	G–I
J–L	M–O	P–R
S–T	U–V	W–Z

SENTENCE SUMMARIES

Directions: Below are four key words or phrases from the article "New Jersey Abolishes the Death Penalty." Your job is to summarize, or restate, what you've learned in this article by using these four words or phrases in two sentences. Then, as a challenge, try to use all four words or phrases in one sentence to summarize the article.

Key Words or Phrases

death penalty   U.S. Supreme Court

cruel and unusual punishment   abolish

Sentence Summaries:

1. _____

   _____

2. _____

   _____

Challenge Summary: (all four words or phrases in one sentence!)

1. _____

   _____

REACTION GUIDE

Directions: Now that you have read and studied information about "New Jersey Abolishes the Death Penalty," reread the statements below, which you responded to before reading the article. Then think about how the author might respond to these statements. If you think the author would agree, put a checkmark on the line before the number. If you think the author would disagree, put an X on the line. Then below the statement, copy the words, phrases, or sentences from the article that provide **evidence** of the views stated by the author. Also note if there is no evidence to support the statement.

_____ **1.** Putting criminals to death keeps others from murdering.

Evidence: _____

_____

_____

_____ **2.** Sometimes innocent people in jail are put to death.

Evidence: _____

_____

_____

_____ **3.** The death penalty is a fair punishment.

Evidence: _____

_____

_____

Name _____ Date _____

TAKE A STAND

Directions: People often have differing feelings or opinions about an issue. When they discuss or argue their opposing views, they are taking part in a debate. A good persuasive argument is based on a claim that is supported by

Facts—statements that can be proven to be true

Statistics—numerical data gotten through research

Examples—instances that support an opinion

You and a partner are going to debate two of your other classmates. The topic you are going to debate is the following:

The death penalty is a fair punishment.

Decide with the other pair who will agree and who will disagree with this statement. Then answer these questions in order to win your debate.

1. What are your two strongest points to persuade the other side? (You can do Internet research to include facts, statistics, and examples.)

   A. _____

   B. _____

2. What might the other side say to argue against point A?

   _____

   _____

3. What might the other side say to argue against point B?

   _____

   _____

4. What will you say to prove the other side's arguments are wrong?

   _____

   _____

   _____

Name _____ Date _____

Comprehension: Answer the questions about the following passage.

Sometimes crime labs or witnesses make mistakes. Even worse, sometimes police lie or lawyers hide information. Americans' opinions about the death penalty are divided. Some states have stopped executions, but not abolished them. Those decisions came from courts or governors. New Jersey is different because the change came from legislators. They decided that the death penalty does not serve the people well, so they made their state the 14th in the nation without it.

1. What makes New Jersey's actions different?

_____

_____

2. Why would people object to the death penalty?

_____

_____

3. What do you think the author is saying by writing this article?

_____

_____

Fluency: The words in the two sentences below are all connected. The sentences are also missing punctuation and capitalization. Draw slash marks (/) between the words. Then rewrite each sentence by filling in the punctuation and capitalization.

1. americansopinionsaboutthedeathpenaltychange

_____

2. in2006newjerseyformedacommissiontostudydeathpenaltycosts

_____

_____

Fluency: Read the three sentences below. Imagine where you would pause within each sentence as you read it aloud. Draw a slash (/) mark between the phrases where you would pause. The first slash is done.

3. The commissioners / looked into a number of questions.

4. Each state in the U.S. can decide whether or not it has a death penalty.

5. Finally, it looked at the risk of executing an innocent person.

Vocabulary: Based on what you have learned in this lesson, match the following words with their definitions. Write the letter of the definition on the blank in front of the word it defines.

1. _____ housing   **A.** in pain

2. _____ abolish   **B.** providing a place to live

3. _____ delay   **C.** a group organized to do something

4. _____ in favor of   **D.** putting someone to death

5. _____ executing   **E.** survey

6. _____ lethal   **F.** to stop permanently

7. _____ poll   **G.** danger

8. _____ suffering   **H.** causing death

9. _____ commission   **I.** to put off for another time

10. _____ risk   **J.** for; in support of

Name _____ Date _____

ANTICIPATION GUIDE

Directions: Before you read the article "Students Were Central Figures in Civil Rights Era," read the statements below. If you agree with a statement, put a checkmark on the line next to it. If you disagree, put an X on the line.

_____ **1.** Schools are not really integrated despite the fact that there are laws to that effect.

_____ **2.** Schools have always been allowed to have non-white students.

_____ **3.** The people responsible for helping integrate schools have been recognized for their efforts.

Once you have responded to the statements above, write in the section below why you agree or disagree with each statement.

1. _____

_____

2. _____

_____

3. _____

_____

In the box below, draw a picture of what you think this article is about.

PREDICTING ABCs

Directions: The article you are going to read is about civil rights. See how many boxes you can fill in below with words relating to this topic. For example, put the word *integration* in the G–I box. Put at least one word in every box, and then try to write a word for every letter.

A–C	D–F	G–I

J–L	M–O	P–R

S–T	U–V	W–Z

LANGUAGE MINI-LESSON

Remember that a **pronoun** is a word that takes the place of a **noun** or another **pronoun**. Pronouns change their forms. In the following statement, the pronoun *he* is used as a subject of a sentence: **He** and Bob talked to Tom.

When a pronoun comes after the verb, it usually changes to the objective. For example: He and Bob talked to **him**. In this case, *him* replaces *Tom*.

A pronoun also changes when it shows ownership, or possession. For example: He and Bob talked to him about **his** skateboard.

Remember also that pronouns can be singular (one person or thing) or plural (more than one). Study the charts below.

Singular	Subject	Object	Possessive
First person	I	me	my, mine
Second person	you	you	your, yours
Third person	he, she, it	him, her, it	his, her, hers, its

Plural	Subject	Object	Possessive
First person	we	us	our, ours
Second person	you	you	your, yours
Third person	they	them	their, theirs

Directions: Replace the **bold nouns** in the paragraph below with the correct pronouns.

Tom was talking to Sara about segregation. (**Tom**) _____ did not know that
segregation _____ was (**Sara's**) _____ essay topic. Tom said that he would
like to make it (**Tom's**) _____ topic. Sara laughed and said, "But that's (**my topic**)
_____." Tom said, "Well, it could be (**Tom and Sara's**) _____ topic." (**Sara
and Tom**) _____ laughed. Sara said, "Okay, let's make (**segregation**) _____
(**Sara and Tom's**) _____ essay topic."

ECHO READING

Directions: When you read, you should make breaks, and sometimes pauses, between groups of words. As your teacher reads each phrase, repeat aloud what is read and put a slash or line after that phrase. Then read the whole sentence aloud as a class. Do the first paragraph together as a class, and then do the second one on your own. The first sentence has been marked for you.

Segregation in schools / had been legal / for a long time. / In 1896 the U.S. Supreme Court had said that schools could be "separate but equal." However, it reversed itself in 1954. In a 9–0 vote it said that segregated schools were "inherently unequal." Few people expected a crisis in Little Rock. The city already had integrated its public library, transportation, and police force. In 1955 Little Rock's schools made a plan to integrate Central High two years later.

Help came from several places. President Eisenhower warned the governor not to interfere, and a judge ordered the governor to remove the troops. Then Little Rock police officers took over while angry white citizens continued to protest. On September 23 police quietly helped the students enter the school. When the protestors began to riot, officers escorted the students out again.

What's Happening
IN THE USA?

BY LAWRENCE GABLE
© 2014 What's Happening Publications

SUBJECT: HUMAN RIGHTS and HISTORY

Students Were Central Figures in Civil Rights Era

1   Until 1957 high school students in Little Rock, Arkansas attended segregated schools. Blacks always had attended the all-Black Horace Mann High School. That changed, though, when nine students showed up at Central High School that September. Fifty years later Americans remembered that first great crisis in the integration of public schools.

2   Segregation in schools had been legal for a long time. In 1896 the U.S. Supreme Court had said that schools could be "separate but equal." However, it reversed itself in 1954. In a 9–0 vote it said that segregated schools were "inherently unequal."

3   Few people expected a crisis in Little Rock. The city already had integrated its public library, transportation and police. In 1955 Little Rock's schools made a plan to integrate Central High two years later.

4   The critical events of September 1957 lasted several weeks. The governor was against integration, so he ordered the Arkansas National Guard to go to the school. When the Black students arrived on September 4, the soldiers blocked their entrance.

5   Help then came from several places. President Eisenhower warned the governor not to interfere, and a judge ordered the governor to remove the troops. Then Little Rock police officers took over while angry White citizens continued to protest. On September 23 the police quietly helped the students enter the school. When the protesters began to riot, officers escorted the students out again.

6   President Eisenhower finally used Army troops at Central High. He sent 1,200 troops to keep the peace and protect the students. On

LITTLE ROCK CENTRAL HIGH
1957-2007
COMMEMORATING
50 YEARS OF INTEGRATION

September 25 soldiers with rifles took the nine students into the school.

7   Problems did not end in September. Troops stayed until the end of the school year. Some White students threatened the Blacks and broke into their lockers. Little Rock closed its public high schools for the 1958–59 school year rather than continue to integrate them.

8   Historians believe that television played a large part in integration. Most Americans were uncomfortable watching the hateful protesters. In addition, the dance show "American Bandstand" showed Black and White teenagers dancing together. Americans saw that integration did not have to cause a crisis.

9   The students who integrated Central High became known as the "Little Rock Nine." People have recognized their courage in the fight for civil rights. In 1999 Congress awarded them the Congressional Gold Medal. Now a statue of them stands outside the Arkansas state capitol, and the U.S. Postal Service put them on a stamp.

10   Several events marked the 50th anniversary. In September 2007 the National Park Service opened its new visitor center across the street from Central High. A soldier escorted each of the Little Rock Nine to the ceremony. That evening President Clinton hosted the Little Rock Nine Foundation's annual scholarship ceremony. Finally, the next day a ceremony took place on Central High's front lawn.

11   When schools reopened in 1959, Black students enrolled. Schools across the nation are integrated now too, but they remain unequal in the quality of education. However, fifty years later Americans can look back with pride on the Little Rock Nine and the integration of Central High.

QUICK READ/DRAW AND WRITE

Directions: First Reading—As you do your first reading of the article, your teacher will time you for one minute. When time is called, write the number of the paragraph where you stopped. **Paragraph # _____**

In the box below, draw a picture summarizing what you read.

Second Reading—As you do your second reading of the article, your teacher will time you for one minute. When time is called, write the number of the paragraph where you stopped. **Paragraph # _____**

Directions: Now continue reading the rest of the article. Below, write five important words that will help you remember the information from the article.

_____ _____ _____ _____ _____

CLOSE READING ANNOTATION

Third Reading—As you reread each paragraph in the article closely, answer the questions by annotating the text. Each numbered question corresponds to a paragraph in the article where the answer can be found. Write your brief answers in the space below each question.

1. What situation in Little Rock does the author refer to as a crisis?

_____

2. Why does the Supreme Court use the word *inherently*?

_____

3. What tells you that the city wasn't entirely against integration?

_____

4. How do you know the governor disagreed with the city's school integration?

_____

5. What words or phrases show you the hatred of some white people?

_____

6. What words or phrases show you how tense the situation was?

_____

7. Why might the public high schools have been closed?

_____

8. How did TV alter some of the public's view of events in Little Rock?

_____

9./10. What purpose did the author have for writing paragraphs 9 and 10?

_____

11. Why does the author say that schools "remain unequal in the quality of education"?

_____

GRAMMAR GAMES

Directions: Reread the two paragraphs below. Words have been left out from the sentences. Think about the information from the article you have read and fill in words that make sense. The part of speech of each missing word is provided.

Segregation in schools had been legal for a long _____.
(1. noun)

In 1896 the U.S. Supreme Court had _____ that schools could
(2. verb)

be "separate but equal." However, it _____ itself in 1954 in a
(3. verb)

decision called *Brown v. Board of Education of Topeka.* _____
(4. pronoun)

ruled that segregated public schools violated _____ Fourteenth
(5. article)

Amendment, which guaranteed _____ American "equal
(6. adjective)

protection of the laws." The _____ said in a 9–0 vote that
(7. proper noun)

_____ schools were "inherently unequal."
(8. adjective)

Few people expected Brown to cause a crisis _____ Little
(9. preposition)

Rock. The _____ had already integrated its public library,
(10. noun)

transportation system, _____ police force. In 1955 Little Rock
(11. conjunction)

schools _____ a plan to integrate _____ High School
(12. verb)   (13. proper noun)

two years later.

CLOSE READING STRUCTURE

Directions: Understanding the structure of a text is important for two reasons. First, understanding the structure of a selection can help you remember the main idea and important details. Second, most academic writing you will encounter uses text structures to organize ideas.

1. Writers often include a statement in the **introduction** that catches the reader's attention. Then, the writer tells what the article will be about. On the space provided, copy the last sentence of the introduction of this article.

   _____

   _____

   _____

2. On the space below, copy the sentence that best states what the author's **claim, main idea,** or **thesis** is for this article.

   _____

   _____

   _____

3. On the space below, copy the sentence that shows where the author introduces the other side's **opinions,** or **opposing claims.**

   _____

   _____

   _____

   _____

4. Near the end of an article, a writer often restates the claim and summarizes the evidence. This is called the **conclusion.** On the space below, write the sentence that best shows where the conclusion to the article begins.

   _____

   _____

   _____

IS THAT A FACT?

Directions: Read the definitions of a fact and an inference below. Then read the paragraph that follows. At the bottom of the page, write an F on the blank if the sentence is a fact. Write an I if the sentence is an inference. Use the following definitions:

Fact—a statement that can be proven true from the paragraph.

Inference—a guess as to what MIGHT be true, based on what you have read and what you already know about the subject.

> Historians believe that television played a large part in integration. Most Americans were uncomfortable watching the hateful protestors. In addition, the dance show "American Bandstand" showed black and white teenagers dancing together. Americans saw that integration did not have to cause a crisis. When schools reopened in 1959, black students enrolled. Schools across the nation are integrated now too, but they remain unequal in the quality of education. However, fifty years later, Americans can look back with pride on the Little Rock Nine and the integration of Central High School.

_____ **1.** Television contributed to school integration.

_____ **2.** Central High School became integrated.

_____ **3.** Many people thought what was going on in Little Rock was terrible.

_____ **4.** All schools across the country are now integrated.

_____ **5.** Just because schools are integrated does not mean they are equal.

_____ **6.** The integration of Central High is important to America.

SUMMARIZING ABCs

Directions: Now that you've read the article on the Little Rock Nine, see how many words about civil rights you can write in the boxes below.

A–C	D–F	G–I
J–L	**M–O**	**P–R**
S–T	**U–V**	**W–Z**

REACTION GUIDE

Directions: Now that you have read and studied information about "Students Were Central Figures in Civil Rights Era," reread the statements below, which you responded to before reading the article. Then think about how the author might respond to these statements. If you think the author would agree, put a checkmark on the line before the number. If you think the author would disagree, put an X on the line. Then below the statement, copy the words, phrases, or sentences from the article that provide evidence of the views stated by the author. Also note if there is no evidence to support the statement.

_____ **1.** Schools are not really integrated despite the fact that there are laws to that effect.

Evidence: _____

_____

_____

_____ **2.** Schools have always been allowed to have nonwhite students.

Evidence: _____

_____

_____

_____ **3.** The people responsible for helping integrate schools have been recognized for their efforts.

Evidence: _____

_____

_____

SENTENCE TRANSITIONS

An informational essay answers questions and provides information. Writers use transitional phrases to link ideas. Some transitional words and phrases include *to show, to prove, because, to explain, to verify, due to, instead of, furthermore, as a result,* and *in order to*.

Directions: Complete the following sentences using the phrases given.

Example: The Little Rock Nine incident is celebrated *to show that the country was able to change its views on segregation of schools*.

1. The Little Rock Nine story is important *to explain*

_____

2. President Eisenhower sent Army troops *in order to*

_____

3. The Little Rock Nine integrated Arkansas schools, and *as a result*

_____

4. The TV show "American Bandstand" was important *to show*

_____

5. The soldiers escorted students to class *because*

_____

PICKING UP PUNCTUATION

Remember that in sentences we use a number of different kinds of **end marks,** such as **periods, question marks,** and **exclamation points.** The rules below tell you when to use which end mark.

Periods: Use a period at the end of a sentence that makes a statement. For example: Few expected a crisis in Little Rock.

Use a period at the end of most abbreviations or after an initial. For example: U.S. Army or M.L. King

Use a period at the end of imperative sentences that give a command. For example: Sit down.

Question Marks: Use a question mark at the end of any question. For example: Why did the President send in army troops?

Exclamation Points: Use an exclamation point after a word or sentence that shows great energy or enthusiasm. For example: Wow! That car is amazing!

Directions: Write the correct end marks on the blanks below.

Segregation in schools had been legal for a long time___ In 1896 the U___S___ Supreme Court had said that schools could be "separate but equal___" Would the Supreme Court reverse itself___ Yes___ In 1954 in a 9–0 vote it said that segregated schools were "inherently unequal___"

The governor was against integration, so he ordered the Arkansas National Guard to go to the school. When the black students arrived on Sept___ 4, the soldiers blocked their entrance___ Pres___ Eisenhower warned the governor not to interfere, and a judge ordered the governor to remove the troops___

ANALYZING A PROMPT

Directions: Read the writing prompt in the box below. Then follow the directions to learn how to analyze and answer it.

> You are planning a new visitor center across from Central High School. You know there are people in the city who do not want the center built. You have been asked to write an open letter for the Little Rock city webpage to explain how the visitor center is important to city and national history. What reasons will you give to persuade opponents that the center is important to the history of civil rights and the city?

1. A writing prompt begins with some background information known as the **set up.** Underline the sentences that set up this assignment.

2. Use the following **R.A.F.T.** technique to finish analyzing the prompt.

Role: What are you supposed to be to answer it? A student? A politician?

Write what you are here: _____

Audience: To whom are you writing? A friend? A particular group?

Write who it is here: _____

Format: Check to see what type of writing you are doing. Is it an essay, a letter, a speech, a story, a description, an editorial, or a report?

Write what it is here: _____

Task: Another sentence in the prompt will tell you what you must do, or your "task." Question words like **why, how,** or **what** may tell the task.

If the question word is **why,** you will *give the reasons* that something is done.

If the question word is **how,** you will *explain the way* that something is done.

If the question word is **what,** you will *identify the thing* that is done.

Below, copy the sentence or question that describes your task.

_____

_____

_____

WHAT'S YOUR POINT?

When writing an essay it is important to have a strong claim. A **claim,** or **thesis statement,** states the main point the writer wants to get across. Once the thesis is introduced, the body of the essay should support that thesis with key points that provide evidence.

The information presented in the article "Students Were Central Figures in Civil Rights Era" is about school integration during the civil rights era in Little Rock, Arkansas. The article explains the difficulties faced by people who wanted to create school integration.

Directions: Which of these sentences provides the best **claim** for an essay on this topic? Circle the number of your choice.

a. Little Rock, Arkansas is an important place for the civil rights movement.

b. A visitor center to memorialize Central High School has historical significance.

c. The courage of the Little Rock Nine helped to integrate schools across America.

In the space below, explain what is weak or wrong about the other two statements.

1. _____

_____

_____

2. _____

_____

_____

ASSESSMENT

1. Circle the letters of the conclusions that are best supported by evidence from the article.

   a. Many white people in the 1950s in Little Rock were prejudiced against blacks.

   b. The governor of Arkansas thought integration was a good idea.

   c. President Eisenhower supported the Supreme Court's decision.

   d. Television had a big effect on Americans' beliefs about racism.

   e. There is little prejudice in our schools today.

2. Circle the letter of the sentence that best explains how paragraph 9 is important to the development of the story of the Little Rock Nine.

   a. Paragraph 9 explains how nine people fought for their civil rights.

   b. Paragraph 9 explains when the Little Rock Nine got their name.

   c. Paragraph 9 gives details of how, years later, the original students were rewarded for their courage.

   d. Paragraph 9 explains how the original students got a statue.

3. Circle the letter of the paragraph that best summarizes the events described in the article.

   a. paragraph 1

   b. paragraph 2

   c. paragraph 7

   d. paragraph 9

   e. paragraph 11

4. Look back through the article. Then on the space below, cite three pieces of evidence from the article to support the claim that President Eisenhower was in favor of the integration of Central High School.

a. _____

_____

b. _____

_____

c. _____

_____

5. A student is writing a report about the Little Rock Nine. Read both sources and the directions that follow.

Source 1: www.ninefromlittlerock.com Three years after the U.S. Supreme Court ruled that separate educational facilities are inherently unequal, nine African American students integrated the all-white Central Rock High School. On September 4, 1957, the first day of school at Central High, a white mob gathered in front of the school. Governor Orval Faubus sent the Arkansas National Guard to stop the black students from entering. With the help of police, the students entered the school through a side entrance on September 23, 1957. Martin Luther King sent a telegram to President Eisenhower stating he must take a stand against the injustice. The President sent in the military to protect the students.

Source 2: www.littlerockequality.com On September 4, 1957, Governor Orval Faubus defied the Supreme Court decision to integrate Central HS. He called in the Arkansas National Guard to prevent nine African American students—"The Little Rock Nine"—from entering the building. The governor told the president he would protect the African American teenagers but instead he dismissed the troops, leaving the African American students exposed to an angry white mob. By noon, local police were forced to evacuate the nine students. President Eisenhower sent 101st Airborne Division paratroopers to Little Rock.

The student took notes about the information in the sources. Circle the letter of the note that correctly paraphrases, or restates, the information in both sources.

a. Governor Faubus lied to the president and didn't protect the students.

b. The Supreme Court ruled that "separate but equal" schools were unequal.

c. Martin Luther King told the president he must act.

d. The president sent in the 101st Airborne Division to protect the students.

Human Rights and History

Quarterly Performance Assessment

The Khmer Rouge Faces Charges

What's Happening

IN THE WORLD?

BY LAWRENCE GABLE
© 2014 What's Happening Publications

QUARTERLY ASSESSMENT

The Khmer Rouge Faces Charges

MYANMAR LAOS

THAILAND

VIETNAM

CAMBODIA

Phnom Penh

South China Sea

1 In 2011 Cambodians began paying close attention to an historic trial. The United Nations helped Cambodia force three former leaders to stand trial in a special court. It accused them of participating in a genocide that killed at least two million Cambodians. In August 2014 that court finally handed down its verdict.

2 The three were part of Cambodia's ruling party called the Khmer Rouge. The party grew in the early 1970s. In April 1975 it finally took control of Phnom Penh and set up its government. Its leader was a man named Pol Pot.

3 The Khmer Rouge wanted to change Cambodia. It wanted a society of farmers in which nobody had advantages over others. The government abolished money and took away private property. It closed stores and banned modern technology. It ended public and private transportation, and closed schools, universities and churches. Rather than traditional or western clothes, Cambodians had to wear simple black clothes.

4 The government also emptied the cities. It forced nearly two million people into the countryside to live on large farms. People could not leave the farm and had no rights. If three people gathered and talked, the government arrested them as enemies. It sent many of them to labor camps, and simply executed others.

5 The Khmer Rouge ruled until 1979, and it killed Cambodians constantly. It killed soldiers and employees from the former government. Many Cambodians died after working long hours without enough food and medicine. The government also executed intellectuals and minorities like Vietnamese and Chinese. It took many of those people to prisons, where soldiers interrogated, tortured and executed them.

6 The government also sent people to their deaths in mass graves. Soldiers led hundreds of thousands of people into fields. There they ordered the people to dig large pits. Then soldiers beat many of them to death, or threw them into the pits and buried them alive. The world now calls those mass graves the "killing fields."

7 When Vietnamese forces took over Cambodia in 1979, the Khmer Rouge fell from power. By then, though, it had killed 25 percent of the population. This kind of killing is "genocide." International law defines it as the destruction of an ethnic, racial, religious or national group.

8 The word "genocide" came into use after World War II. In Germany Nazis stood trial for the killing of six million Jews. Unfortunately other genocides have followed. One was in 1994 in Rwanda, where there were mass killings of 800,000 people. Then in July 1995 the army in Bosnia killed more than 8,000 Muslims. Already there has been a genocide in the 21st century. It took place in Sudan, and it resulted in the deaths of at least 500,000 people.

9 The three former officials went on trial in 2011. Pol Pot was not among them, because he died in 1998. The three men, all in their 80s, faced charges of crimes against humanity, war crimes and genocide. They denied all charges. Unfortunately one of these men died in 2013.

10 The court held a series of smaller trials before this one. In 2010 it sent an official of the Khmer Rouge to prison. However, Cambodians and the whole world waited for this verdict so that they could see how one of the deadliest chapters in history would end. When the verdict came three years later, they found out. The court sentenced the two surviving defendants to spend what remains of their lives in prison.

QUARTERLY PERFORMANCE ASSESSMENT

1. Support the claim that the Khmer Rouge wanted to create a country in which nobody had advantages over others. Then on the space below, cite three pieces of evidence from the article to support this claim.

    a. _____

    _____

    b. _____

    _____

    c. _____

    _____

    _____

2. Circle the letters of the conclusions below that are best supported by evidence from the article.

    a. Pol Pot and his government did not value the life of Cambodians.

    b. The Vietnamese ended the rule of Pol Pot.

    c. What the Khmer Rouge did is a rare example of genocide.

    d. Many Cambodians escaped from the horrors of the "killing fields."

    e. Genocide can be defined as the killing of a large number of people.

3. Reread the last paragraph in the article. Explain below how the author completes the ideas with which he began.

    _____

    _____

    _____

    _____

Unit 1: Human Rights and History

4. Circle the letter of the paragraph which illustrates that Pol Pot is not the only person to wage war on a large group of people.

   a. paragraph 5

   b. paragraph 6

   c. paragraph 7

   d. paragraph 8

5. A student has made a plan for research. Read the plan and the directions below.

Research Report Plan

Topic: genocide in modern times

Audience: social studies class

Research Question: Does absolute power by one person
or one group corrupt, or make evil, those in power?

The student needs to find a credible, or trustworthy, source with relevant, or up to date, information. Circle the letter of the source below that would **most likely** have credible and relevant information.

a. www.PolPotshorror.com Put together by the World Justice Association, this site exposes the horrors of the Pol Pot regime as his government killed over a million of the country's citizens.

b. www.whoshouldgovern.com Sponsored by the War Institute, this site explains how some dictators in power should be removed, yet often it is in the world's best interest to let other absolute rulers continue to govern.

c. www.endingmassmurder.com What happens when one person or group of people gain absolute power over others? From World War II to the present day in Sudan, governments with absolute power seek to destroy their enemies. The subject of genocide is explored in this site that looks at dictatorships, corrupt governments, and the genocides some have practiced.

d. www.Bosniasgenocide.com Sponsored by the Muslim Association for Truth, this site provides a detailed report of the killing of thousands of Muslims during the war in Bosnia before the UN stepped in.

Unit 2

Science and Environment

154

Name _____ Date _____

ANTICIPATION GUIDE

Directions: Before you read the article "Plastic Swirls in the Pacific," read the statements below. If you agree with a statement, put a checkmark on the line next to it. If you disagree, put an X on the line.

_____ **1.** The Pacific Ocean is so big that trash is not causing a problem.

_____ **2.** The United States is responsible for keeping oceans clean.

_____ **3.** If the ocean gets polluted, it can eventually be cleaned up.

Once you have responded to the statements above, write in the section below why you agree or disagree with each statement.

1. _____

_____

2. _____

_____

3. _____

_____

In the box below, draw a picture of what you think this article is about.

PREDICTING ABCs

Directions: The article you are going to read is about pollution in the ocean. See how many boxes you can fill in below with words relating to the topic. For example, put the word *oil* in the M–O box. Put at least one word in every box, and then try to write a word for every letter.

A–C	D–F	G–I
J–L	**M–O**	**P–R**
S–T	**U–V**	**W–Z**

TIME MY READ #1

Directions: With a partner, see how many words you can read correctly in 45 seconds. As you read, your partner will put an X through any word read incorrectly on his or her copy. When you are finished, trade your books or papers, and let your partner read while you keep score. Count the total number of words you read correctly. Write this score at the bottom of your page.

remote gyre researchers current rarely mainland swirls circulates	8
creatures hunting surface plastic containers experts seabirds drains	16
unflattering wind floating unusual packaging brittle waters millimeters	24
remote gyre researchers current rarely mainland swirls circulates	32
creatures hunting surface plastic containers experts seabirds drains	40
unflattering wind floating unusual packaging brittle waters millimeters	48
remote gyre researchers current rarely mainland swirls circulates	56
creatures hunting surface plastic containers experts seabirds drains	64
unflattering wind floating unusual packaging brittle waters millimeters	72
remote gyre researchers current rarely mainland swirls circulates	80

Number of words read correctly _____

ECHO READING

Directions: When you read, you should make breaks, and sometimes pauses, between groups of words. As your teacher reads each phrase, repeat aloud what is read and put a slash or line after that phrase. Then read the whole sentence aloud as a class. Do the first paragraph together as a class, and then do the second one on your own. The first sentence has been marked for you.

The area lies / about 1,000 miles west / of the U.S. mainland / and 1,000 miles north / of Hawaii. / It is called the North Pacific Gyre. Now it also has unflattering names like "the garbage patch" and "the plastic soup." It forms the largest mass of trash on Earth. It stretches thousands of miles and 100 feet deep.

A sailor named Charles Moore discovered it in 1997. On his return from Hawaii to California he sailed through the North Pacific Gyre. Sailors rarely go there because for hundreds of miles there is no wind and the ocean's surface is smooth. It took him a week to cross it, and trash surrounded him the entire time.

Most of what floats in the gyre is plastic. About one-fifth of it comes from ships and oil platforms. The rest comes from land, where it goes from storm drains into streams, and then into the ocean. The water's circulating motion finally pulls the trash from the coasts of Asia and North America into the "plastic soup."

What's Happening
IN THE WORLD?

BY LAWRENCE GABLE
© 2014 What's Happening Publications

SUBJECT: SCIENCE and ENVIRONMENT

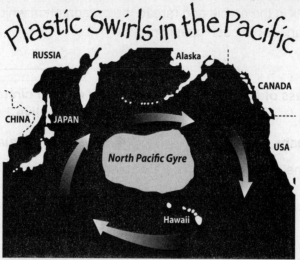

Plastic Swirls in the Pacific

RUSSIA — Alaska — CANADA — CHINA — JAPAN — North Pacific Gyre — USA — Hawaii

1 Plastic became popular in the 1950s. Since then a lot of plastic trash has gone into the oceans. In 1997 a sailor sailed through a remote part of the Pacific Ocean and found it covered with trash. At the time he said the plastic covered an area the size of Texas. Now it has grown to the size of Australia.

2 The area lies about 1,000 miles west of the U.S. mainland and 1,000 miles north of Hawaii. It is called the North Pacific Gyre. Now it also has unflattering names like "the garbage patch" and "the plastic soup." It forms the largest mass of trash on Earth. It stretches thousands of miles and 100 feet deep.

3 A sailor named Charles Moore discovered it. On his return from Hawaii to California he sailed through the North Pacific Gyre. Sailors rarely go there because for hundreds of miles there is no wind and the ocean's surface is smooth. It took him a week to cross it, and trash surrounded him the entire time.

4 Four Pacific currents bring the trash to that spot. They move in a clockwise pattern near Japan, up toward Alaska, down along North America, and south of Hawaii. The currents push two masses of water together, and where they meet the water circulates and sinks. That is why the area is called a gyre. Water swirls like water in a toilet that will not flush, and anything that floats stays on the surface.

5 Researchers have found all kinds of plastic things there. They find many plastic bags, bottles and containers. Large numbers of unusual things are floating there too, like umbrella handles, huge fishing nets, toolboxes and orange traffic cones.

6 Under normal circumstances the things that float are alive. The small animal life that other creatures feed on makes the gyre a fine hunting ground for seabirds. However, researchers have found almost none of those small floating animals.

7 Birds and fish mistake plastic for food. Experts estimate that it kills more than a million seabirds and 100,000 marine mammals every year. When researchers have opened up dead seabirds in the Pacific, they have found cigarette lighters, bottle caps and toothbrushes in their stomachs.

8 Most of what floats in the gyre is plastic. About one-fifth of it comes from ships and oil platforms. The rest comes from land, where it goes from storm drains into streams, and then into the ocean. The water's circulating motion finally pulls the trash from the coasts of Asia and North America into the "plastic soup."

9 The trash in the gyre does not form a solid mass. Much of it floats, but even more hangs suspended in the water. Sunlight makes plastic brittle, so it breaks into tiny pieces and even into a plastic dust. Researchers from the United Nations estimate that there are a million pieces of plastic per square mile. Most of them are only a few millimeters across.

10 About 90 percent of all trash floating in the oceans is plastic. Cleaning up the gyre will be nearly impossible. It lies in international waters, so no single country will clean it up. For now people must handle plastic objects more responsibly. They can use less plastic packaging, recycle more plastic, and dispose of it properly so that it never reaches the ocean.

GET A CONTEXT CLUE

Directions: Below are sentences from "Plastic Swirls in the Pacific." First, read the sentence. Then, look back in the article and reread the paragraph in which the sentence is found. Circle the best answer to each question.

"It forms the largest *mass* of trash on Earth."

1. The word *mass* means

    A. collection of something
    B. pollution
    C. picture
    D. island

"Four Pacific *currents* bring the trash to that spot."

2. The word *current* is best described as

    A. the movement of water
    B. a bolt of electricity
    C. occurring at this moment
    D. electricity

"*Researchers* have found all sorts of plastic things there."

3. The word *researchers* means

    A. people in government
    B. people trying to gather information
    C. polluters
    D. people involved in shipping

"Under normal *circumstances* the things that float are alive."

4. The word *circumstances* means

    A. places
    B. oceans
    C. events or conditions
    D. problems

"Sunlight makes plastic *brittle*, so it breaks into tiny pieces and even into a plastic dust."

5. The word *brittle* means

    A. thick
    B. strong
    C. breaks easily
    D. sticky

"For now people must handle plastic objects more *responsibly*."

6. The word *responsibly* is related to

    A. quickly
    B. with good judgment; reliably
    C. easily
    D. badly

WORD MAP

Directions: Follow the directions to map the word in the box below.

pollution

List two more words that mean the same.

garbage

List two more examples of pollution.

smog

List two more words that mean the opposite.

clean air

Draw a picture below to help you remember the meaning.

Write a definition IN YOUR OWN WORDS.

LOOK WHO'S TALKING

Directions: Below are sentences that relate to "Plastic Swirls in the Pacific." Look back in the article and reread the paragraph in which you find the reference. Circle the best answer to each question.

1. In the third sentence of paragraph 1, the word *it* best refers to

    A. the plastic
    B. the ocean
    C. a remote area
    D. the trash

2. In the last sentence of paragraph 3, the first *it* refers to

    A. the area
    B. the ocean
    C. the North Pacific gyre
    D. the amount of time he took

3. In the third sentence of paragraph 4, the word *they* refers to

    A. the currents
    B. the trash
    C. the oceans
    D. the gyre

4. In the last sentence of paragraph 7, the word *they* refers to

    A. the plastic
    B. the seabirds
    C. the countries
    D. the researchers

5. In the third sentence in paragraph 9, the word *it* refers to

    A. the plastic
    B. the mass
    C. the ocean
    D. the estimate

6. In the last sentence of paragraph 10, the word *they* refers to

    A. the people
    B. the countries
    C. the plastic
    D. the gyre

HOW'S IT ORGANIZED?

This article is organized as a **problem that needs solving.**

Directions: Answer these questions in the spaces at the bottom.

1. What is the problem?

2. Who discovered the problem of the gyre?

3. What is causing the problem in the Pacific Ocean?

4. What are the effects of the problem?

5. Is anyone trying to solve the problem? If yes, who?

6. Why is the North Pacific Gyre a challenging problem to solve?

7. What solutions are recommended?

Answers:

1.	
2.	
3.	
4.	
5.	
6.	
7.	

*On a separate sheet of paper, write a summary of what your notes say about the problems with plastic in the ocean.

IS THAT A FACT?

Directions: Read the definitions of a fact and an inference below. Then read the paragraph that follows. At the bottom of the page, write an F on the blank if a sentence is a fact or an I if it is an inference. Use the following definitions:

Fact—a statement that can be proven true from the paragraph

Inference—a guess as to what MIGHT be true, based on what you have read and what you already know about the subject

> Most of what floats in the gyre is plastic. About one-fifth of it comes from ships and oil platforms. The rest comes from land, where it goes from storm drains into streams, and then into the ocean. The water's circulating motion finally pulls the trash from the coasts of Asia and North America into the "plastic soup."

_____ **1.** Two of the largest polluters are Asia and North America.

_____ **2.** The ocean's current pulls the trash out to sea.

_____ **3.** People tend to be careless about how they dispose of trash.

_____ **4.** Most of the pollution comes from plastic.

_____ **5.** Owners of some ships and oil platforms don't care about pollution.

_____ **6.** Since so many people drink water out of plastic bottles, the North Pacific Gyre will only grow larger.

MAKE A SPACE

Directions: Below are sentences that are missing punctuation and capitalization. First, draw slash marks (/) between the words. Then, rewrite each sentence in the space below it, filling in the missing punctuation and capitalization.

An example is provided:

> eleven / years / ago / a / sailor / sailed / through / a / remote / part / of / the /
>
> pacific / ocean
>
> Eleven years ago a sailor sailed through a remote part of the
>
> Pacific Ocean.

1. fourpacificcurrentsbringthetrashtothatspot

_____

_____

2. researchershavefoundallkindsofplasticthingsdownthere

_____

_____

3. thewaterscirculatingmotionfinallypullsthetrashfromthecoastsofasia
andnorthamericaintotheplasticsoup

_____

_____

4. about90percentofthetrashfloatingintheoceanisplastic

_____

_____

Name _____ Date _____

TIME MY READ #2

Directions: With a partner, see how many words you can read correctly in 45 seconds. As you read, your partner will put an X through any word read incorrectly on his or her copy. When you are finished, trade your books or papers, and let your partner read while you keep score. Count the total number of words you read correctly. Write this score at the bottom of your page.

remote gyre researchers current rarely mainland swirls circulates	8
creatures hunting surface plastic containers experts seabirds drains	16
unflattering wind floating unusual packaging brittle waters millimeters	24
remote gyre researchers current rarely mainland swirls circulates	32
creatures hunting surface plastic containers experts seabirds drains	40
unflattering wind floating unusual packaging brittle waters millimeters	48
remote gyre researchers current rarely mainland swirls circulates	56
creatures hunting surface plastic containers experts seabirds drains	64
unflattering wind floating unusual packaging brittle waters millimeters	72
remote gyre researchers current rarely mainland swirls circulates	80

Number of words read correctly _____

Is the score higher than it was in Time My Read #1? _____

Name _____ Date _____

WORD PARTS

Directions: The Latin word *circulus* means "circle." Read the definitions below. Then draw a picture of what each word means.

1. circle—(noun) a ring, a continuous curve that ends where it begins

2. circus—(noun) a group of performers with clowns and animals who travel and usually perform under a large round tent

3. circulate—(verb) to move from place to place or from person to person

4. circumference—(noun) the distance around something

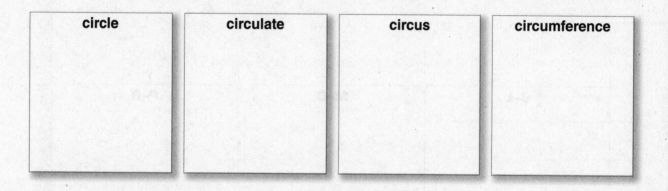

| circle | circulate | circus | circumference |

Directions: The Latin word *marinus* means "sea" or "ocean." Read the sentences below. Then write a definition for each **bold** word.

1. The **marines** normally travel on ships to the places where they will fight for their country.

_____

2. The city of Norfolk is a large port with many **maritime** businesses such as shipbuilders, fish markets, sailmakers, and seafood restaurants.

_____

3. There were many expensive boats and yachts docked in the **marina**.

_____

4. Some examples of **marine** animals are fish, seals, and whales.

_____

SUMMARIZING ABCs

Directions: Now that you've read the article about the trash in the Pacific Ocean, see how many words you can write about pollution in the boxes below.

A–C	D–F	G–I
J–L	**M–O**	**P–R**
S–T	**U–V**	**W–Z**

SENTENCE SUMMARIES

Directions: Below are four key words from the article "Plastic Swirls in the Pacific." Your job is to summarize, or restate, what you've learned in this article by using these four words in two sentences. Then, as a challenge, try to use all four words in one sentence to restate the article.

Key Words

gyre   currents

international   responsibility

Sentence Summaries:

1. _____

_____

2. _____

_____

Challenge Summary (all four words in one sentence!):

1. _____

_____

_____

REACTION GUIDE

Directions: Now that you have read and studied information about "Plastic Swirls in the Pacific," reread the statements below, which you responded to before reading the article. Then think about how the author might respond to these statements. If you think the author would agree, put a checkmark on the line before the number. If you think the author would disagree, put an X on the line. Then below the statement, copy the words, phrases, or sentences from the article that provide **evidence** of the views stated by the author. Also note if there is no evidence to support the statement.

_____ **1.** The Pacific Ocean is so big that trash is not causing a problem.

Evidence: _____

_____

_____

_____ **2.** The United States is responsible for keeping oceans clean.

Evidence: _____

_____

_____

_____ **3.** If the ocean gets polluted, it can eventually be cleaned up.

Evidence: _____

_____

_____

TAKE A STAND

Directions: People often have differing feelings or opinions about an issue. When they discuss or argue their opposing views, they are taking part in a debate. A good persuasive argument is based on a claim that is supported by

Facts—statements that can be proven to be true

Statistics—numerical data gotten through research

Examples—instances that support an opinion

You and a partner are going to debate two of your other classmates. The topic you are going to debate is the following:

The huge plastic gyre in the Pacific is everyone's problem.

Decide with the other pair who will agree and who will disagree with this statement. Then answer these questions in order to win your debate.

1. What are your two strongest points to persuade the other side? (You can do Internet research to include facts, statistics, and examples.)

  A. _____

  B. _____

2. What might the other side say to argue against point A?

_____

_____

3. What might the other side say to argue against point B?

_____

_____

4. What will you say to prove the other side's arguments are wrong?

_____

_____

_____

ASSESSMENT

Comprehension: Answer the questions about the following passage.

The area lies about 1,000 miles west of the U.S. mainland and 1,000 miles north of Hawaii. It is called the North Pacific Gyre. Now it also has unflattering names like "the garbage patch" and "the plastic soup." It forms the largest mass of trash on Earth. It stretches thousands of miles and is 100 feet deep. Most of what floats in the gyre is plastic. About one-fifth of it comes from ships and oil platforms. The rest comes from land, where it goes from storm drains into streams, and then into the ocean. The water's circulating motion finally pulls the trash from the coasts of Asia and North America.

1. What are two causes of the gyre?

_____

_____

2. Why might the gyre be a tremendous problem?

_____

_____

3. What was the author's purpose for writing about the gyre?

_____

_____

Fluency: The words in the two sentences below are all connected. The sentences are also missing punctuation and capitalization. Draw slash marks (/) between the words. Then rewrite each sentence by filling in the punctuation and capitalization.

1. thegyreresultsfromfourcurrentsthatpullthetrashtooneplace

_____

2. thegyreisininternationalwatersandnocountryacceptsresponsibility

_____

_____

Fluency: Read the three sentences below. Imagine where you would pause within each sentence as you read it aloud. Draw a slash (/) mark between the phrases where you would pause. The first slash is done.

3. Birds and fish / mistake the plastic for food.

4. It took him a week to cross the area, and the entire time he was surrounded by trash.

5. Although much of it floats, even more hangs suspended in the water.

Vocabulary: Based on what you have learned in this lesson, match the following words with their definitions. Write the letter of the definition on the blank in front of the word it defines.

1. _____ circulate   **A.** the distance around something

2. _____ brittle   **B.** soldiers who travel aboard ships

3. _____ marina   **C.** harmful stuff put in the environment

4. _____ pollution   **D.** a ring or continuous curve

5. _____ circumference   **E.** breaks easily

6. _____ responsibly   **F.** having to do with the ocean or sea

7. _____ current   **G.** to move in a circle from one place to another

8. _____ circle   **H.** a place to dock or store ships

9. _____ maritime   **I.** the movement of water

10. _____ marines   **J.** with good judgment; reliably

Name _____ Date _____

ANTICIPATION GUIDE

Directions: Before you read the article "Japan Struggles with its Nuclear Future," read the statements below. If you agree with a statement, put a checkmark on the line next to it. If you disagree, put an X on the line.

_____ **1.** Nuclear energy is essential to the world's future.

_____ **2.** Although nuclear energy has risks, it is worth them.

_____ **3.** Each country's government is responsible for keeping its citizens safe.

Once you have responded to the statements above, write in the section below why you agree or disagree with each statement.

1. _____

_____

2. _____

_____

3. _____

_____

In the box below, draw a picture of what you think this article is about.

WORDSTORM

Directions: It's good to know more than just the dictionary definition of a word. Completing a wordstorm lets you write down information to help you understand what a word means, how it's related to other words, and how to use it in different ways.

What is the word?

energy

Here is the sentence from the text in which the word is used:

"Japan uses large amounts of energy to support its industries and modern lifestyle."

What are some other words or phrases that mean the same thing?

_____ _____ _____

What are three things you know about energy?

1. _____ 2. _____ 3. _____

Name three people other than teachers who would likely use this word.

1. _____ 2. _____ 3. _____

Draw a picture below that reminds you of the word *energy*.

LANGUAGE MINI-LESSON

You probably remember that a **noun** is any person, place, or thing in a sentence. We often use a **pronoun** in place of a noun to make language more interesting. Pronouns are words like *I*, *them*, *our*, *who*, *we*, *it*, *themselves*, and *this*.

Directions: Write five more pronouns on the lines below.

_____   _____   _____   _____   _____

The **subject** of any sentence is made up of the words that tell what the sentence is about. A **pronoun** that stands for a subject is said to be in the **nominative case**.

Directions: In each of the sentences below, draw a line from the **pronoun** (in **bold**) back to the word or words it replaces. The first one has been done for you.

1. In March 2011 an earthquake and a tsunami struck Japan. **They** took lives and did tremendous damage.

2. On March 11, 2011, an earthquake struck Japan's northeastern coast. **It** was the largest in Japan's history.

3. The tsunami's high water struck Japan's coast almost immediately. In some places **it** rose 50 feet high and rushed ten miles inland.

4. Together the earthquake and tsunami killed 15,839 people, injured 5,950 and left 3,642 missing. **They** also caused a disaster at the Fukushima Daiichi Nuclear Power Plant.

5. A report about the disaster came out in July 2012. **It** states that Fukushima's operators made serious mistakes and covered up problems.

6. In September 2012 the Japanese government announced its new nuclear policy. **It** wanted to stop using nuclear power completely by 2040.

7. Japan's government finds itself in a difficult position now. **It** certainly does not want to damage the economy. On the other hand, **it** must pay attention to the Japanese people's anti-nuclear feelings.

Name _____ Date _____

ECHO READING

Directions: When you read, you should make breaks, and sometimes pauses, between groups of words. As your teacher reads each phrase, repeat aloud what is read and put a slash or line after that phrase. Then read the whole sentence aloud as a class. Do the first paragraph together as a class, and then do the second one on your own. The first sentence has been marked for you.

Japan uses / large amounts of energy / to support its industries / and modern lifestyle. Japan has few fossil fuels of its own, so it must import large amounts of natural gas, oil, and coal. Since the 1970s it also has built nuclear power plants. In March 2011, Japan had 54 nuclear reactors. They supplied 30 percent of the country's electricity. Then things changed when the earthquake and tsunami hit.

On March 11, 2011, an earthquake struck Japan's northeastern coast. It was the largest in Japan's history. It destroyed buildings and caused fires in the region. It also caused skyscrapers to sway 150 miles away in Tokyo. Even worse, the earthquake caused a tsunami that did more damage than the earthquake itself. Most people in Japan no longer feel that nuclear power plants are safe. The government shut down the last of the country's nuclear reactors in May 2012. When it started up two reactors in July 2012, people began protesting in the streets. The protests continued every week, and some of them attracted 75,000 people.

What's Happening
IN THE WORLD?

BY LAWRENCE GABLE
© 2014 What's Happening Publications

SUBJECT: SCIENCE and ENVIRONMENT

Japan Struggles with its Nuclear Future

1 In March 2011 an earthquake and tsunami struck Japan. They took lives and did tremendous damage. They also led to a disaster at a nuclear power plant. Ever since then the Japanese people have lost faith in the safety of nuclear power. Now the government is struggling with how to make the country's energy.

2 Japan uses large amounts of energy to support its industries and modern lifestyle. Japan has few fossil fuels of its own, so it must import large amounts of natural gas, oil and coal. Since the 1970s it also has built nuclear power plants.

3 In March 2011 Japan had 54 nuclear reactors. They supplied 30 percent of the country's electricity. The government also had plans to increase that amount to 50 percent by the year 2050. Then things changed when the earthquake and tsunami hit.

4 On March 11, 2011 an earthquake struck Japan's northeastern coast. It was the largest in Japan's history. It destroyed buildings and caused fires in the region. It also caused skyscrapers to sway 150 miles away in Tokyo. Even worse, the earthquake caused a tsunami that did more damage than the earthquake itself.

5 The tsunami's high water struck Japan's coast almost immediately. In some places it rose 50 feet high and rushed ten miles inland. It wiped out entire towns, and swept away buildings, trains and cars. Together the earthquake and tsunami killed 15,839 people, injured 5,950 and left 3,642 missing. They also caused a disaster at the Fukushima Daiichi Nuclear Power Plant.

6 The power plant has six reactors. On March 11 three of them were not working because they were getting regular service. The other three reactors shut down automatically when the earthquake struck. The earthquake probably damaged the emergency cooling systems, but 30 minutes later the tsunami certainly damaged them. Within three days the reactors suffered meltdowns. When radiation went into the air, the government evacuated 150,000 people from their homes. The region will take many years to recover.

7 A report about the disaster came out in July 2012. It stated that Fukushima's operators had made serious mistakes and covered up problems. It accused the government's nuclear agency of ignoring problems at Fukushima. It also found that officials could have prevented the disaster.

8 Most people in Japan no longer feel that nuclear power plants are safe. The government shut down the last of the country's nuclear reactors in May 2012. When it started up two reactors in July 2012, people began protesting in the streets. They continued every week, and some of them attracted 75,000 people.

9 In September 2012 the Japanese government announced its new nuclear policy. It wanted to stop using nuclear power completely by 2040. It would replace nuclear power with fossil fuels, solar and wind energy, and programs to save energy. However, big business complained that this would hurt the economy. A week later the government reversed its policy.

10 Japan's government finds itself in a difficult position now. It certainly does not want to damage the economy. On the other hand, it must pay attention to the Japanese people's anti-nuclear feelings. No amount of money is worth sacrificing their health and safety.

QUICK READ/DRAW AND WRITE

Directions: First Reading—As you do your first reading of the article, your teacher will time you for one minute. When time is called, write the number of the paragraph where you stopped. **Paragraph #** _____

In the box below, draw a picture summarizing what you read.

Second Reading— As you do your second reading of the article, your teacher will time you for one minute. When time is called, write the number of the paragraph where you stopped. **Paragraph #** _____

Directions: Now continue reading the rest of the article. Below write five important words that will help you remember the information from the article.

_____ _____ _____ _____ _____

CLOSE READING ANNOTATION

Third Reading—As you reread each paragraph in the article closely, answer the
questions by annotating the text. Each numbered question corresponds to a paragraph
in the article where the answer can be found. Write your brief answers in the space
below each question.

1. What made the Japanese people lose faith in their safety?

_____

2. What are three types of fossil fuels?

_____

3. What does the last sentence in this paragraph do for the reader?

_____

4. Why do you think the writer chose the word *sway*?

_____

5. What does the last sentence in this paragraph do for the reader?

_____

6. What happened to the reactors on March 11, 2011?

_____

7. How would you summarize the government's caretaking of the power plant?

_____

8. What sentences show you the intense feelings some have about nuclear power?

_____

9. What does the next-to-last sentence tell you about the government?

_____

10. How does the author explain the problems that the Japanese government
has now?

_____

GRAMMAR GAMES

Directions: Reread the two paragraphs below. Words have been left out from the sentences. Think about the information from the article you have read and fill in a word that makes sense. The part of speech of the missing word is provided.

In March 2011 an earthquake and tsunami struck Japan. They

took lives and _____ tremendous damage. They also led
           (1. verb)

to a disaster at one of Japan's _____ power plants. Ever since
          (2. adjective)

then the Japanese people have _____ faith in the safety of
          (3. verb)

nuclear power, and the government _____ struggled with how
          (4. verb)

to make the country's nuclear _____ safe.
          (5. noun)

    Japan consumes large amounts of energy to _____ its
          (6. verb)

industries and modern lifestyle. However, it has few fossil

_____ of its own, so it must _____ huge amounts
(7. plural noun)   (8. verb)

_____ natural _____ , oil, and coal. _____
(9. preposition)   (10. noun)   (11. pronoun)

also built a number of nuclear power _____ in the 1970s.
          (12. plural noun)

HOW'S IT ORGANIZED?

This article is organized as a **problem that needs solving.**

Directions: Answer these questions in the spaces at the bottom.

1. What made the Japanese people lose faith in the safety of nuclear power?

2. Why did Japan rely on nuclear power for 30 percent of their electricity?

3. What two things made the damage on March 11, 2011, so extensive?

4. What were some of the effects of the damage to the reactors?

5. What was the government's first reaction to the nuclear disaster?

6. What is the new nuclear policy of the Japanese government?

Answers:

1.	
2.	
3.	
4.	
5.	
6.	

The main idea of a selection reflects what the paragraph or sentences are about. Put an X on the space next to the sentence that best states the main idea of the article.

_____ 1. The earthquake and Tsunami in Japan caused many people to consider the risks of using nuclear energy.

_____ 2. The need for energy is increasing in countries with a lot of industry.

_____ 3. The Japanese government changed its mind about energy to satisfy its people.

Explain why your choice is the best main idea. _____

_____

IS THAT A FACT?

Directions: Read the definitions of a fact and an inference below. Then read the paragraph that follows. At the bottom of the page, write an F on the blank if the sentence is a fact. Write an I if the sentence is an inference. Use the following definitions:

Fact—a statement that can be proven true from the paragraph

Inference—a guess as to what MIGHT be true, based on what you have read and what you already know about the subject

Japan is one of the world's leading industrialized countries and it consumes large amounts of energy. Japan has few fossil fuels of its own, so it must import huge amounts of natural gas. In the 1970s it built a number of nuclear power plants. Since then, Japan has been getting much of its electricity from nuclear power. But now the Japanese people no longer trust the safety of nuclear power because of the earthquake and tsunami that damaged a nuclear power plant and released radiation into the air and water. Japan's government finds itself in a difficult situation, because without nuclear power their economy might suffer.

_____ **1.** Nuclear energy is a sign of progress for Japan.

_____ **2.** Japan's nuclear program was very successful.

_____ **3.** The Japanese government supports the use of nuclear power.

_____ **4.** The Japanese have been using nuclear energy since the 1970s.

_____ **5.** Some Japanese are not on good terms with their government.

_____ **6.** Part of Japan's nuclear energy issue is the effect it has on the country's economy.

TIC-TAC-TOE SUMMARIZING

When you **summarize** in writing, you present all the key points the author is trying to make.

Directions: Write four sentences to summarize the article about Japan's nuclear future. To help you, there are nine words or phrases in the Tic-Tac-Toe graphic organizer below. To write a sentence, you must use three words or phrases in a row. The row can be horizontal (—), vertical (I), or diagonal (/).

disaster	earthquake	meltdown
Japanese government	Fukushima Nuclear Reactor	energy
government policy	many deaths	tsunami

1. _____

_____

2. _____

_____

3. _____

_____

4. _____

REACTION GUIDE

Directions: Now that you have read and studied information about "Japan Struggles with its Nuclear Future," reread the statements below, which you responded to before reading the article. Then think about how the author might respond to these statements. If you think the author would agree, put a checkmark on the line before the number. If you think the author would disagree, put an X on the line. Then below the statement, copy the words, phrases, or sentences from the article that provide evidence of the views stated by the author. Also note if there is no evidence to support the statement.

_____ **1.** Nuclear energy is essential to the world's future.

Evidence: _____

_____

_____

_____ **2.** Although nuclear energy has risks, it is worth them.

Evidence: _____

_____

_____

_____ **3.** Each country's government is responsible for keeping its citizens safe.

Evidence: _____

_____

_____

TAKE A STAND

Directions: People often have differing feelings or opinions about an issue. When they discuss or argue their opposing views, they are taking part in a debate. A good persuasive argument is based on a claim that is supported by

Facts—statements that can be proven true

Statistics—numerical data gotten through research

Examples—instances that support an opinion

You and a partner are going to debate two of your other classmates. The topic you are going to debate is the following:

Although nuclear energy has risks, it is worth it.

Decide with the other pair who will agree and who will disagree with this statement. Then answer these questions in order to win your debate.

1. What are your two strongest points to persuade the other side? (You can do Internet research to include facts, statistics, and examples.)

   A. _____

   B. _____

2. What might the other side say to argue against point A?

   _____

   _____

3. What might the other side say to argue against point B?

   _____

   _____

4. What will you say to prove the other side's arguments are wrong?

   _____

   _____

   _____

WHAT'S THE COMBINATION?

Writing is more interesting when the writer joins, or combines, short sentences. Follow the directions below to learn different ways to combine two sentences.

What to do: You can join two sentences using the words *and*, *but*, *or*, or *so*. This method works well when the subject (the person, people, thing, or things doing the action) is the SAME for both sentences. In the example below, *mother* is the subject of both sentences.

Example: My *mother* loves to cook. My *mother* loves to play softball. My mother loves to cook **and** play softball.

Directions: Combine these sentences using the method above. Use the word in parentheses at the end to join the two sentences.

1. In March 2011 an earthquake and tsunami struck Japan. The earthquake and tsunami caused much damage. (and)

_____

_____

2. Japan is one of the leading industrialized countries. Japan consumes large amounts of energy to support its lifestyle. (but)

_____

_____

3. Japan has few fossil fuels of its own. Japan decided to increase its use of nuclear energy. (so)

_____

_____

4. Japan's government does not want to endanger the environment. Japan's government does not want to have a shortage of energy. (but)

_____

_____

5. Japan will have to figure out how to get energy safely. Japan will continue to face serious risks. (or)

_____

_____

ANALYZING A PROMPT

Directions: Read the writing prompt in the box below. Then follow the directions to learn how to analyze and answer it.

> You are a citizen who lived near the Fukushima Daiichi Nuclear Power Plant. During the disaster you lost your home and your property. You have been asked to write an essay that will convince the government's nuclear commission that the country should no longer use nuclear power. What evidence will you include to support your argument?

1. A writing prompt begins with some background information known as the **set up.** Underline the sentences that set up this assignment.

2. Use the following **R.A.F.T.** technique to finish analyzing the prompt.

Role: What are you supposed to be to answer it? A student? A politician?

Write what you are here: _____

Audience: To whom are you writing? A friend? A particular group?

Write who it is here: _____

Format: Check to see what type of writing you are doing. Is it an essay, a letter, a speech, a story, a description, an editorial, or a report?

Write what it is here: _____

Task: Another sentence in the prompt will tell you what you must do, or your "task." Question words such as **why, how,** or **what** may tell the task.

If the question word is **why,** you will *give the reasons* that something is done.

If the question word is **how,** you will *explain the way* that something is done.

If the question word is **what,** you will *identify the thing* that is done.

Below, copy the sentence or question that describes your task.

_____

_____

ANALYZING INFORMATIONAL TEXT

1. Informational articles are written to provide data or descriptions that explain something. Below name three groups that might be interested in reading this article besides students and teachers.

a. _____ b. _____ c. _____

2. What main point is the author making in this article?

_____

_____

3. Give two of the most important facts you learned in this article.

a. _____

b. _____

4. **Domain-specific vocabulary** consists of words used in a specific subject such as math, science, or social studies. Reread the article and list six domain-specific words used with this subject. After you select the words, write their definitions on the lines provided

a. _____ : _____

b. _____ : _____

c. _____ : _____

d. _____ : _____

e. _____ : _____

f. _____ : _____

ASSESSMENT

1. The author claims that the tsunami was more destructive than the earthquake that caused it. Below, cite three pieces of evidence from the article to support this claim.

   a. _____

   _____

   b. _____

   _____

   c. _____

   _____

2. Circle the letters of the conclusions below that are the two **best** supported by evidence from the article.

   a. Tsunamis can be very powerful forces of nature.

   b. The major way Japan creates electricity is through nuclear power.

   c. Many people did not have time to escape the tsunami.

   d. Radiation killed more people than the actual tsunami did.

   e. The Japanese government should have been watching the Fukushima Nuclear Plant more closely.

3. Circle the letter of the paragraph where the author indicates that businesses in Japan have a lot of influence on the country's government.

   a. paragraph 1

   b. paragraph 7

   c. paragraph 8

   d. paragraph 9

4. The author explains that Japan has few fossil fuels. Underline the sentence in the paragraph below that names three fossil fuels.

"Japan uses large amounts of energy to support its industries and modern

lifestyle. Japan has few fossil fuels of its own, so it must import large amounts of

natural gas, oil, and coal. Since the 1970s it also has built nuclear power plants. In

March 2011 Japan had 54 nuclear reactors."

5. A student has made a plan for research. Read the plan and the directions below.

Research Report Plan

Topic: pros and cons of nuclear power

Audience: readers of a science magazine

Research Question: Do the benefits of nuclear power outweigh the

dangers that come from creating and using it?

The student needs to find a credible, or trustworthy, source with relevant information (information related to the topic being discussed). Circle the letter of the source below that would **most likely** have credible and relevant information.

a. www.thefutureofenergy.com—Nuclear power provides the energy the world needs "to go and to grow." On this site, the Nuclear Industry Association presents the facts about using nuclear energy.

b. www.radiationreduction.com—This *Say-No-to-Radiation* site explains both the short- and long-term hazards of nuclear energy.

c. www.naturesradioactivepower.com—The power of nature is shown vividly in these video clips of the destruction by the tsunami that hit Japan and its nuclear reactor.

d. www.canlivewiththeatom.com—Our world needs nuclear energy. It powers our homes, factories, schools, city lights—just about everything—but it also has real dangers. This site presents a scientific analysis of nuclear energy.

Name _____ Date _____

ANTICIPATION GUIDE

Directions: Before you read the article "Venice Puts Up a Defense," read the statements below. If you agree with a statement, put a checkmark on the line next to it. If you disagree, put an X on the line.

_____ **1.** Flooding is caused only by heavy rains.

_____ **2.** Sometimes, people trying to improve a place can cause more problems.

_____ **3.** People should try to prevent nature from destroying historic places.

Once you have read and responded to the statements above, write in the section below why you agree or disagree with each statement.

1. _____

_____

2. _____

_____

3. _____

_____

In the box below, draw a picture of what you think this article is about.

WORDSTORM

Directions: It's good to know more than just the dictionary definition of a word. Completing a wordstorm lets you write down information to help you understand what a word means, how it's related to other words, and how to use it in different ways.

What is the word?

defense

Here is the sentence from the text in which the word is used:

"Venice puts up a defense."

What are some other words or phrases that mean the same thing?

_____

What are three examples of how the word *defense* is used?

1. _____ 2. _____ 3. _____

Name three people other than teachers who would likely use this word.

1. _____ 2. _____ 3. _____

Draw a picture below that reminds you of the word *defense*.

TIME MY READ #1

Directions: With a partner, see how many words you can read correctly in 45 seconds. As you read, your partner will put an X through any word read incorrectly on his or her copy. When you are finished, trade your books or papers, and let your partner read while you keep score. Count the total number of words you read correctly. Write this score at the bottom of your page.

global canals century lagoon sewage canals flowing elevated	8
underground sandbars sewage residents tide unfortunately tourists treasures	16
damage seawater flooding climate architecture forecast experts diverted	24
global canals century lagoon sewage canals flowing elevated	32
underground sandbars sewage residents tide unfortunately tourists treasures	40
damage seawater flooding climate architecture forecast experts diverted	48
global canals century lagoon sewage canals flowing elevated	56
underground sandbars sewage residents tide unfortunately tourists treasures	64
damage seawater flooding climate architecture forecast experts diverted	72
global canals century lagoon sewage canals flowing elevated	80

Number of words read correctly _____

ECHO READING

Directions: When you read, you should make breaks, and sometimes pauses, between groups of words. As your teacher reads each phrase, repeat aloud what is read and put a slash or line after that phrase. Then read the whole sentence aloud as a class. Do the first paragraph together as a class, and then do the second one on your own. The first sentence has been marked for you.

Venice has a long history / of high water / known as *acqua alta*. The water flows onto the city's squares and above the buildings' foundations. A century ago it happened about seven times a year. Now it happens a hundred times. People have to wear rubber boots and walk on elevated wooden boards.

Two things cause the increase in high water. One is that the city has been sinking. In the 16th century the city diverted the major rivers from flowing into the lagoon. That kept the silt from settling in the canals. The second reason is that global warming is causing the sea level to rise. Venice feels the effects of global warming because it sits at sea level. Experts expect the sea to rise twelve inches a year.

What's Happening

IN THE WORLD?

BY LAWRENCE GABLE
© 2014 *What's Happening Publications*

SUBJECT: *SCIENCE and ENVIRONMENT*

Venice Puts Up a Defense

1. Venice is one of the world's most beautiful cities. It lies in northeastern Italy on the Adriatic Sea. Its streets are canals, so people travel around in boats. Unfortunately high tides push water into Venice too often, so the city is building a barrier against the sea.

2. The city's 118 small islands lie in the center of a lagoon. A long sandbar divides the lagoon from the sea, but water enters the lagoon at three inlets. Every six hours the sea's tides either send some water in or pull it back out naturally.

3. Natural protection from the tides has almost vanished. Salt marshes once filled much of the lagoon, but most of them are gone. The government dug deep channels that replaced the gentle shallow waters. That has brought powerful water movement that erodes the marshland, islands and sandbars.

4. Venice has a long history of high water known as *acqua alta*. The water flows onto the city's squares and above the buildings' foundations. A century ago it happened about seven times a year. Now it happens a hundred times. People have to wear rubber boots and walk on elevated wooden boards.

5. The water rises high enough to damage buildings. It eats away at the brick walls above the stone foundations. That weakens them and makes them crumble. Now water seeps into homes and shops through the sewage pipes. Most Venetians no longer live on the ground floors.

6. Two things cause the increase in high water. One is that the city has been sinking. In the 16th century the city diverted major rivers from flowing into the lagoon. That kept silt from settling in the canals. Also, last century the city pumped fresh groundwater and gas from underground. The water table decreased and Venice's islands sank 11 inches.

7. The other thing is that global warming is causing the sea level to rise. Venice feels the effects of it because it lies at sea level. Experts expect a rise in the seas of at least 12 inches in this century.

8. A flood in November 1966 changed everything. Heavy rain and high tides pushed the water in the lagoon four feet higher than normal. Then the *sirocco* winds prevented it from flowing back out. When the next high tide came, it put Venice under six feet of water. People were trapped for three days without power or heat. Sewage and dead rats floated in the canals. That flood led to a law to save Venice.

9. In 2003 the government began the MOSE project. It is putting 79 hollow mobile gates at the three inlets. Normally they will lie flat on the sea floor and not affect the flow of water. However, during high waters managers will pump air into them. That will make them rise and form a barrier against the entering tide.

10. The gates will close when the forecast calls for a tide to rise 43 inches above normal. That will happen only about five times a year. The gates will be able to hold back seawater that is six feet higher than the level of the lagoon.

11. High waters in Venice have become too frequent for comfort. Many Venetians have moved away from the city, but about 20 million tourists visit Venice every year. MOSE will be finished in 2016. Then high waters and flooding may be a thing of the past for the residents and tourists in Venice, one of the world's great treasures.

GET A CONTEXT CLUE

Directions: Below are sentences from "Venice Puts Up a Defense." First, read the sentence. Then, look back in the article and reread the paragraph in which the sentence is found. Circle the best answer to each question.

"Unfortunately high tides push water into Venice too often, so the city is building a *barrier* against the sea."

1. The word *barrier* means

   A. tower to see over something
   B. wall to block something
   C. island
   D. ship to sail away on

"Natural protection from the tides has almost *vanished*."

2. The word *vanished* means

   A. grown
   B. disappeared
   C. finished
   D. opened

"Venice has a long history of high water known as *acqua alta*."

3. The phrase *acqua alta* means

   A. sewage
   B. crumbling buildings
   C. canals
   D. high tides or water

"People have to wear rubber boots and walk on *elevated* wooden boards."

4. The word *elevated* means

   A. lowered
   B. rotten
   C. raised or lifted up
   D. antiqued

"In the 16th century the city *diverted* major rivers from flowing into the lagoon."

5. The word *diverted* means

   A. stopped
   B. increased
   C. turned away
   D. started

"It is putting 79 hollow *mobile* gates at the three inlets."

6. The term *mobile* means

   A. movable
   B. strong
   C. waterproof
   D. new

WORD CHOICE

Directions: The sentences below contain blanks for missing words. Three answer choices are listed after each blank. Read the sentence past the blank and choose the correct word. Write it in the blank.

Venice is one of the most beautiful cities in the world. It _____ *(lie, lied, lies)* in northeastern Italy on the Adriatic Sea. Instead of streets it _____ *(had, have, has)* canals, so people travel around in boats. Because high tides _____ *(pushing, pushes, push)* water into Venice too often, the city _____ *(is, are, were)* building a barrier against the sea.

The city's 118 small islands lie in the center of a lagoon. A long strip of sandbars _____ *(divide, divided, divides)* the lagoon from the sea, but water does _____ *(entrance, enter, enters)* the lagoon. Every six hours the Adriatic Sea's tides either rise or _____ *(fell, fall, fill)*, sending some water into the lagoon or _____ *(pulled, pulls, pulling)* it back out naturally.

Natural protection from the Adriatic's tides _____ *(has, have, having)* almost vanished. Salt marshes once _____ *(occupy, occupies, occupied)* much of the lagoon, but most of them are gone.

LOOK WHO'S TALKING

Directions: Below are sentences that relate to "Venice Puts Up a Defense." Look back in the article and reread the paragraph in which you find the reference. Circle the best answer to each question.

1. In the third sentence of paragraph 1, the word *its* refers to

    A. the city of Venice
    B. the country of Italy
    C. the buildings
    D. the sea

2. In the last sentence of paragraph 2, the word *it* refers to

    A. the sea
    B. the tides
    C. the water
    D. the city

3. In the second sentence of paragraph 3, the word *them* refers to

    A. the tides
    B. the salt marshes
    C. the lagoons
    D. the channels

4. In paragraph 7, the phrase *the other thing* refers to

    A. the only cause of increasing water
    B. the city sinking
    C. diverting the rivers
    D. one of the reasons the water rises

5. The fourth sentence of paragraph 8 says, "When the next high tide came, it put Venice under six feet of water." The word *it* refers to

    A. the tide
    B. the city
    C. global warming
    D. the flood

6. In the last sentence in paragraph 10, *that* refers to

    A. the rising tide
    B. the gates
    C. the seawater
    D. the lagoon

NOTE MAKING

Directions: Read the boldfaced key words on the left side of the chart below. Then add notes that answer the question in parentheses under the key word.

Venice
(Where is it?)

Acqua alta
(What is it?)

Flooding
(Why? Give two reasons.)

Law to save Venice
(When was the law
established?)

MOSE
(What is it?)

*On a separate sheet of paper write a summary of what your notes say about the problems with the Venice canals.

Unit 2: Science and Environment

IS THAT A FACT?

Directions: Read the definitions of a fact and an inference below. Then read the paragraph that follows. At the bottom of the page, write an F on the blank if a sentence is a fact. Write an I if the sentence is an inference. Use the following definitions:

Fact—a statement that can be proven true from the paragraph

Inference—a guess as to what MIGHT be true, based on what you have read and what you already know about the subject

A flood in November of 1966 changed everything. Heavy rain and high tides pushed the water in the lagoon four feet higher than normal. Then high winds prevented it from flowing back out. When the next high tide came, it put Venice under six feet of water. People were trapped for three days without power or heat. Sewage and dead rats floated in the canals. That flood led Venice to begin the MOSE project, which could save the city from flooding.

_____ **1.** Winds can affect flooding.

_____ **2.** The city of Venice is not prepared for large floods.

_____ **3.** The water level around Venice is always changing.

_____ **4.** The MOSE project is designed to combat the rising water.

_____ **5.** Venice is not a very sanitary, or clean, place.

_____ **6.** The November 1966 flood was a turning point.

MAKE A SPACE

Directions: Below are sentences that are missing punctuation and capitalization. First, draw slash marks (/) between the words. Then rewrite each sentence in the space below it, filling in the missing punctuation and capitalization.

> Example:
>
> flooding / happens / more / often / today / than / a / century / ago
>
> Flooding happens more often today than a century ago.

1. globalwarmingiscausingthesealeveltorise

_____

_____

2. asandbardividesthelagoonfromtheseabutwatercomesinfrominlets

_____

_____

3. heavyrainsandhightidespushedwaterintothelagoon

_____

_____

4. thewatercaneatawayatbrickwallsandatthefoundationsofhomes

_____

_____

TIME MY READ #2

Directions: With a partner, see how many words you can read correctly in 45 seconds. As you read, your partner will put an X through any word read incorrectly on his or her copy. When you are finished, trade your books or papers, and let your partner read while you keep score. Count the total number of words you read correctly. Write this score at the bottom of your page.

global canals century lagoon sewage canals flowing elevated	8
underground sandbars sewage residents tide unfortunately tourists treasures	16
damage seawater flooding climate architecture forecast experts diverted	24
global canals century lagoon sewage canals flowing elevated	32
underground sandbars sewage residents tide unfortunately tourists treasures	40
damage seawater flooding climate architecture forecast experts diverted	48
global canals century lagoon sewage canals flowing elevated	56
underground sandbars sewage residents tide unfortunately tourists treasures	64
damage seawater flooding climate architecture forecast experts diverted	72
global canals century lagoon sewage canals flowing elevated	80

Number of words read correctly _____

Is the score higher than it was in Time My Read #1? _____

WORD PARTS

Directions: Read the definitions below. In each box on the map, write the number of the word that matches the map feature the box points to.

sandbar—(noun) a thin strip of land formed by waves and currents of water

lagoon—(noun) an area of shallow water separated from the sea by a sandbar or strip of land

canal—(noun) an artificial waterway used for irrigation or navigation

channel—(noun) a wide, deep waterway

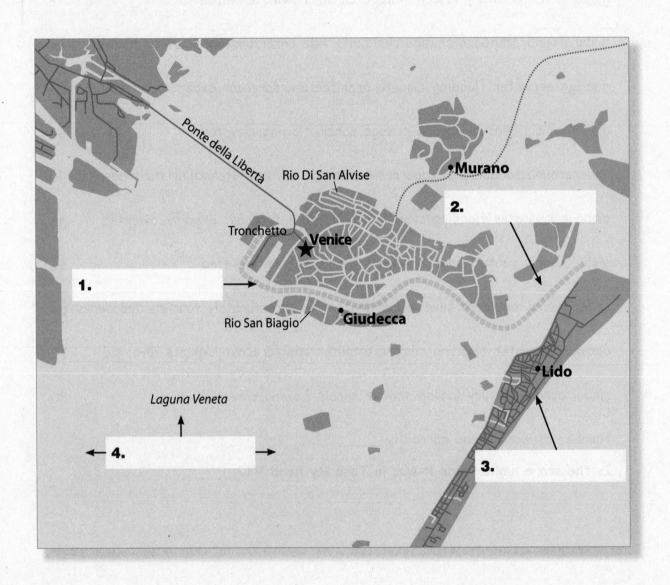

VENICE WORD PUZZLE

Directions: Complete the crossword puzzle.

Word List
CANAL
DIVERTED
SANDBAR
DEFENSE
VANISHED
BARRIER
CHANNEL
MOBILE
LAGOON
ELEVATED

Across
2 a wide, deep waterway
4 a thin strip of land formed by waves
6 turned away
7 disappeared
9 movable

Down
1 an area of shallow water separated from the sea
2 an artificial waterway
3 raised or lifted up
5 a wall to block something
8 protection

WRITING FRAME

Directions: Use your knowledge and information from the article to complete the writing frame below.

Venice, Italy is a unique city consisting of 118 small islands that lie in the center of a lagoon. Residents use _____ instead of _____ to travel around town. Changing tides and rain cause high water that results in _____. The water overflows from the sewers and into people's homes. Flooding happens more often today than it did a hundred years ago. Two reasons are _____ and _____.

In some years the floods are worse than others. For example, in 1966 the water rose four feet higher than normal because

_____.

In order to stop the water, the city _____.

In 2003 the government began to solve the problem by establishing the _____, which is designed to_____.

REACTION GUIDE

Directions: Now that you have read and studied information about "Venice Puts Up a Defense," reread the statements below, which you responded to before reading the article. Then think about how the author might respond to these statements. If you think the author would agree, put a checkmark on the line before the number. If you think the author would disagree, put an X on the line. Then below the statement, copy the words, phrases, or sentences from the article that provide evidence of the views stated by the author. Also note if there is no evidence to support the statement.

_____ **1.** Flooding is caused only by heavy rains.

Evidence: _____

_____

_____

_____ **2.** Sometimes, people trying to improve a place can cause more problems.

Evidence: _____

_____

_____

_____ **3.** People should try to prevent nature from destroying historic places.

Evidence: _____

_____

_____

Name _____ Date _____

TAKE A STAND

Directions: People often have differing feelings or opinions about an issue. When they discuss or argue their opposing views, they are taking part in a debate. A good persuasive argument is based on a claim that is supported by

Facts—statements that can be proven to be true

Statistics—numerical data gotten through research

Examples—instances that support an opinion

You and a partner are going to debate two of your other classmates. The topic you are going to debate is the following:

People should try to prevent nature from destroying historic places.

Decide with the other pair who will agree and who will disagree with this statement. Then answer these questions in order to win your debate.

1. What are your two strongest points to persuade the other side? (You can do Internet research to include facts, statistics, and examples.)

   A. _____

   B. _____

2. What might the other side say to argue against point A?

   _____

   _____

3. What might the other side say to argue against point B?

   _____

   _____

4. What will you say to prove the other side's arguments are wrong?

   _____

   _____

ASSESSMENT

Comprehension: Answer the questions about the following passage.

In 2003 the government began the MOSE project. It is putting 79 hollow mobile gates at the three inlets. Normally the gates will lie flat on the sea floor and not affect the flow of water. However, during high waters managers will pump air into them. That will make them rise and form a barrier, or wall, against the entering tide. High waters in Venice have become too frequent for comfort. About 20 million tourists visit the city every year. MOSE is supposed to be finished in 2016, and then maybe high waters and flooding will be a thing of the past.

1. What problem does the high water cause in Venice?

_____

_____

2. What are Venetians doing to stop flooding?

_____

_____

3. What was the author's purpose for writing about Venice and floods?

_____

_____

Fluency: The words in the following two sentences are all connected. The sentences are also missing punctuation and capitalization. Draw slash marks (/) between the words. Then rewrite each sentence by filling in the punctuation and capitalization.

1. mostvenetiansnolongerliveonthegroundfloor

_____

2. **thegateswillrisewhenthelevelreachesfortythreeinchesabovenormal**

_____

_____

Fluency: Read the three sentences below. Imagine where you would pause within each sentence as you read it aloud. Draw a slash (/) mark between the phrases where you would pause. The first slash is done.

3. Natural protection / from the tides has all but vanished.

4. Two things cause the increase in high water.

5. Climate change experts predict a rise in the seas of at least 12 inches in this century.

Vocabulary: Based on what you have learned in this lesson, match the following words with their definitions. Write the letter of the definition on the blank in front of the word it defines.

1. _____ canal
A. disappeared

2. _____ elevated
B. protection

3. _____ defense
C. movable

4. _____ diverted
D. an artificial waterway

5. _____ lagoon
E. turned away

6. _____ sandbar
F. a thin strip of land formed by waves

7. _____ barrier
G. raised or lifted up

8. _____ vanished
H. a wide, deep waterway

9. _____ mobile
I. a wall to block something

10. _____ channel
J. an area of shallow water separated from the sea by a strip of land

Name _____ Date _____

ANTICIPATION GUIDE

Directions: Before you read the article "Brazil Counts Trees in the Amazon Basin," read the statements below. If you agree with a statement, put a checkmark on the line next to it. If you disagree, put an X on the line.

_____ **1.** Governments don't have an interest in saving rainforests.

_____ **2.** People overestimate how important the rainforest is.

_____ **3.** Saving the environment is more important than saving a few people.

Once you have responded to the statements above, write in the section below why you agree or disagree with each statement.

1. _____

_____

2. _____

_____

3. _____

_____

In the box below, draw a picture of what you think this article is about.

PREDICTING ABCs

Directions: The article you are going to read is about saving the Amazon rainforest. See how many boxes you can fill in below with words relating to this topic. For example, put the word *jungle* in the J–L box. Try to put at least one word in every box, and then try to write a word for every letter.

A–C	D–F	G–I
J–L	**M–O**	**P–R**
S–T	**U–V**	**W–Z**

Name _____ Date _____

LANGUAGE MINI-LESSON

You probably remember that a **verb** is a word that shows action. A verb in the **present tense** shows something happening now. A verb in the **past tense** shows something that happened in the past. Past-tense verbs are usually formed by adding **-d** or **-ed** to the verb. For example: Today I **use** the bike. Yesterday I **used** the bike.

Some verbs change when they become past tense. For example, the past tense of the verb **bring** is **brought**. Today I **bring** you a gift. Yesterday I **brought** you a gift.

Directions: Work with a partner to fill in the past tense of each verb. If you don't know it, use a dictionary. The past tense is usually given after the present.

Present Tense	Past Tense
cover	
increase	
take	
do	
dig	
influence	
pay	
announce	
reduce	
sweep	
come	
make	
suffer	

ECHO READING

Directions: When you read, you should make breaks, and sometimes pauses, between groups of words. As your teacher reads each phrase, repeat aloud what is read and put a slash or line after that phrase. Then read the whole sentence aloud as a class. Do the first paragraph together as a class, and then do the second one on your own. The first sentence has been marked for you.

The Amazon River / carries more water / than any other river / in the world. / It is also home to the Amazon rainforest. Although the rainforest covers parts of nine countries, most of it is in Brazil. Recently Brazil announced that it will take a census of the Amazon's trees.

This census will provide information in a number of areas. One is the deforestation that has reduced the size of the rainforest. Another is climate change. A third area regards Brazil's efforts to protect the rainforest. Finally, the census will increase understanding of plant, animal, and human life in the rainforest. Brazil's environment agency is taking the census.

It will employ researchers from government and universities. In teams they will go to 22,000 sites in the rainforest. At each site they will record the number, size, and species of trees. In addition, they will record the local people's interactions with the forest. The census will take four years to complete.

What's Happening
IN THE WORLD?

BY LAWRENCE GABLE
© 2014 What's Happening Publications

SUBJECT: SCIENCE and ENVIRONMENT

Brazil Counts Trees in the Amazon Basin

1 The Amazon River carries more water than any other river in the world. It is also home to the Amazon rainforest. Although the rainforest covers parts of nine countries, most of it is in Brazil. In 2013 Brazil announced that it will take a census of the Amazon's trees.

2 This census will provide information in a number of areas. One is the deforestation that has reduced the size of the rainforest. Another is climate change. A third area regards Brazil's efforts to protect the rainforest. Finally, the census will increase understanding of plant, animal and human life in the rainforest.

3 Brazil's environment agency is taking the census. It will employ researchers from government and universities. In teams they will go to 22,000 sites in the rainforest. At each site they will record the number, size and species of trees. In addition, they will record the local people's interactions with the forest. The census will take four years to complete.

4 Deforestation lies at the core of the rainforest's problems. The clearing has been done illegally for logging, ranching and farming. Landowners cut down trees. Then they set fires that sweep through the forest. Tractors then dig up the roots. Cattle ranchers have been responsible for most of the Amazon's deforestation.

5 In 2004 Brazil announced that it would reduce deforestation by 80 percent by 2020. The government began using satellites to find illegal logging and clearing. Then teams go in to arrest the people. Those efforts have paid off too. The rate of deforestation already has fallen by almost 80 percent.

6 Slowing down deforestation also is helping Brazil keep a promise to the international commu-

nity. Brazil produces a lot of carbon dioxide (CO_2) that adds to global warming. Much of that comes from burning the rainforest. In 2009 it promised to reduce its CO_2 emissions by at least 36 percent by 2020. Slowing the burning of rainforest already has helped.

7 The Amazon rainforest influences Earth's climate. The trees absorb carbon dioxide. This is part of the reason that the international community wants Brazil to protect the forest. Scientists say that 17 percent of the Amazon rainforest already has been cleared.

8 The Amazon is also critical to Earth's water resources. The water cycle there affects rainfall throughout South America and in much of the Northern Hemisphere. Unfortunately the Amazon has suffered two long droughts since 2005. They have slowed the growth of trees, so the rainforest is absorbing less CO_2. They also make forest fires more likely, which release CO_2 into the air.

9 Brazil also recognizes that the Amazon Basin is home to 25 million people. It cannot expect those people to live in poverty just to help the environment. Somehow it must convince people that keeping the rainforest is more advantageous than clearing it is. For example, Brazil has some programs that pay landowners for the trees that grow on their land. It also must help towns and cities to grow, but do little damage to the rainforest.

10 The last big census of trees took place in the 1970s. This new census will give the government accurate information. The government will use it to make new laws that protect the rainforest for the benefit of Brazilians and the rest of the world.

Lesson 12: Brazil Counts Trees in the Amazon Basin

215

© Houghton Mifflin Harcourt Publishing Company

QUICK READ/DRAW AND WRITE

Directions: First Reading—As you do your first reading of the article, your teacher will time you for one minute. When time is called, write the number of the paragraph where you stopped.   **Paragraph #** _____

In the box below, draw a picture summarizing what you read.

Second Reading—As you do your second reading of the article, your teacher will time you for one minute. When time is called, write the number of the paragraph where you stopped.   **Paragraph #** _____

Directions: Now continue reading the rest of the article. Below, write five important words that will help you remember the information from the article.

_____   _____   _____   _____   _____

Unit 2: Science and Environment

CLOSE READING ANNOTATION

Third Reading—As you reread each paragraph in the article closely, answer the questions by annotating the text. Each numbered question corresponds to a paragraph in the article where the answer can be found. Write your brief answers in the space below each question.

1. What is the meaning of the word *census*?

_____

2. What is the author's purpose for writing paragraph 2?

_____

3. Why will the census take four years to complete?

_____

4. Why are cattle ranchers blamed for the Amazon rainforest's problems?

_____

5. What was the effect of having people arrested?

_____

6. Why does Brazil feel it owes it to the international community to stop deforestation?

_____

7. How is climate connected to the rainforest?

_____

8. Why does the author begin the third sentence with the word *unfortunately*?

_____

9. What is the connection between people living in poverty and deforestation?

_____

10. How will the government use the information from the census?

_____

Name _____ Date _____

GRAMMAR GAMES

Directions: Reread the two paragraphs below. Words have been left out from the
sentences. Think about the information from the article you have read and fill in words
that make sense. The part of speech of each missing word is provided.

> The Amazon River carries more water than any other
>
> _____ in the world. _____ is also home to the Amazon
>   (1. noun)   (2. pronoun)
>
> rainforest, and most of it is _____ Brazil. Recently,
>   (3. preposition)
>
> _____ announced it will _____ a census of the
> (4. proper noun)   (5. verb)
>
> Amazon's trees.
>
>
>   This _____ will provide information in a number of areas.
>   (6. noun)
>
> One is the deforestation that has _____ the size of the
>   (7. verb)
>
> rainforest. Finally, the census will increase understanding of plant,
>
> _____, and human life in the _____.
>   (8. noun)   (9. noun)

          Unit 2: Science and Environment

Name _____ Date _____

CLOSE READING STRUCTURE

Directions: Understanding the structure of a text is important for two reasons. First, understanding the structure of a selection can help you remember the main idea and important details. Second, most academic writing you will encounter uses text structures to organize ideas.

1. Writers often include a statement in the **introduction** that catches the reader's attention. Then, the writer tells what the article will be about. On the space provided, copy the last sentence of the introduction of this article.

_____

_____

2. On the space below, copy the sentence that best states what the author's **claim, main idea,** or **thesis** is for this article.

_____

_____

3. On the space below, copy the sentence that shows where the author introduces another side to the issue of deforestation in Brazil.

_____

_____

4. Near the end of an article, a writer often restates the claim and summarizes the evidence. This is called the **conclusion.** On the space below, copy the sentence that best shows where the conclusion to the article begins.

_____

_____

IS THAT A FACT?

Directions: Read the definitions of a fact and an inference below. Then read the paragraph that follows. At the bottom of the page, write an F on the blank if the sentence is a fact. Write an I if the sentence is an inference. Use the following definitions:

<u>Fact</u>—a statement that can be proven true from the paragraph

<u>Inference</u>—a guess as to what MIGHT be true, based on what you have read and what you already know about the subject

Deforestation lies at the core of the rainforest's problem. The clearing for logging, ranching, and farming has been done illegally. Landowners cut down trees. Then they set fires that sweep through the forest. Tractors then dig up the roots. Cattle ranchers have been responsible for most of the Amazon's deforestation. Brazil produces a lot of carbon dioxide that adds to global warming, and most of that comes from burning the rainforest. Slowing down deforestation is helping Brazil keep a promise to the international community.

_____ **1.** A lot of illegal activity is the cause for much deforestation.

_____ **2.** People who own land don't want the trees to grow back.

_____ **3.** There has been a lot of pressure on Brazil from other countries.

_____ **4.** Carbon dioxide is adding to global warming.

_____ **5.** Many farmers and ranchers in the Amazon Basin don't care about the environment.

_____ **6.** Brazil understands its responsibility to stop global warming.

Name _____ Date _____

SUMMARIZING ABCs

Directions: Now that you've read the article about saving the Amazon rainforest, see how many words you can write about this topic in the boxes below.

A–C	D–F	G–I
J–L	**M–O**	**P–R**
S–T	**U–V**	**W–Z**

Name _____ Date _____

REACTION GUIDE

Directions: Now that you have read "Brazil Counts Trees in the Amazon Basin," reread the statements below, which you responded to before reading the article. Then think about how the author might respond to these statements. If you think the author would agree, put a checkmark on the line before the number. If you think the author would disagree, put an X on the line. Then, below the statement, copy the words, phrases, or sentences from the article that provide evidence of the views stated by the author. Also note if there is no evidence to support the statement.

_____ **1.** Governments don't have an interest in saving rainforests.

Evidence: _____

_____

_____

_____ **2.** People overestimate how important the rainforest is.

Evidence: _____

_____

_____

_____ **3.** Saving the environment is more important than saving a few people.

Evidence: _____

_____

_____

SENTENCE TRANSITIONS

An informational essay answers questions and provides information. Writers use transitional phrases to link ideas. Some transitional words and phrases include *to show, to prove, because, to explain, to verify, due to, instead of, furthermore, as a result,* and *in order to*.

Directions: Complete the following sentences using the phrases given.

Example: The Brazilian government started counting trees. The Brazilian government started counting trees *in order to stop deforestation*.

1. Deforestation of the rainforest is happening *due to*

_____

2. Brazil wants to reduce the amount of carbon dioxide *to prove*

_____

3. Scientists say that 17 percent of the rainforest has been cleared *to show*

_____

4. Brazil won't expect help from people who live in the rainforest *because*

_____

5. Brazil started programs to pay landowners and *as a result*

_____

PICKING UP PUNCTUATION

An **apostrophe** (') can be used for a number of purposes. An apostrophe is used most often to show possession, or who owns what. Apostrophes are used with nouns, which can be persons, places, or things. Apostrophes are also used with pronouns, because pronouns often replace nouns: *Maria* (noun) is my sister. *She* (pronoun) is nine years old.

Here's how to use apostrophes with **singular nouns** (just one). The noun is in **bold.**

    Carlo's pencil   a **student's** phone   the **dog's** bone

Here's how to use apostrophes with **plural nouns** (more than one).

    the **boys'** bathroom   some of the **students'** tests   the **tigers'** food

You can also use an apostrophe to show that a **pronoun** owns something.

    everyone's dinner   **someone's** desk   **no one's** hall pass

Don't use an apostrophe with **personal pronouns** to show possession. These are:

    hers   **ours**   **its**   **yours**   **theirs**

Finally, you use an apostrophe in a contraction to show a letter has been left out.

    it's (it is)   **they're** (they are)   **didn't** (did not)

Directions: Rewrite the bold word on the blank with an apostrophe in place.

1. The **Amazons** trees are disappearing. _____

2. A **landowners** land can be used to grow crops. _____

3. **Earths** climate is changing. _____

4. Many people think climate change is **everyones** business. _____

5. Illegal loggers **shouldnt** be chopping down trees. _____

ANALYZING A PROMPT

Directions: Read the writing assignment in the box below. Then follow the directions to learn how to analyze and answer it.

> You are an environmentalist who is concerned about how the rainforest is being affected by deforestation and why this problem is increasing. You have been asked to write a report to a group of industrialists and landowners. You want to inform them about the effects of their chopping down and burning trees, because you want to protect the environment by convincing them to stop doing it. What information will you use from the article?

1. A writing prompt begins with some background information known as the **set up.** Underline the sentences that set up this assignment.

2. Use the following **R.A.F.T.** technique to finish analyzing the prompt.

Role: What are you supposed to be to answer it? A student? A politician?

Write what you are here: _____

Audience: To whom are you writing? A friend? A particular group?

Write who it is here: _____

Format: Check to see what type of writing you are doing. Is it an essay, a letter, a speech, a story, a description, an editorial, or a report?

Write what it is here: _____

Task: Another sentence in the prompt will tell you what you must do, or your "task." Question words like **why, how,** or **what** may tell the task.

If the question word is **why,** you will *give the reasons* that something is done.

If the question word is **how,** you will *explain the way* that something is done.

If the question word is **what,** you will *identify the thing* that is done.

Below, copy the sentence or question below that describes your task.

_____

_____

Name _____ Date _____

WHAT'S YOUR POINT?

When writing an essay it is important to have a strong claim. A **claim,** or **thesis statement,** states the main point the writer wants to get across. Once the thesis is introduced, the body of the essay should support that thesis with key points that provide evidence.

The article "Brazil Counts Trees in the Amazon Basin" is about the deforestation of the Amazon rainforest in Brazil. The article explains the effects of deforestation and cites Brazil's efforts to cope with this issue.

Directions: Which of these sentences provides the best **claim** for an essay on this topic? Circle the letter of your choice.

a. Brazil has a tropical rainforest that is disappearing at an alarming rate.

b. The deforestation of the rainforest is having significant negative effects on the environment.

c. The fires from the deforestation of the rainforest cause a buildup of carbon dioxide.

In the space below, explain what is weak or wrong about the other two statements.

1. _____

_____

_____

2. _____

_____

_____

Name _____ Date _____

ASSESSMENT

1. This question has two parts. First, answer **Part A.** Then, answer **Part B.**

Part A: Circle the letter of the sentence below that states the author's main purpose in "Brazil Counts Trees in the Amazon Basin."

   a. The author wants people to realize carbon dioxide is causing climate change and that trees help soak up carbon dioxide.

   b. The author wants South American ranchers who cut down trees so that they can raise cattle to sell for beef.

   c. The author wants people to know that Brazil is studying the rainforest to prevent climate change and to better understand plant, animal, and human life.

   d. The author wants people to understand that Brazil has promised the world that they will slow down the deforestation of the Amazon rainforest.

Part B: Underline the pair of sentences below that supports your answer to part A.

   a. One area is climate change and another regards Brazil's efforts to protect the rainforest. The census will increase understanding of plant, animal, and human life in the rainforest.

   b. Deforestation lies at the core of the rainforest's problems. The clearing has been done illegally for logging, ranching, and farming.

   c. The Amazon rainforest influences Earth's climate. The trees absorb carbon dioxide.

   d. Slowing down deforestation is helping Brazil keep a promise to the international community. Brazil produces a lot of carbon dioxide that adds to global warming.

2. Circle the letter of the paragraph that explains the impact trees have on our climate.

   a. paragraph 4

   b. paragraph 5

   c. paragraph 7

   d. paragraph 8

3. Support the claim that Brazil's government understands that it must balance protecting the rainforest with protecting people and the economy. Below, cite three pieces of evidence from the article.

a. _____

_____

b. _____

_____

c. _____

_____

4. A student is writing an informative report about the rainforest for a science fair. Read the paragraph below from the draft of the student's report and complete the task that follows.

Destroying the Amazon rainforest will have a negative effect on people all over the earth. Because the rainforest is very large, it has a large impact on climate change. Trees absorb carbon dioxide, and it's carbon dioxide that is causing the earth to warm. Cattle spend a lot of time grazing on land near the rainforest. Warming sea and air temperatures are melting the ice caps in the North and South Poles, and the sea levels around the world are rising. The Brazilian government must look after people living in the rainforest. Eventually people living in low-lying areas around the world will experience flooding because of the deforestation of the Amazon rainforest.

Below, copy the two sentences that do not support the underlined sentence and should be removed from this paragraph.

a. _____

_____

_____

b. _____

_____

_____

Name _____ Date _____

ANTICIPATION GUIDE

Directions: Before you read the article "Bike Sharing Gets Rolling," read the statements below. If you agree with a statement, put a checkmark on the line next to it. If you disagree, put an X on the line.

_____ **1.** People in cities are willing to share things.

_____ **2.** If bikes were free to use in cities, people would steal them.

_____ **3.** Cities should not allow cars in their downtown areas.

Once you have responded to the statements above, write in the section below why you agree or disagree with each statement.

1. _____

_____

2. _____

_____

3. _____

_____

In the box below, draw a picture of what you think this article is about.

PREDICTING ABCs

Directions: The article you are going to read is about bike-sharing programs in cities. See how many boxes you can fill in below with words relating to this topic. For example, put the word *accident* in the A–C box. Try to put at least one word in every box, and then try to write a word for every letter.

A–C	D–F	G–I
J–L	**M–O**	**P–R**
S–T	**U–V**	**W–Z**

TIME MY READ #1

Directions: With a partner, see how many words you can read correctly in 45 seconds. As you read, your partner will put an X through any word read incorrectly on his or her copy. When you are finished, trade your books or papers, and let your partner read while you keep score. Count the total number of words you read correctly. Write this score at the bottom of your page.

stations advertising exchange anti-theft thieves electronic recyclable steal	8
residents popular unlock high-tech membership annual aluminum speed	16
vandals thieves computerized standard credit European struggling plan	24
stations advertising exchange anti-theft thieves electronic recyclable steal	32
residents popular unlock high-tech membership annual aluminum speed	40
vandals thieves computerized standard credit European struggling plan	48
stations advertising exchange anti-theft thieves electronic recyclable steal	56
residents popular unlock high-tech membership annual aluminum speed	64
vandals thieves computerized standard credit European struggling plan	72
stations advertising exchange anti-theft thieves electronic recyclable steal	80

Number of words read correctly _____

Name _____ Date _____

ECHO READING

Directions: When you read, you should make breaks, and sometimes pauses, between groups of words. As your teacher reads each phrase, repeat aloud what is read and put a slash or line after that phrase. Then read the whole sentence aloud as a class. Do the first paragraph together as a class, and then do the second one on your own. The first sentence has been marked for you.

Cities around the world / are struggling / with traffic jams / in their downtown areas. / Traffic jams waste people's time, and they fill the areas with noise and pollution. Some European cities have improved things through bike sharing, and their success is leading to more programs in Europe and North America.

Bike sharing programs use high-tech methods. Some use credit cards and some use smart cards at computerized bike stands. Some even send text messages with a code that unlocks the bike. There are limited problems with theft because the programs know who the bike riders are.

What's Happening
IN THE WORLD?

BY LAWRENCE GABLE
© 2014 What's Happening Publications

SUBJECT: SCIENCE and ENVIRONMENT

Bike Sharing Gets Rolling

1 Cities around the world are struggling with traffic in their downtown areas. Traffic jams waste people's time, and they fill the areas with noise and pollution. Some European cities have improved things through bike sharing programs. Their success is leading to more programs in Europe and North America too.

2 Bike sharing began in the Netherlands. In 1968 Amsterdam's "White Bicycles" plan put simple bicycles around the city. Residents could use a bike for free and then leave it for someone else to use. However, within a month people had stolen most of the bikes or thrown them into the canals.

3 Programs like Amsterdam's asked too little of the riders. In 1994 Portland, Oregon, started one like Amsterdam's. Its "Yellow Bike Project" fit the city's green image nicely. It was popular, but thieves and vandals also brought that program to an end.

4 Then bike sharing programs started to require some sort of payment. In 1995 Copenhagen, Denmark, put locked bikes at stations around the city. Riders used coins to unlock the bikes, and they got their money back when they returned the bikes. The program still exists today. Thieves do not steal the bikes because they look different from standard bikes and have different parts.

5 New bike sharing programs use high-tech methods. Some take credit cards. Others use electronic smart cards at computerized bike stands. Some even send text messages with the code that unlocks a bike. There are few problems with theft, because the programs know who the riders are.

6 The best of the new programs began in 2007 in Paris, France. It began with 10,000 bikes and was successful from the start. In the first 40 days people made two million trips, and in the first year they made 29 million. It grew to 20,000 silver bikes at 1,450 stations across the city.

7 Paris covers its costs in a number of ways. Riders use a credit card to pay about $2.00 for a day. Also, more than 250,000 people have annual memberships that cost only $44. An advertising company supports the program in exchange for ad space on city-owned places like bus stops. Finally, the program puts global positioning and anti-theft devices on the bikes to reduce the number of thefts.

8 In August 2008 Washington, D.C., became the first major American city with bike sharing. "SmartBike DC" has 120 red, three-speed bicycles at ten stations downtown. Quickly the program had 900 members. They swipe a magnetic membership card that unlocks a bike and assigns it to them for three hours.

9 Canada is also setting up programs in its cities. In April 2009 Montreal opened an environmentally friendly new program. "Bixi" (from "bike" and "taxi") has recyclable aluminum bikes and stations. The electronic system for locking and paying for bikes at the stations runs on solar power. Radio frequency ID tags prevent theft of the 2,400 bikes.

10 Bike sharing programs are finding their place in transportation. Residents and visitors are saving money on gas and saving time on short trips. The exercise they get makes them healthier, and the cities get healthier too. As these programs grow, they create a cleaner, more peaceful environment by reducing traffic, noise and pollution.

GET A CONTEXT CLUE

Directions: Below are sentences from "Bike Sharing Gets Rolling." First, read the sentence. Then, look back in the article and reread the paragraph in which the sentence is found. Circle the best answer to each question.

"*Residents* could use a bike for free and then leave it for someone else to use."

1. The word *residents* means

   A. pedestrians
   B. people who live in an area
   C. office people
   D. passengers

"Then bike sharing programs started to *require* some form of payment."

2. The word *require* means

   A. to need; must have
   B. having a choice
   C. no limits
   D. undecided

"There are limited problems with *theft* because the programs know who the riders are."

3. The word *theft* means

   A. accidents
   B. citizens
   C. weather
   D. stealing

"Paris *covers* its costs in a number of ways."

4. The word *covers* means

   A. gets paid back
   B. takes a loss
   C. bets
   D. counts

"Bixi has *recyclable* aluminum bikes and stations."

5. The word *recyclable* means

   A. brand new
   B. old
   C. can be used again and again
   D. good for one time use

"Bike sharing programs are *finding their place* in transportation."

6. The phrase *finding their place* means

   A. they have been discovered
   B. they are put in place
   C. are not wanted
   D. becoming more common

WORD MAP

Directions: Follow the directions to map the word in the box below.

> **recycle**

List two more words that
mean the same.

List two more things
that people recycle.

List two more words that mean
the opposite.

| reprocess | glass bottle | trash |

Draw a picture below to help
you remember the meaning.

Write a definition
IN YOUR OWN WORDS.

LOOK WHO'S TALKING

Directions: Below are sentences that relate to "Bike Sharing Gets Rolling." Look back in the article and reread the paragraph in which you find the reference. Circle the best answer to each question.

1. In the last sentence of paragraph 2, the word *them* refers to

   A. the European cities
   B. the commuters
   C. the bikes
   D. the people

2. In the third sentence of paragraph 4, both uses of the word *they* refer to

   A. the riders
   B. the bikes
   C. the program
   D. the different parts

3. In the last sentence of paragraph 6, the word *it* refers to

   A. the city of Paris
   B. the program in Paris
   C. the riders
   D. the stations

4. In the first sentence of paragraph 7, the word *its* refers to

   A. the riders
   B. the actual number of bikes
   C. the memberships
   D. Paris

5. In the last sentence of paragraph 8, the word *they* refers to

   A. the bikes
   B. the members
   C. the locks
   D. the magnetic cards

6. In the last sentence of paragraph 10, the word *they* refers to

   A. the residents
   B. the bikes
   C. the programs
   D. the traffic and pollution

HOW'S IT ORGANIZED?

This article is organized as **problem-solution** AND in **chronological order,** or in the order in time that things happened.

Directions: Answer these questions in the spaces at the bottom.

1. Which city first tried to start bike sharing in 1968?

2. What happened after only a month?

3. What city next tried to start bike sharing in 1994?

4. What happened to the program in that city?

5. What did Copenhagen do differently in 1995?

6. How did Paris improve the bike-sharing program in 2007?

7. What did Washington, DC, do with SmartBike DC in 2008?

8. Finally, how did Montreal improve the program in 2009?

Answers:

1.	
2.	
3.	
4.	
5.	
6.	
7.	
8.	

*On a separate sheet of paper write a summary of what your notes say about bike sharing.

IS THAT A FACT?

Directions: Read the definitions of a fact and an inference below. Then read the paragraph that follows. At the bottom of the page, write an F on the blank if the sentence is a fact. Write an I if the sentence is an inference. Use the following definitions:

Fact—a statement that can be proven true from the paragraph

Inference—a guess as to what MIGHT be true, based on what you have read and what you already know about a subject

Washington, D.C., became the first major American city to begin a bike-sharing program. The program, "SmartBike DC," began with 120 red, three-speed bicycles at ten stations downtown. The program started with 900 members. They swiped a magnetic membership card that unlocked a bike and assigned it to them for three hours. Bike-sharing programs are finding their place in transportation. Residents and visitors are saving money on gas and saving time on short trips. As these programs grow, they create a cleaner and more peaceful environment by reducing noise and pollution. People and cities get healthier as a result.

_____ **1.** Bike sharing became popular very quickly.

_____ **2.** Washington, DC, was the first American city to have bike sharing.

_____ **3.** Technology makes it less likely that the bikes will be stolen.

_____ **4.** Bike sharing can make someone healthy.

_____ **5.** Bike-sharing programs help make the air cleaner.

MAKE A SPACE

Directions: Below are sentences that are missing punctuation and capitalization. First draw slash marks (/) between the words. Then rewrite each sentence in the space below it, filling in the missing punctuation and capitalization.

Example:

cities / around / the / world / are / struggling / with / traffic

Cities around the world are struggling with traffic.

1. itwaspopularbutthievesandvandalsbroughttheprogramtoanend

_____

_____

2. nowbikesharingprogramsusehightechmethodsandcomputers

_____

_____

3. washingtondcbecamethefirstamericancitywithbikesharing

_____

_____

4. astheseprogramsgrowtheycreateacleanerandhealthierenvironment

_____

_____

TIME MY READ #2

Directions: With a partner, see how many words you can read correctly in 45 seconds. As you read, your partner will put an X through any word read incorrectly on his or her copy. When you are finished, trade your books or papers, and let your partner read while you keep score. Count the total number of words you read correctly. Write this score at the bottom of your page

stations advertising exchange anti-theft thieves electronic recyclable steal	8
residents popular unlock high-tech membership annual aluminum speed	16
vandals thieves computerized standard credit European struggling plan	24
stations advertising exchange anti-theft thieves electronic recyclable steal	32
residents popular unlock high-tech membership annual aluminum speed	40
vandals thieves computerized standard credit European struggling plan	48
stations advertising exchange anti-theft thieves electronic recyclable steal	56
residents popular unlock high-tech membership annual aluminum speed	64
vandals thieves computerized standard credit European struggling plan	72
stations advertising exchange anti-theft thieves electronic recyclable steal	80

Number of words read correctly _____

Is the score higher than it was in Time My Read #1?_____

WORD PARTS

Directions: The prefix *trans-* means *across, beyond,* or *through.* Match the following words with their definitions. Look the words up if you are not sure. Check your answers with a classmate.

1. _____ transfer

A. a business agreement between people

2. _____ transaction

B. to turn from one language into another

3. _____ transport

C. to change from one shape to another

4. _____ translate

D. to move from one place to another

5. _____ transform

E. to carry something or someone

Directions: The Greek word *kyklos* means *cycle, circle,* or *wheel.* A *cycle* is a series of events that repeats itself and can be thought of as one full turn of a wheel. We use the root *cycle* in words like *bicycle* or *motorcycle.* We also use the word *cycle* in science to explain natural events. Look up on the Internet the **water cycle,** the **rock cycle,** or the **carbon cycle,** which is part of global warming. Draw a picture of the carbon cycle on the circle below.

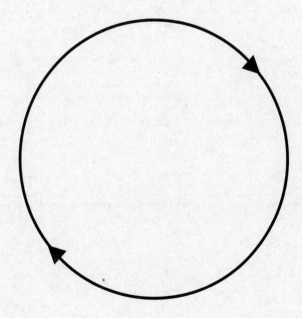

SUMMARIZING ABCs

Directions: Now that you've read the article about bike-sharing programs in cities, see how many words about bike sharing you can write in the boxes below.

A–C	D–F	G–I
J–L	M–O	P–R
S–T	U–V	W–Z

Name _____ Date _____

SENTENCE SUMMARIES

Directions: Below are four key words from the article "Bike Sharing Gets Rolling." Your job is to summarize, or restate, what you've learned in this article by using these four words in two sentences. Then, as a challenge, try to use all four words in one sentence to summarize the article.

Key Words

traffic   theft

bicycles   payment

Sentence Summaries:

1. _____

_____

2. _____

_____

Challenge Summary (all four words in one sentence!):

1. _____

_____

Name _____ Date _____

REACTION GUIDE

Directions: Now that you have read and studied information about "Bike Sharing Gets Rolling," reread the statements below, which you responded to before reading the article. Then think about how the author might respond to these statements. If you think the author would agree, put a checkmark on the line before the number. If you think the author would disagree, put an X on the line. Then below the statement, copy the words, phrases, or sentences from the article that provide evidence of the views stated by the author. Also note if there is no evidence to support the statement.

_____ **1.** People in cities are willing to share things.

Evidence: _____

_____

_____

_____ **2.** If bikes were free to use in cities, people would steal them.

Evidence: _____

_____

_____

_____ **3.** Cities should not allow cars in their downtown areas.

Evidence: _____

_____

_____

TAKE A STAND

Directions: People often have differing feelings or opinions about an issue. When they discuss or argue their opposing views, they are taking part in a debate. A good persuasive argument is based on a claim that is supported by

Facts—statements that can be proven to be true

Statistics—numerical data gotten through research

Examples—instances that support an opinion

You and a partner are going to debate two of your other classmates. The topic you are going to debate is the following:

Cities should not allow cars in their downtown areas.

Decide with the other pair who will agree and who will disagree with this statement. Then answer these questions in order to win your debate.

1. What are your two strongest points to persuade the other side? (You can do Internet research to include facts, statistics, and examples.)

    A. _____

    B. _____

2. What might the other side say to argue against point A?

_____

_____

3. What might the other side say to argue against point B?

_____

_____

4. What will you say to prove the other side's arguments are wrong?

_____

_____

_____

© Houghton Mifflin Harcourt Publishing Company

ASSESSMENT

Comprehension: Answer the questions about the following passage.

Bike sharing began in the Netherlands. Programs at first asked too little of the riders and there was theft, but now there are new high-tech methods to keep track of the bikes. Computerized programs can text-message a rider with an activation code, and the program knows who is riding the bike. Washington, DC, became the first American city to have a bike-sharing program.

These programs are finding their place in transportation. Residents and visitors are saving money and time on short trips. The exercise they get makes the riders and the cities healthier and keeps the environment cleaner.

1. Why might it be a good idea to have a bike-sharing program?

_____

_____

2. What was needed to prevent abuse and theft of the bikes?

_____

_____

3. What was the author's purpose for writing this article about bike sharing?

_____

_____

Fluency: The words in the following two sentences are all connected. The sentences are also missing punctuation and capitalization. Draw slash marks (/) between the words. Then rewrite each sentence by filling in the punctuation and capitalization.

1. pariscoversitscostsinanumberofways

_____

ASSESSMENT

2. itbeganwithtenthousandbikesandwasverysuccessfulfromthestart

_____

_____

Fluency: Read the three sentences below. Imagine where you would pause within each sentence as you read it aloud. Draw a slash (/) mark between the phrases where you would pause. The first slash is done.

3. Riders / use credit cards to pay about $2.00 a day to ride the bikes.

4. There are few problems with theft because the program knows who is riding the bikes.

5. The electronic system for locking and paying for bikes at the stations runs on solar power.

Vocabulary: Based on what you have learned in this lesson, match the following words with their definitions. Write the letter of the definition on the blank in front of the word it defines.

1. _____ transform   **A.** people who live in an area

2. _____ residents   **B.** a business agreement between people

3. _____ recycle   **C.** to change shape or form; convert

4. _____ transport   **D.** to need; must have

5. _____ translate   **E.** to carry something or someone

6. _____ theft   **F.** to turn from one language into another

7. _____ transaction   **G.** gets paid back

8. _____ covers   **H.** reuse or reprocess

9. _____ transfer   **I.** stealing

10. _____ require   **J.** to move something or someone from one place to another

Name _____ Date _____

ANTICIPATION GUIDE

Directions: Before you read the article "Fracking Raises Serious Concerns," read the statements below. If you agree with a statement, put a checkmark on the line next to it. If you disagree, put an X on the line.

_____ **1.** Our nation's need for energy is more important than protecting the environment.

_____ **2.** If the United States ran out of energy, we could always find more.

_____ **3.** Natural gas is a good energy substitute for buying oil from other countries.

Once you have responded to the statements above, write in the section below why you agree or disagree with each statement.

1. _____

_____

2. _____

_____

3. _____

_____

In the box below, draw a picture of what you think this article is about.

WORDSTORM

Directions: It's good to know more than just the dictionary definition of a word. Completing a wordstorm lets you write down information to help you understand what a word means, how it's related to other words, and how to use it in different ways.

What is the word?

environmentalists

Here is the sentence from the text in which the word is used:

"Environmentalists argue that companies always should clean the wastewater or bury it safely in closed wells."

What are some other words or phrases that mean the same thing?

_____

What are three things you know about environmentalists?

1. _____ 2. _____ 3. _____

Name three people other than teachers who would likely use this word.

1. _____ 2. _____ 3. _____

Draw a picture below that reminds you of the word *environmentalists*.

LANGUAGE MINI-LESSON

Every **verb** has four basic forms. The **present** and **present participle** tenses show something happening now. The **past** and **past participle** tenses show something that happened in the past. See how they are formed in the chart below.

Present	Present Participle	Past	Past Participle
walk	(is) walk**ing**	walk**ed**	(has/have) walk**ed**

There are five groups of "irregular" verbs that do not change to the past and past participle tenses by adding –ed or –d. Some of these verbs are shown in the chart below. The first one is filled in for you. Fill in the other examples yourself.

	Present	Past	Past Participle
Group 1: The forms of the present, past, and past participle are the same.	cut	cut	has cut
	hit		
	hurt		
	let		
Group 2: The past and past participle forms are the same.	buy	bought	has bought
	catch		
	feel		
	keep		
	leave		
Group 3: The past participle is formed by adding -n or -en to the **past** tense.	break	broke	has broken
	choose		
	speak		
	steal		
Group 4: The past participle is formed by adding -n or -en to the **present** tense.	blow	blew	has blown
	know		
	drive		
	eat		
	give		
Group 5: The last vowel changes from i to a in the past and to u in the past participle.	ring	rang	has rung
	drink		
	swim		
	begin		

ECHO READING

Directions: When you read, you should make breaks, and sometimes pauses, between groups of words. As your teacher reads each phrase, repeat aloud what is read and put a slash or line after that phrase. Then read the whole sentence aloud as a class. Do the first paragraph together as a class, and then do the second one on your own. The first sentence has been marked for you.

One way / that oil companies / get natural gas / from the ground / is called / hydraulic fracturing. / People often shorten that name to "fracking." In the last few years oil companies have been fracking more often. While it leads to more oil and natural gas, it also raises concerns about the damage it does.

Fracking reaches oil and gas that is trapped in rock deep in the ground. It starts by drilling a hole about 10,000 feet down. When it reaches shale, the drill turns horizontally and drills another mile through that rock. Then a small explosive makes tiny cracks in the shale. After that the company blasts millions of gallons of water, sand and chemicals into the hole. That opens the cracks further and allows the trapped oil and gas to escape.

What's Happening

IN THE USA?

BY LAWRENCE GABLE
© *2014 What's Happening Publications*

SUBJECT: SCIENCE and ENVIRONMENT

Fracking Raises Serious Concerns

1 One way that oil companies get natural gas from the ground is called hydraulic fracturing. People often shorten that name to "fracking." In the last few years oil companies have been fracking more often. While it leads to more oil and natural gas, it also raises concerns about the damage it does.

2 Fracking reaches oil and gas that is trapped in rock deep in the ground. It starts by drilling a hole about 10,000 feet down. When it reaches shale, the drill turns horizontally and drills another mile through that rock. Then a small explosive makes tiny cracks in the shale. After that the company blasts millions of gallons of water, sand and chemicals into the hole. That opens the cracks further and allows the trapped oil and gas to escape.

3 The second largest natural gas deposit in the world is the Marcellus Shale. It stretches from New York across parts of Pennsylvania, Ohio, Maryland, West Virginia and Virginia. Oil companies are increasing their use of hydraulic fracturing in those states. In Pennsylvania, for example, the number of wells grew from 27 in 2007 to 1,445 in 2010.

4 For a long time environmentalists have liked natural gas. In comparison to the pollution that comes from mining coal and burning it at power plants, natural gas is cleaner. It produces fewer gases that cause global warming. However, now environmentalists are changing their minds.

5 A report by Cornell University found that fracking is leading to more global warming than coal does. Methane is a gas that escapes into the air from drilling normal gas wells. However, twice as much methane escapes from wells drilled by hydraulic fracturing.

Methane is also getting into groundwater. Some landowners near wells have been able to light their water on fire as it comes out the faucet.

6 There are also serious concerns about chemicals in groundwater. Fracking uses 40,000 gallons of different chemicals for each well. The U.S. government reports that some of them are poison, and some cause cancer. The oil industry says that fracking does not pollute water. However, already there are many places where people and animals have gotten sick. Chemicals in water also have killed fish and plants in ponds and streams.

7 Fracking always creates wastewater. Some stays in the ground, and some returns to the surface. When companies leave it there to evaporate, harmful chemicals enter the air. Environmentalists argue that companies always should clean the wastewater or bury it safely in closed wells.

8 The U.S. Geological Survey has studied fracking too. It connects fracking directly to recent earthquakes in Ohio and Oklahoma. It also fears the effect of tens of millions of gallons of water and chemicals that remain in the ground.

9 Protests against fracking are increasing. New York has banned it. Maryland has stopped it while it studies the environmental damage. Now Pennsylvania is forcing companies to identify the chemicals that they use.

10 The advantages of fracking are obvious. It could lead to jobs, profits and enough oil and natural gas for 100 years. However, its disadvantages are troubling. State governments hesitate to allow fracking if it is going to damage people's health and the environment around them.

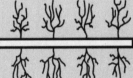

QUICK READ/DRAW AND WRITE

Directions: First Reading—As you do your first reading of the article, your teacher will time you for one minute. When time is called, write the number of the paragraph where you stopped.   **Paragraph #** _____

In the box below, draw a picture summarizing what you read.

Second Reading—As you do your second reading of the article, your teacher will time you for one minute. When time is called, write the number of the paragraph where you stopped.   **Paragraph #** _____

Directions: Now continue reading the rest of the article. Below, write five important words that will help you remember the information from the article.

_____   _____   _____   _____   _____

CLOSE READING ANNOTATION

Third Reading—As you reread each paragraph in the article closely, answer the questions by annotating the text. Each numbered question corresponds to a paragraph in the article where the answer can be found. Write your brief answers in the space below each question.

1. What is the author's purpose for writing the first paragraph?

_____

2. How does fracking work?

_____

3. Why is fracking increasing in some states?

_____

4. What is the purpose of the last sentence in paragraph 4?

_____

5. What was the reason that environmentalists changed their minds?

_____

6. Why is there so much concern about the chemicals used in fracking?

_____

7. What are the problems caused by wastewater?

_____

8. Why do you think people relate fracking and earthquakes?

_____

9. What have been the results of some of the protests about fracking?

_____

10. What is the author's purpose in writing paragraph 10?

_____

GRAMMAR GAMES

Directions: Reread the two paragraphs below. Words have been left out from the sentences. Think about the information from the article you have read and fill in words that make sense. The part of speech of each missing word is provided.

Fracking reaches gas that _____ trapped in rock deep in
(1. verb)

the ground. It starts by drilling a _____ about 10,000 feet
(2. noun)

down. When _____ reaches shale, the drill turns horizontally
(3. pronoun)

and drills another mile _____ that rock. Then a small explosive
(4. preposition)

makes tiny _____ in the shale. After that the company blasts
(5. plural noun)

millions of gallons of water, sand _____ chemicals into the hole.
(6. conjunction)

That opens the cracks further and allows the trapped oil and gas to

_____ .
(7. verb)

The second largest natural gas _____ in the world is the
(8. noun)

Marcellus Shale. It stretches from New York _____ parts of
(9. preposition)

Pennsylvania, Ohio, Maryland, West Virginia and Virginia. _____
(10. adjective)

companies are increasing their _____ of hydraulic fracturing in
(11. noun)

_____ states.
(12. pronoun)

HOW'S IT ORGANIZED?

This article is organized as causes followed by their effects.

Directions: Answer these questions in the spaces at the bottom.

1. What is hydraulic fracturing?

2. What has the size of the Marcellus Shale caused?

3. What are some of the problems caused by fracking?

4. What problem does the escape of methane gas cause?

5. What effect has fracking had in Oklahoma and Ohio?

6. How have some states responded to concerns about fracking?

Answers:

1.	
2.	
3.	
4.	
5.	
6.	

The main idea of a selection reflects what the paragraph or sentences are about. Put an X on the space next to the sentence that best states the main idea of the article.

_____ **1.** Fracking is an efficient way to get energy from natural gas.

_____ **2.** Fracking produces cheap energy but has risks for the environment.

_____ **3.** The benefits of fracking outweigh the many consequences.

Explain below why your choice is the best main or central idea.

_____

_____

IS THAT A FACT?

Directions: Read the definitions of a fact and an inference below. Then read the paragraphs that follow. At the bottom of the page, write an F on the blank if the sentence is a fact. Write an I if the sentence is an inference. Use the following definitions:

Fact—a statement that can be proven true from the paragraphs

Inference—a guess as to what MIGHT be true, based on what you have read and what you already know about the subject

> For a long time environmentalists have liked natural gas. In comparison to the pollution that comes from mining coal and burning it at power plants, natural gas is cleaner. It produces fewer gases that cause global warming. However, now environmentalists are changing their minds.
>
> A recent study found that fracking is leading to more global warming than coal does. Methane is a gas that escapes into the air from drilling normal gas wells. However, twice as much methane escapes from wells drilled by hydraulic fracturing. Methane is also getting into groundwater. Some landowners near wells have been able to light their water on fire as it comes out the faucet.

_____ **1.** Fracking is worse for the environment than burning coal.

_____ **2.** Environmentalists were in favor of fracking.

_____ **3.** Methane gas is harmful to the environment.

_____ **4.** Methane gas can catch fire.

_____ **5.** People who own land allow the wells to be drilled on their property.

TIC-TAC-TOE SUMMARIZING

When you **summarize** in writing, you present all the key points the author is trying to make.

Directions: Write four sentences to summarize the article about the future of fracking. To help you, there are nine words or phrases in the Tic-Tac-Toe graphic organizer below. To write a sentence, you must use three words or phrases in a row. The row can be horizontal (—), vertical (I), or diagonal (/).

fracking	environmentalists	wells
wastewater	methane	shale
protests	drilling	oil companies

1. _____

_____

2. _____

_____

3. _____

_____

4. _____

_____

REACTION GUIDE

Directions: Now that you have read and studied information about "Fracking Raises Serious Concerns," reread the statements below, which you responded to before reading the article. Then think about how the author might respond to these statements. If you think the author would agree, put a checkmark on the line before the number. If you think the author would disagree, put an X on the line. Then below the statement, copy the words, phrases, or sentences from the article that provide evidence of the views stated by the author. Also note if there is no evidence to support the statement.

_____ **1.** Our nation's need for energy is more important than protecting the environment.

Evidence: _____

_____

_____

_____ **2.** If the United States ran out of energy, we could always find more.

Evidence: _____

_____

_____

_____ **3.** Natural gas is a good energy substitute for buying oil from other countries.

Evidence: _____

_____

_____

Name _____ Date _____

TAKE A STAND

Directions: People often have differing feelings, or opinions, about an issue. When they discuss or argue their opposing views, they are taking part in a debate. A good persuasive argument is based on a claim that is supported by

Facts—statements that can be proven true

Statistics—numerical data gotten through research

Examples—instances that support an opinion

You and a partner are going to debate two of your other classmates. The topic you are going to debate is the following:

Our nation's energy needs are more important than the environment.

Decide with the other pair who will agree and who will disagree with this statement. Then answer these questions in order to win your debate.

1. What are your two strongest points to persuade the other side? (You can do Internet research to include facts, statistics, and examples.)

A. _____

B. _____

2. What might the other side say to argue against point A?

_____

_____

3. What might the other side say to argue against point B?

_____

_____

4. What will you say to prove the other side's arguments are wrong?

_____

_____

WHAT'S THE COMBINATION?

Writing is more interesting when the writer joins, or combines, short sentences. Follow the directions below to learn different ways to combine two sentences.

What to do: You can join two sentences by taking an infinitive phrase from one sentence and putting it inside another sentence that has the same subject (the same noun or a pronoun that stands for that noun). An infinitive phrase is a group of words that begins with *to* followed by a verb and adverbs, nouns, pronouns, and other words that work with the verb. The infinitive phrase in the sentence below is *to try new plays*.

Example: The team is on the field. They are there *to try new plays*.
New sentence: The team is on the field *to try new plays*.

Directions: Combine these sentences using the method above.

1. The oil companies wanted to dig more wells. They wanted to increase gas production.

_____

2. Environmental groups held protests. They wanted to get fracking stopped.

_____

3. Companies have been leaving chemicals in wastewater. They leave them to save money.

_____

4. The U.S. Geological Survey studied fracking. They wanted to determine if fracking was connected to earthquakes in Oklahoma.

_____

5. Maryland and North Carolina stopped fracking. They wanted to study the environmental damage.

_____

Name _____ Date _____

ANALYZING A PROMPT

Directions: Read the writing prompt in the box below. Then follow the directions to learn how to analyze and answer it.

> You work for a major oil company. You have been sent to talk to a farmer about paying him so your company can dig a well on his property. You will need to create notes on what you'll say to persuade this farmer that the benefits of fracking outweigh the possible risks. Use information from the article to help make your case and convince him.

1. A writing prompt begins with some background information known as the **set up.** Underline the sentences that set up this assignment.

2. Use the following **R.A.F.T.** technique to finish analyzing the prompt.

Role: What are you supposed to be to answer it? A student? A politician?

Write what you are here: _____

Audience: To whom are you writing? A friend? A particular group?

Write who it is here: _____

Format: Check to see what type of writing you are doing. Is it an essay, a letter, a speech, a story, a description, an editorial, or a report?

Write what it is here: _____

Task: Another sentence in the prompt will tell you what you must do, or your "task." Question words such as **why, how,** or **what** may tell the task.

If the question word is **why,** you will *give the reasons* that something is done.

If the question word is **how,** you will *explain the way* that something is done.

If the question word is **what,** you will *identify the thing* that is done.

Below, copy the sentence or question that describes your task.

_____

_____

ANALYZING INFORMATIONAL TEXT

1. Informational articles are written to provide data or descriptions that explain something. Below name three groups that might be interested in reading this article besides students and teachers.

   a. _____ b. _____ c. _____

2. What main point is the author making in this article?

   _____

   _____

3. Give two of the most important facts you learned in this article.

   a. _____

   b. _____

4. **Domain-specific vocabulary** consists of words used in a specific subject such as math, science, or social studies. Reread the article and list six domain-specific words used with this subject. After you select the words, write their definitions on the lines provided

   a. _____ : _____

   b. _____ : _____

   c. _____ : _____

   d. _____ : _____

   e. _____ : _____

   f. _____ : _____

ASSESSMENT

1. Circle the letter of the paragraph that explains why fracking is such an abundant source of natural gas.

   a. paragraph 2

   b. paragraph 3

   c. paragraph 8

   d. paragraph 10

2. Circle the letters of the two conclusions below that are best supported by evidence from the article.

   a. Oil and natural gas companies are limiting their use of fracking.

   b. Some environmentalists have been in favor of fracking.

   c. Fracking is linked to earthquakes.

   d. The growth of drilling for new wells has been slow over the last few years.

   e. Fracking can cause faucet water to catch fire.

3. Reread the last paragraph in the article. Explain below how the author completes the ideas he began with.

_____

_____

_____

_____

4. The author describes a number of dangers caused by fracking. Circle the letters of those dangers that are described in the article.

a. Twice as much methane escapes from wells drilled by hydraulic fracturing as from normal wells.

b. There are serious concerns about chemicals in groundwater.

c. The explosions used to get to natural gas have killed many.

d. Fracking is directly connected to earthquakes.

e. Natural gas wells are known to explode and cause great damage.

5. A student is writing a report about fracking. Read both sources below and the directions that follow.

Source 1: www.oilindustryreports.com Of the chemicals used to blast into shale deposits, water accounts for about 90 percent of the fracturing mixture. Sand accounts for about 9.5 percent. This leaves only about one half of one percent of other chemicals in the mixture. There are several ways oil and natural gas companies manage the use of fracturing fluids. How companies manage the wastewater depends on what specifically is in it, the presence of usable groundwater or surface water, the local geography, and government regulations. The bulk of water used in fracturing stays trapped tens of thousands of feet below the surface with little chance of chemicals reaching the surface or going into the air.

Source 2: www.firefromthefaucet.com Oil and gas companies pump millions of gallons of water into shale deposits to release natural gas, which is needed to power our country. Within this water are many chemicals that can potentially contaminate ground water. Companies that use fracking are required to follow local, state, and federal government regulations, which are meant to protect our ground and drinking water. Contaminated drinking water is only one potential risk. Other risks include the worsening of air quality, the possibility of the process triggering earthquakes, and the migration of gases and hydraulic-fracturing chemicals to the surface.

The student took notes about the information in the sources. Circle the letters of the notes that show disagreements in the facts presented by the two sources.

a. Companies pump millions of gallons of water underground to release natural gas.

b. Fracking produces much-needed natural gas to power the nation.

c. Companies are required to follow government regulations.

d. Fracking can worsen air quality and trigger earthquakes.

e. There is little chance dangerous chemicals can reach the surface.

Name _____ Date _____

ANTICIPATION GUIDE

Directions: Before you read the article "The Outlook Is Improving for Right Whales," read the statements below. If you agree with a statement, put a checkmark on the line next to it. If you disagree, put an X on the line.

_____ **1.** Right whales are nearly extinct and should be protected.

_____ **2.** Human hunters kill most right whales.

_____ **3.** Endangered animals need laws to protect them.

Once you have responded to the statements above, write in the section below why you agree or disagree with each statement.

1. _____

_____

2. _____

_____

3. _____

_____

In the box below, draw a picture of what you think this article is about.

Name _____ Date _____

WORDSTORM

Directions: It's good to know more than just the dictionary definition of a word. Completing a wordstorm lets you write down information to help you understand what a word means, how it's related to other words, and how to use it in different ways.

What is the word?

endangered

Here is the sentence from the text in which the word is used:

"The North Atlantic right whale is an endangered species."

What are some other words or phrases that mean the same thing?

_____

What are three reasons why living things might be endangered?

1. _____ 2. _____ 3. _____

Name three people other than teachers who would likely use this word.

1. _____ 2. _____ 3. _____

Draw a picture below that reminds you of the word *endangered*.

TIME MY READ #1

Directions: With a partner, see how many words you can read correctly in 45 seconds. As you read, your partner will put an X through any word read incorrectly on his or her copy. When you are finished, trade your books or papers, and let your partner read while you keep score. Count the total number of words you read correctly.

population underside dorsal calves filter serious whaler regulations	8
survival collisions shipping plates distinctive estimate researchers oil	16
extinction species damage endangered aquarium commercial vessels mobility	24
population underside dorsal calves filter serious whaler regulations	32
survival collisions shipping plates distinctive estimate researchers oil	40
extinction species damage endangered aquarium commercial vessels mobility	48
population underside dorsal calves filter serious whaler regulations	56
survival collisions shipping plates distinctive estimate researchers oil	64
extinction species damage endangered aquarium commercial vessels mobility	72
population underside dorsal calves filter serious whaler regulations	80

Number of words read correctly _____

ECHO READING

Directions: When you read, you should make breaks, and sometimes pauses, between groups of words. As your teacher reads each phrase, repeat aloud what is read and put a slash or line after that phrase. Then read the whole sentence aloud as a class. Do the first paragraph together as a class, and then do the second one on your own. The first sentence has been marked for you.

The right whale's name / came from whalers. / The whales are easy targets because they are slow, swim close to shore, and float when they are dead. In addition, their bodies contain large amounts of oil, meat and whalebone. Whalers thought they were "right" for hunting.

Whalers from America almost hunted the right whale to extinction. By 1750, the North Atlantic right whale's numbers were so low that whalers moved to the South Atlantic and South Pacific. By the early 20th century, whalers had killed about 40,000 right whales in each ocean. They had also taken 15,000 in the North Atlantic.

BY LAWRENCE GABLE
© 2014 What's Happening Publications

SUBJECT: SCIENCE and ENVIRONMENT

THE OUTLOOK IS IMPROVING FOR RIGHT WHALES

1 The North Atlantic right whale is an endangered species. Researchers estimate their population at only around 325. However, in 2009 they got good news when they saw a record number of calves. They counted 39, and that was the best sign in centuries for the right whale's survival.

2 The right whale is easy to identify. It has a black body, and may have white patches on its underside. It can grow to 55 feet long and 70 tons. It does not have a dorsal fin on its back, but it has two blowholes that form a V-shaped blow of water and air. Growths on its head make one right whale look different from another.

3 Right whales prefer shallow waters. They swim slowly along the coastline and in large bays. They have no teeth. Instead they have large jaws made of whalebone. Hundreds of whalebone plates hang from their upper jaw. As the whale opens its mouth to feed, the plates filter food from the water.

4 The right whale's name came from whalers. The whales were easy targets because they are slow, swim close to shore and float when they are dead. In addition, their bodies contain large amounts of oil, meat and whalebone. Whalers thought they were "right" for hunting.

5 Whalers from America almost hunted the right whale to extinction. By 1750 the North Atlantic right whale's numbers were so low that whalers moved to the South Atlantic and South Pacific. By the early 20th century whalers had killed about 40,000 right whales in each ocean. They also had taken 15,000 in the North Atlantic.

6 The world decided to protect the right whale. A worldwide ban on commercial hunting took effect in 1935. That stopped the population from getting smaller. Now Canadian and U.S. laws protect right whales. The U.S. put the right whale on the Endangered Species list in the 1970s.

7 The North Atlantic right whale still faces serious threats. They have only two predators, killer whales and humans. Researchers believe that killer whales do little damage. Even though humans no longer hunt the right whale, still their activities have killed too many.

8 Collisions with ships are the largest cause of right whale deaths along the Atlantic coast. Ships going in and out of harbors kill at least two or three a year. In 2008 new regulations went into effect. Now ships over 65 feet long must slow down. They also must sail in new shipping lanes that avoid areas where whales are.

9 The other great danger to right whales is entanglement in commercial fishing lines. Some whales drown because they get wrapped in thick ropes and nets. Others suffer from decreased mobility and infection. The number of entanglements has risen sharply in recent years.

10 Research and environmental organizations cooperate to help right whales. They use boats and planes to locate them, then report their locations so that ships can avoid them. They also have teams that free whales from fishing lines. Whenever possible, they take photos and enter them into a computer system.

11 According to the New England Aquarium, not a single North Atlantic right whale died because of humans in 2008. That was probably the first time since the 1600s. Although there are still dangers for them and their survival, the increased number of calves provides hope.

GET A CONTEXT CLUE

Directions: Below are sentences from "The Outlook Is Improving for Right Whales." First, read the sentence. Then, look back in the article and reread the paragraph in which the sentence is found. Circle the best answer to each question.

"Researchers *estimate* their population at only around 325."

1. The word *estimate* means

    A. wish
    B. firmly believe
    C. guess based on information
    D. hate

"Right whales prefer *shallow* waters."

2. The word *shallow* means

    A. deep
    B. cold
    C. fast
    D. not deep

"A worldwide ban on commercial hunting *took effect* in 1935."

3. The phrase *took effect* means

    A. began
    B. fell apart
    C. ended
    D. restarted

"The other great danger to right whales is *entanglement* in commercial fishing lines."

4. The word *entanglement* means

    A. being trapped
    B. swimming
    C. sleeping
    D. being found

"In 2008 new *regulations* went into effect."

5. The word *regulations* means

    A. statements
    B. laws or rules
    C. ideas
    D. projects

"Research and environmental organizations *cooperate* to help right whales."

6. The word *cooperate* means

    A. argue about
    B. try
    C. work together
    D. do research

WORD CHOICE

Directions: The sentences below contain blanks for missing words. Three answer choices are listed after each blank. Read the sentence past the blank and choose the correct word. Write it in the blank.

The world _____ (*decides, deciding, decided*) to protect the right whale. A worldwide ban on commercial hunting _____ (*took, takes, taking*) effect in 1935. That _____ (*stopped, stops, stopping*) the population from _____ (*gets, got, getting*) smaller. Now Canadian and U.S. laws _____ (*protect, protects, protecting*) right whales. The U.S. put the right whale on the _____ (*endangering, endangers, endangered*) list in the 1970s. The whales _____ (*have, has, having*) only two predators, killer whales and humans. Researchers _____ (*belief, believe, believing*) that killer whales do little damage. Even though humans no longer _____ (*hunting, hunters, hunt*) the right whale, still _____ (*there, their, they're*) activities have _____ (*killed, kills, kill*) too many.

Unit 2: Science and Environment

LOOK WHO'S TALKING

Directions: Below are sentences that relate to "The Outlook Is Improving for Right Whales." Look back in the article and reread the paragraph in which you find the reference. Circle the best answer to each question.

1. In the third sentence of paragraph 1, the word *they* best refers to

   A. the whales

   B. the researchers

   C. the calves

   D. the population

2. In paragraph 4, the second use of the word *they* refers to

   A. the whales

   B. the whalers

   C. the bodies

   D. the heads

3. In the second sentence of paragraph 7, the word *they* refers to

   A. the whalers

   B. the whales

   C. the humans

   D. the researchers

4. In the last sentence of paragraph 8, the word *they* refers to

   A. the ships

   B. the researchers

   C. the whales

   D. the shipping lanes

5. In paragraph 10, the word *they* refers each time to

   A. the whales

   B. the ships

   C. the organizations

   D. the locations

6. In the last sentence of paragraph 11, the word *them* refers to

   A. the whales

   B. the New England Aquarium

   C. the dangers

   D. the humans

NOTE MAKING

Directions: Read the boldfaced key words on the left side of the chart below. Then add notes that answer the question in parentheses under the key word.

Right whales (What do they look like?)	
Their name (How did they get their name?)	
Hunted (Where and why?)	
Endangered (By what?)	
Saved from extinction (How?)	

*On a separate sheet of paper write a summary of what your notes say about the recovery efforts for right whales.

IS THAT A FACT?

Directions: Read the definitions of a fact and an inference below. Then read the paragraph that follows. At the bottom of the page, write an F on the blank if the sentence is a fact. Write an I if the sentence is an inference. Use the following definitions:

Fact—a statement that can be proven true from the paragraph

Inference—a guess as to what MIGHT be true, based on what you have read and what you already know about the subject

Research and environmental organizations cooperate to help right whales. They use boats and planes to locate them and then report that information so that ships can avoid them. They also have teams that free whales from fishing lines. Whenever possible, they take photos and enter them in their computer system. According to the New England Aquarium, not a single right whale died because of humans in 2008. That was probably the first time since the 1600s.

_____ **1.** People are getting more concerned about the right whale.

_____ **2.** Agencies are using high-level technology to help the whales.

_____ **3.** The number of right whale deaths at the hands of humans is declining.

_____ **4.** Whales can die when they encounter fishing lines.

_____ **5.** No whales died at the hands of human beings in 2008.

_____ **6.** If ships get reports in time, they can avoid hitting whales.

MAKE A SPACE

Directions: Below are sentences that are missing punctuation and capitalization. First draw slash marks (/) between the words. Then rewrite each sentence in the space below it by filling in the missing punctuation and capitalization.

> Example:
>
> now / the / whales / are / swimming / north / to / Canada
>
> Now the whales are swimming north to Canada.

1. thenumberofentanglementshasrisensharplyinthelastdecade

_____

_____

2. researchandenvironmentalorganizationscooperatetohelprightwhales

_____

_____

3. nowshipsmustsailinlanestoavoidareaswherethewhalesare

_____

_____

4. aworldwidebanonhuntingtookplacein1935

_____

_____

TIME MY READ #2

Directions: With a partner, see how many words you can read correctly in 45 seconds. As you read, your partner will put an X through any word read incorrectly on his or her copy. When you are finished, trade your books or papers, and let your partner read while you keep score. Count the total number of words you read correctly. Write this score at the bottom of your page

population underside dorsal calves filter serious whaler regulations	8
survival collisions shipping plates distinctive estimate researchers oil	16
extinction species damage endangered aquarium commercial vessels mobility	24
population underside dorsal calves filter serious whaler regulations	32
survival collisions shipping plates distinctive estimate researchers oil	40
extinction species damage endangered aquarium commercial vessels mobility	48
population underside dorsal calves filter serious whaler regulations	56
survival collisions shipping plates distinctive estimate researchers oil	64
extinction species damage endangered aquarium commercial vessels mobility	72
population underside dorsal calves filter serious whaler regulations	80

Number of words read correctly _____

Is the score higher than it was in Time My Read #1?_____

WORD PARTS

Directions: A **base word** is a word that can stand alone. A **suffix** is a word part added to the end of a base word to change how the word is used in the sentence. The suffixes *-tion, -ation, -sion,* and *-cion* all change **verbs** to abstract **nouns.** The new noun can *express action* (revolution) or *tell what state something is in* (starvation). Write a definition of the words below. Try not to use the base word in the definition. If you don't know the base word, such as *revolt* in *revolution,* look it up in a dictionary or ask a partner.

1. **extinction—** _____

2. **suspicion—** _____

3. **population—** _____

4. **confusion—** _____

5. **imagination—** _____

6. **organization—** _____

7. **decision—** _____

8. **instruction—** _____

9. **coercion—** _____

10. **regulation—** _____

11. **possession—** _____

12. **exploration—** _____

13. **aggression—** _____

14. **temptation—** _____

15. **exclusion—** _____

WHALES WORD PUZZLE

Directions: Complete the crossword puzzle.

Word List

ESTIMATE

EXTINCTION

ENDANGER

SHALLOW

ENTANGLEMENT

REGULATION

ORGANIZATION

COOPERATE

POPULATION

TOOK EFFECT

Across

1. to expose to harm

4. the total number of something, such as people or animals

7. to guess based on information

8. not deep

9. the state of being completely killed off

10. began (2 words)

Down

2. getting trapped or tied up

3. to work together

5. a group of people united for a purpose

6. a law or rule

WRITING FRAME

Directions: Use your knowledge and information from the article to complete the writing frame below.

The North Atlantic right whale is an endangered species.

Researchers estimate that _____ . However,

_____ have appeared, and that is good news.

The right whale is easy to spot because _____

_____ _____ , and

_____ . The right whale was given that name

because _____ . Whalers from America almost

_____ , but now the world has decided to

_____ . There now is a _____

on commercial hunting that took effect in _____ .

That resulted in the population's getting _____ .

Now Canadian and U.S. laws protect the whales by putting them

_____ _____ . Environmental

and research organizations _____ . They use boats

and planes to locate the whales so that ships avoid them.

REACTION GUIDE

Directions: Now that you have read and studied information about "The Outlook is Improving for Right Whales," reread the statements below, which you responded to before reading the article. Then think about how the author might respond to these statements. If you think the author would agree, put a checkmark on the line before the number. If you think the author would disagree, put an X on the line. Then below the statement, copy the words, phrases, or sentences from the article that provide evidence of the views stated by the author. Also note if there is no evidence to support the statement.

_____ **1.** Right whales are nearly extinct and should be protected.

Evidence: _____

_____

_____

_____ **2.** Human hunters kill most right whales.

Evidence: _____

_____

_____

_____ **3.** Endangered animals need laws to protect them.

Evidence: _____

_____

_____

TAKE A STAND

Directions: People often have differing feelings or opinions about an issue. When they discuss or argue their opposing views, they are taking part in a debate. A good persuasive argument is based on a claim that is supported by

Facts—statements that can be proven true

Statistics—numerical data gotten through research

Examples—instances that support an opinion

You and a partner are going to debate two of your other classmates. The topic you are going to debate is the following:

Commercial whaling should be outlawed worldwide.

Decide with the other pair who will agree and who will disagree with this statement. Then answer these questions in order to win your debate.

1. What are your two strongest points to persuade the other side? (You can do Internet research to include facts, statistics, and examples.)

   A. _____

   B. _____

2. What might the other side say to argue against point A?

   _____

   _____

3. What might the other side say to argue against point B?

   _____

   _____

4. What will you say to prove the other side's arguments are wrong?

   _____

   _____

   _____

ASSESSMENT

Comprehension: Answer the questions about the following passage.

Whalers from America almost hunted the right whale to extinction. By 1750 the North Atlantic right whale's numbers were so low that whalers moved to the South Atlantic and the South Pacific. By the early 20th century whalers had killed about 40,000 right whales in each ocean. They also had taken 15,000 in the North Atlantic. Entanglements in nets from commercial fishing ships are now one of the largest causes of right whale deaths. They get wrapped in thick nets and drown, or they suffer from infections. The number of entanglements has risen recently.

1. What caused right whales to become nearly extinct in the past?

_____

_____

2. What dangers do right whales face today?

_____

_____

3. What was the author's purpose for writing about right whales?

_____

_____

Fluency: The words in the following two sentences are all connected. The sentences are also missing punctuation and capitalization. Draw slash marks (/) between the words. Then rewrite each sentence by filling in the punctuation and capitalization.

1. **shipsgoinginandoutofharborskilltwoorthreewhaleseachyear**

_____

2. indecembernewregulationswentintoeffectandnowshipsmust
sailinshippinglanesthatavoidthewhales

_____

_____

Fluency: Read the three sentences below. Imagine where you would pause within each sentence as you read it aloud. Draw a slash (/) mark between the phrases where you would pause. The first slash is done.

3. Hundreds of whalebone plates / hang from their upper jaw.

4. Now ships over sixty-five feet must slow down.

5. The North Atlantic right whale still faces serious threats.

Vocabulary: Based on what you have learned in this lesson, match the following words with their definitions. Write the letter of the definition on the blank in front of the word it defines.

1. _____ endanger   **A.** to work together

2. _____ regulation   **B.** being trapped or wrapped

3. _____ estimate   **C.** not deep

4. _____ organization   **D.** to guess based on information

5. _____ cooperate   **E.** expose to harm

6. _____ took effect   **F.** a group of people united for a purpose

7. _____ population   **G.** a law or rule

8. _____ entanglement   **H.** the total number of something

9. _____ shallow   **I.** began

10. _____ extinction   **J.** the state of being completely killed off

Name _____ Date _____

ANTICIPATION GUIDE

Directions: Before you read the article "DNA Sampling Goes to Court," read the statements below. If you agree with a statement, put a checkmark on the line next to it. If you disagree, put an X on the line.

_____ **1.** DNA can be used to tell one individual from another.

_____ **2.** Police should have a right to take a person's DNA if they think he or she committed a crime.

_____ **3.** DNA is an effective way to find out who committed a crime.

Once you have responded to the statements above, write in the section below why you agree or disagree with each statement.

1. _____

_____

2. _____

_____

3. _____

_____

In the box below, draw a picture of what you think this article is about.

PREDICTING ABCs

Directions: The article you are going to read is about using DNA to solve crimes. See how many boxes you can fill in below with words relating to this topic. For example, put the word *defendant* in the D–F box. Try to put at least one word in every box, and then try to write a word for every letter.

A–C	D–F	G–I
J–L	**M–O**	**P–R**
S–T	**U–V**	**W–Z**

LANGUAGE MINI-LESSON

The main verb in a sentence often needs a **helping verb** to show action or more precise meaning. A **verb phrase** consists of at least one verb and one or more helping verbs. For example: the verb phrase in the sentence below is *am going*.

Helping verb *am*   **I am going to the store.**   Verb phrase *am going*

The main **helping verbs** are shown in the chart below.

Forms of the verb *be*	be, am, is, are, was, were, being, been
Forms of the verb *do*	do, does, did
Forms of the verb *have*	have, has, had
Other helping verbs	could, should, would, may, might, must, can, shall, will

Directions: Circle the helping verb and draw a line under the verb phrase. Note: Sometimes there is more than one helping verb!

1. Police have used DNA evidence to solve crimes for years.

2. Police can take DNA samples from people when they are arrested.

3. A DNA sample can be something like blood, saliva, or skin cells.

4. The DNA might be sent to a government database of known criminals.

5. All states must send the DNA from certain kinds of criminals.

6. The police may conduct a search if they have suspected a crime has been committed.

7. When a person has been arrested, the police will take photographs and fingerprints.

8. DNA has become an important part of criminal investigations.

9. DNA has helped prove people's innocence or guilt.

ECHO READING

Directions: When you read, you should make breaks, and sometimes pauses, between groups of words. As your teacher reads each phrase, repeat aloud what is read and put a slash or line after that phrase. Then read the whole sentence aloud as a class. Do the first paragraph together as a class, and then do the second one on your own. The first sentence has been marked for you.

At crime scenes / investigators almost always find / a DNA sample. / It could be something like blood, saliva or skin cells. If the police already have a suspect, they compare that person's DNA to what was at the scene. They can also send it to the government's database of DNA from known criminals. If it matches, then they instantly learn who was at the crime scene.

The U.S. government set up a DNA database in the late 1980s. It holds DNA samples of criminals from around the country. This system compares a new DNA sample to samples it already has. It also can compare the new sample to evidence from other crime scenes. All fifty states must send the DNA from certain kinds of criminals to the database.

What's Happening

IN THE USA?

BY LAWRENCE GABLE
© 2014 What's Happening Publications

SUBJECT: SCIENCE and ENVIRONMENT

DNA Sampling Goes to Court

1   For some years the police have been using DNA evidence to solve crimes. In 2013, though, the U.S. Supreme Court heard a case about taking DNA samples. It questioned whether police can take samples from people at the time of their arrest.

2   Human DNA (deoxyribonucleic acid) is a molecule that holds a person's genetic information. It is nearly identical in most humans, but each human's DNA is also unique. Scientists can use it to identify one individual from another.

3   At crime scenes investigators almost always find a DNA sample. It could be something like blood, saliva or skin cells. If the police already have a suspect, they compare that person's DNA to what was at the scene. They also can send it to the government's database of DNA from known criminals. If it matches, then they instantly learn who was at the crime scene.

4   The U.S. government set up a DNA database in the late 1980s. It holds DNA samples of criminals from around the country. This system compares a new DNA sample to samples it already has. It also can compare the new sample to evidence from other crime scenes. All fifty states must send the DNA from certain kinds of criminals to the database.

5   The case before the Supreme Court in 2013 dealt with a man from Maryland. In 2009 the police had arrested Alonzo King and had used a cotton swab to collect a DNA sample. A few months later the database linked him to an unsolved rape case six years earlier. He stood trial and received a sentence of life in prison.

6   The Maryland Court of Appeals reversed his conviction though. It agreed that taking his DNA sample had violated his freedom from "unreasonable searches and seizures." In general, the police must have a search warrant from a judge to look for something specific. They also may conduct a search if they have immediate cause for suspicion, like seeing drugs on the seat of a car during a traffic stop. Maryland's court objected to taking DNA from an innocent person.

7   Police can do many things when making arrests. They search people, put them in handcuffs and hold them in jail. At the police station they take photographs and fingerprints to verify their identity. Police also check records to see whether people have a criminal history.

8   The State of Maryland appealed the court's decision to the Supreme Court. Its lawyers argued that using a cotton swab is a modern form of fingerprinting. They also argued that it is a harmless act during an arrest. They reminded the Court too that Maryland destroys the sample if the person is innocent.

9   Mr. King's lawyers made different arguments, of course. They disagreed that a DNA sample resembles fingerprinting, since it is not used for identification. They agreed with the police's right to take DNA samples from guilty people. However, if Mr. King was not yet guilty of the crime in 2009, then taking his DNA invaded his privacy.

10   DNA has become an important part of criminal investigations. Before the 2013 case, more than half of the states allowed police to collect samples at the time of an arrest. The Supreme Court made its ruling in June 2013. It ruled that police may take DNA samples in order to identify people. So now taking a sample is just like taking fingerprints and photographs, and it is legal under the Fourth Amendment.

QUICK READ/DRAW AND WRITE

Directions: First Reading—As you do your first reading of the article, your teacher will time you for one minute. When time is called, write the number of the paragraph where you stopped.   **Paragraph #** _____

In the box below, draw a picture summarizing what you read.

Second Reading—As you do your second reading of the article, your teacher will time you for one minute. When time is called, write the number of the paragraph where you stopped.   **Paragraph #** _____

Directions: Now continue reading the rest of the article. Below, write five important words that will help you remember the information from the article.

_____   _____   _____   _____   _____

CLOSE READING ANNOTATION

Third Reading—As you reread each paragraph in the article closely, answer the questions by annotating the text. Each numbered question corresponds to a paragraph in the article where the answer can be found. Write your brief answers in the space below each question.

1. What question does the first paragraph ask?

_____

2. What is DNA, or deoxyribonucleic acid?

_____

3. What are some of the forms of DNA found at crime scenes?

_____

4. How does the government keep track of people's DNA?

_____

5. What happened with the case of the man in Maryland?

_____

6. What does the phrase "unreasonable searches and seizures" mean?

_____

7. What is the author's purpose for writing paragraph 7?

_____

8. What argument did the Maryland lawyers use to support using DNA?

_____

9. What was the counterargument that Mr. King's lawyers made?

_____

10. What is the author's purpose of the final paragraph?

_____

GRAMMAR GAMES

Directions: Reread the two paragraphs below. Words have been left out from the sentences. Think about the information from the article you have read and fill in words that make sense. The part of speech of each missing word is provided.

At crime scenes investigators almost always _____ a
(1. verb)

DNA sample. _____ could be something like blood, saliva
(2. pronoun)

_____ skin cells. If the _____ already have a suspect,
(3. conjunction)   (4. noun)

they compare that person's DNA to what was _____ the scene.
(5. preposition)

They also can _____ it to the government's database of DNA of
(6. verb)

known criminals. If it matches, then they _____ learn who was
(7. verb)

at the _____ scene.
(8. adjective)

The U.S. government set up a _____ database in the late
(9. adjective)

1980s. It holds DNA _____ from criminals from around the
(10. plural noun)

country. This system _____ a new DNA sample to samples it
(11. verb)

already has. _____ also can compare the new sample to
(12. pronoun)

evidence from other crime _____.
(13. plural noun)

Unit 2: Science and Environment

CLOSE READING STRUCTURE

Directions: Understanding the structure of a text is important for two reasons. First, understanding the structure of a selection can help you remember the main idea and important details. Second, most academic writing you will encounter uses text structures to organize ideas.

1. Writers often include a statement in the **introduction** that catches the reader's attention. Then, the writer tells what the article will be about. On the space provided, copy the last sentence of the introduction to the article.

_____

_____

2. On the space below, copy the sentence that best states what the author's **claim, main idea,** or **thesis** is for this article.

_____

_____

3. On the space below, copy the sentence that shows where the author introduces the other side's **opinions,** or **opposing claims.**

_____

_____

4. Near the end of an article, a writer often restates the claim and summarizes the evidence. This is called the **conclusion.** On the space below, copy the sentence that best shows where the conclusion to the article **begins.**

_____

_____

IS THAT A FACT?

Directions: Read the definitions of a fact and an inference below. Then read the paragraph that follows. At the bottom of the page, write an F on the blank if the sentence is a fact. Write an I if the sentence is an inference. Use the following definitions:

Fact—a statement that can be proven true from the paragraph

Inference—a guess as to what MIGHT be true, based on what you have read and what you already know about the subject

At crime scenes investigators almost always find a DNA sample. It could be something like blood, saliva or skin cells. If the police already have a suspect, they compare that person's DNA to what was at the scene. They also can send it to the government's database of DNA from known criminals. If it matches, then they instantly learn who was at the crime scene. The U.S. government set up a DNA database in the late 1980s. It holds DNA samples of criminals from around the country. This system compares a new DNA sample to samples it has.

_____ **1.** The government is interested in knowing who commits crimes across the country.

_____ **2.** It's difficult to commit a crime and not leave DNA.

_____ **3.** Police can compare a person's DNA to what is found at the scene of a crime.

_____ **4.** If a person's DNA matches a crime, he or she is automatically going to be found guilty.

_____ **5.** Every criminal in the country might be in the government's DNA database.

SUMMARIZING ABCs

Directions: Now that you've read the article on DNA sampling, see how many words about crime evidence you can write in the boxes below.

A–C	D–F	G–I
J–L	**M–O**	**P–R**
S–T	**U–V**	**W–Z**

REACTION GUIDE

Directions: Now that you have read and studied information about "DNA Sampling Goes to Court," reread the statements below, which you responded to before reading the article. Then think about how the author might respond to these statements. If you think the author would agree, put a checkmark on the line before the number. If you think the author would disagree, put an X on the line. Then below the statement, copy the words, phrases, or sentences from the article that provide evidence of the views stated by the author. Also note if there is no evidence to support the statement.

_____ **1.** DNA can be used to tell one individual from another.

Evidence: _____

_____

_____

_____ **2.** Police should have a right to take a person's DNA if they think he or she committed a crime.

Evidence: _____

_____

_____

_____ **3.** DNA is an effective way to find out who committed a crime.

Evidence: _____

_____

_____

SENTENCE TRANSITIONS

An informational essay answers questions and provides information. Writers use transitional phrases to link ideas. Some transitional words and phrases include *to show, to prove, because, to explain, to verify, due to, instead of, furthermore, as a result of,* and *in order to*.

Directions: Complete the following sentences using the phrases given.

Example: The Court of Appeals in Maryland reversed a conviction. The Court of Appeals in Maryland reversed a conviction *due to a violation of Mr. King's freedom*.

1. Police are using DNA sampling *in order to*

_____

2. A person's DNA is gathered by the police *because*

_____

3. DNA can be collected at a crime scene *as a result of*

_____

4. Police must have a search warrant *in order to*

_____

5. Mr. King's lawyers disagreed with the court's decision, and *as a result*

_____

PICKING UP PUNCTUATION

Remember that **commas** can be used to separate parts of a sentence. Here are some rules that tell you when to use commas.

1. Use a comma after every item in a series except the last one. For example: A DNA sample could be something like bone, blood, saliva, or skin cells.

2. Use a comma between two or more adjectives of equal rank that describe the same noun. For example: The lawyers made **important, different** arguments.

3. Sometimes, however, a comma is not needed between two adjectives that describe the same noun. For example: The lawyers argued that a **soft cotton** swab is illegal.

Here's how you decide whether to put a comma between two adjectives.

Place the word *and* between the two adjectives. If the sentence still makes sense, then put in the comma. For example: The lawyers made important *and* different arguments.

If the sentence does **not** make sense, leave the comma out. For example: The lawyers argued that a soft *and* cotton swab is illegal.

Directions: This paragraph needs six commas. Fill them in where you think they should go.

> The police must have a legal search warrant from a judge to look into a car truck boat or house. The police can do many things when making arrests. They search people ask them questions put them in handcuffs and put them in a jail cell. The police also check records to see whether people have a violent criminal history.

ANALYZING A PROMPT

Directions: Read the writing prompt in the box below. Then follow the directions to learn how to analyze and answer it.

> You are a police investigator who believes that a suspect is guilty of a
> crime. The court says that you cannot get a DNA sample from the
> suspect. Your task is to write a request informing the court as to the
> value of the DNA sample that needs to be obtained from the suspect to
> make the case. Give an explanation of how and why DNA can be useful.
> Provide information from the article to support your request and
> convince the court that the evidence is vital to proving your case.

1. A writing prompt begins with some background information known as the **set up.** Underline the sentences that set up this assignment.

2. Use the following **R.A.F.T.** technique to finish analyzing the prompt.

Role: What are you supposed to be to answer it? A student? A lawyer?

Write what you are here: _____

Audience: To whom are you writing? A friend? A particular group?

Write who it is here: _____

Format: Check to see what type of writing you are doing. Is it an essay, a letter, a speech, a story, a description, an editorial, or a report?

Write what it is here: _____

Task: Another sentence in the prompt will tell you what you must do, or your "task." Question words like **why, how,** or **what** may tell the task.

If the question word is **why,** you will *give the reasons* that something is done.

If the question word is **how,** you will *explain the way* that something is done.

If the question word is **what,** you will *identify the thing* that is done.

Below, copy the sentence or question that describes your task.

_____

_____

WHAT'S YOUR POINT?

When writing an essay it is important to have a strong **claim**. A **claim,** or **thesis statement**, states the main point the writer wants to get across. Once the thesis is introduced, the body of the essay should support that thesis with key points that provide evidence.

The information presented in the article "DNA Sampling Goes to Court" explains the value of using DNA to identify criminals. There is an issue about when a person's DNA can be taken. Some feel that collecting a person's DNA is a violation of that person's freedom. Others feel that using DNA to identify criminals is an effective tool, since everyone's DNA is unique.

Directions: Which of these sentences provides the best **claim** for an essay on this topic? Circle the letter of your choice.

a. Using DNA provides effective evidence about a person's criminal involvement, even though some feel it shouldn't be taken from suspects.

b. Police have many tools other than DNA, such as videotape and eyewitnesses, that they can use to identify suspects.

c. The U.S. government has a database that is used to match criminals to crimes all over the country.

In the space below, explain what is weak or wrong about the other two statements.

1. _____

_____

_____

2. _____

_____

_____

ASSESSMENT

1. This question has two parts. First, answer **Part A.** Then, answer **Part B.**

Part A: The Maryland Court of Appeals said that taking a DNA sample from Mr. King violated his protection from "unreasonable searches and seizures." Circle the letter of the statement below that explains what was unreasonable.

a. Maryland's Court of Appeals objected to taking DNA from an innocent person.

b. If the police already have a suspect, they compare that person's DNA to what was at the scene.

c. At crime scenes investigators almost always find a DNA sample.

d. If it matches, then they instantly learn who was at the crime scene.

Part B: Circle the letter of the one statement that does NOT support your answer to Part A.

a. In 2009 the police had arrested Alonzo King and had used a cotton swab to take a DNA sample.

b. A few months later the database linked him to an unsolved rape case six years earlier.

c. The State of Maryland argued that using a DNA sample is a form of fingerprinting.

d. If Mr. King was not yet guilty of the crime in 2009, then taking his DNA invaded his privacy.

2. On the lines below, summarize the arguments that the State of Maryland made to the Supreme Court supporting the use of DNA to find Mr. King guilty.

_____

_____

_____

_____

_____

ASSESSMENT

3. Reread paragraph 10. Based on what the Supreme Court decided, circle the letters of the conclusions that can be made.

   a. Taking a swab of someone's DNA is just like fingerprinting and therefore legal.

   b. Mr. King was found innocent since the police had taken his DNA six years after the crime.

   c. The Supreme Court reversed the Maryland Court of Appeals decision that Mr. King was innocent.

   d. DNA samples can now be used to prove that people were at the scene of past crimes and therefore may be found guilty.

4. A student is writing a report to explain why DNA should be used to establish the guilt or innocence of people who might be connected with a crime. Read the first draft below and then follow the directions.

The use of DNA samples has become a valuable and legal tool in discovering who commits crime in America. Many police don't know what they're doing when they collect evidence. But today, thanks to DNA, police have a tool that is as individual as one's fingerprints to discover who was at a crime scene. People who commit crimes are a danger to our society. When one commits a crime, there is almost always a sample of that person's DNA left at the scene. The sample may come from blood, saliva, or skin cells. Because everyone's DNA is unique, it is possible to connect the DNA at a crime scene to the criminal who committed the crime.

On the lines below, copy the two sentences that do not provide specific evidence to support the underlined sentence.

a. _____

_____

b. _____

_____

Unit

2

Quarterly Performance Assessment

New Ban Targets Giant Snakes

What's Happening
IN THE USA?

BY LAWRENCE GABLE
© 2014 What's Happening Publications

New Ban Targets Giant Snakes

1   In January 2012 the U.S. Fish and Wildlife Service announced a ban on four snakes. They are the Burmese python, yellow anaconda, and North African and South African pythons. The ban mainly protects Everglades National Park in Florida, where the Burmese python is killing many animals that are native species.

2   The U.S. has a long history of dealing with exotic species. In 1900 the Lacey Act stopped people from hunting for profit and killing birds for the feather trade. It also stopped the introduction of harmful exotic species into the U.S. The recent ban is a new part of the Lacey Act.

3   The Burmese python is causing the most problems. It can grow to 26 feet long and weigh more than 200 pounds. They were not in the Everglades before the 1990s, but 1,825 of them have been caught since 2000. Nobody knows how many live in South Florida now, but wildlife experts believe that there are tens of thousands. They are an invasive species, one whose introduction causes harm to its new environment.

4   Experts think that Burmese pythons arrived in South Florida two ways. One is that some python owners just got rid of their pets by releasing them in the Everglades. The other is that the snakes came from the exotic pet industry. When Hurricane Andrew struck Florida in 1992, it destroyed many pet stores and warehouses. About 900 Burmese pythons escaped.

5   The pythons are with alligators at the top of the Everglades' food chain. Since the mid-1990s they have been feasting on animals that are native to the region. A team studied animal populations in the Everglades from 2003–2011. They compared their numbers with those from 1996 and 1997.

6   The study shows that populations of medium-sized animals have suffered. Where the snakes have been living the longest, rabbits and foxes have disappeared completely. The raccoon population has fallen by 99.3 percent, opossums by 98.9 percent, and bobcats by 87.5 percent. The snakes are also eating large numbers of birds and rodents.

7   Burmese pythons are constrictors. They bite their prey just to hold it, then kill it by wrapping themselves around it. When pythons constrict their muscles, they suffocate their prey. Then they open their jaws and eat the animal whole. In October 2011 authorities found a 16-foot python resting after it had eaten a deer.

8   Experts worry that the snakes will migrate. They have adapted to salt water in the Everglades and they are excellent swimmers. Already people have caught several of them in the Florida Keys, islands 15 miles away. Experts predict that the python also will adapt to colder climates to the north.

9   This is not the first ban on snakes. Florida passed a law in 2010 that bans future ownership of seven different snakes. This ban took effect in March 2012. Originally the federal government wanted to ban nine snakes. However, under pressure from the reptile industry, it reduced the number to four. That decision disappointed many people because the other five snakes remain a threat.

10   Now the ban covers eight snakes. It will not get rid of large snakes in South Florida, but it will control their numbers. The balance of nature allows native animal populations to do well in the Everglades. This ban protects them from huge snakes that do not belong there in the first place.

Name _____ Date _____

QUARTERLY PERFORMANCE ASSESSMENT

1. This question has two parts. First, answer **Part A.** Then, answer **Part B.**

Part A: What is the author's main purpose in "New Ban Targets Giant Snakes"?

a. The author wants people to learn more about the Burmese pythons.

b. The author wants readers to understand why the ban on snakes is needed.

c. The author wants readers to know about the Everglades.

d. The author wants readers to know how the python was introduced to Florida.

Part B: Which sentence from the text supports your answer to **Part A**?

a. Originally the federal government wanted to ban nine snakes.

b. Experts worry that the snakes will migrate.

c. They bite their prey just to hold it, then kill it by wrapping themselves around it.

d. Nobody knows how many live in South Florida now, but wildlife experts believe that there are tens of thousands.

2. The author is trying to explain the effect of the number of pythons in Florida. Which **two** paragraphs below give the best description of the problems?

a. paragraph 2

b. paragraph 3

c. paragraph 6

d. paragraph 7

e. paragraph 9

3. Support the claim that the pythons are creating an environmental problem. On the lines below, cite two pieces of evidence from the article to support this claim.

a. _____

_____

_____

b. _____

_____

_____

4. A student is writing a report on the situation with pythons in Florida. Read the draft of the introduction below and the directions that follow.

What would happen if many parts of the country were overrun with dangerous animals that threatened our existence? Because there have been so many pythons introduced into the Everglades in South Florida, the animals—and even the people—who live in the Everglades are in danger of losing their lives. There are four different types of pythons that are causing the problem. These are the Burmese python, the African and South African pythons, and the yellow anaconda. Pythons are a deadly predator to other animals.

The student took these notes from reliable sources:

—Pythons are constrictors.

—The ban took effect in March of 2012 to control the numbers of snakes.

—Then they suffocate their prey and eat the animal whole.

—Experts worry that the snakes will migrate as they have adapted to salt water.

—They bite their prey to hold it, and then they kill it by wrapping themselves around it.

—Populations of some animals like rabbits have been wiped out.

—Pythons are excellent swimmers and can adapt to salt water.

—There are four types of pythons: Burmese, North African, and South African pythons, and the yellow anaconda.

Directions: Using information from the student's notes, write one paragraph developing the idea that is presented in the last sentence of the introduction.

_____

_____

_____

_____

Global Issues

Quarterly Performance Assessment
Sharks Find Themselves in Danger

Name _____ Date _____

ANTICIPATION GUIDE

Directions: Before you read the article "Space Is Filling with Junk," read the statements below. If you agree with a statement, put a checkmark on the line next to it. If you disagree, put an X on the line.

_____ **1.** Outer space is too big for us to worry about old satellites.

_____ **2.** If outer space is polluted, it can be cleaned up easily.

_____ **3.** Pollution in outer space is a problem for all countries.

Once you have responded to the statements above, write in the section below why you agree or disagree with each statement.

1. _____

_____

2. _____

_____

3. _____

_____

In the box below, draw a picture of what you think this article is about.

PREDICTING ABCs

Directions: The article you are going to read is about outer space. See how many boxes you can fill in below with words relating to this topic. For example, put the word *planet* in the P–R box. Put at least one word in every box, and then try to write a word for every letter.

A–C	D–F	G–I

J–L	M–O	P–R

S–T	U–V	W–Z

Name _____ Date _____

Directions: With a partner, see how many words you can read correctly in 45 seconds. As you read, your partner will put an X through any word read incorrectly on his or her copy. When you are finished, trade your books or papers, and let your partner read while you keep score. Count the total number of words you read correctly. Write this score at the bottom of your page.

debris dumping exploration satellites burnt travel engines distant	8
orbits explosion diameter atmosphere operators dented pieces fallen	16
fuel objects location missile functioned collision astronauts NASA	24
debris dumping exploration satellites burnt travel engines distant	32
orbits explosion diameter atmosphere operators dented pieces fallen	40
fuel objects location missile functioned collision astronauts NASA	48
debris dumping exploration satellites burnt travel engines distant	56
orbits explosion diameter atmosphere operators dented pieces fallen	64
fuel objects location missile functioned collision astronauts NASA	72
debris dumping exploration satellites burnt travel engines distant	80

Number of words read correctly _____

ECHO READING

Directions: When you read, you should make breaks, and sometimes pauses, between groups of words. As your teacher reads each phrase, repeat aloud what is read and put a slash or line after that phrase. Then read the whole sentence aloud as a class. Do the first paragraph together as a class, and then do the second one on your own. The first sentence has been marked for you.

Space junk / presents a danger / to spacecraft / and to humans in them. / Most objects travel in "low orbit" 500–1,200 miles above Earth. They reach a speed of 22,300 miles per hour, so even the smallest bits of debris can damage a spacecraft. The space shuttle and other spacecraft have gotten dents from collisions. In 1983 a speck of paint cracked the space shuttle's windshield.

Certain locations in space are especially crowded. Some satellites must keep the same location over Earth, so they travel at the same speed as Earth turns. As more satellites go into space, those locations are getting more crowded. A collision costs money and creates more debris. Although only three known collisions between two satellites have ever occurred, the risk is growing all the time.

What's Happening

IN THE USA?

BY LAWRENCE GABLE
© 2014 What's Happening Publications

SUBJECT: GLOBAL ISSUES

1   The Soviet Union launched its satellite *Sputnik* in October 1957. Since then space has become more crowded. Unfortunately much of what orbits Earth now is junk.

2   As a result of space exploration, space debris now circles the planet. The objects are as large as rocket engines and as small as nuts and bolts. Astronauts also have lost things like coffee cups and a camera.

3   Space junk presents a danger. Most objects travel in "low orbit" 500–1,200 miles above Earth. They reach a speed of 22,300 miles per hour, so even the smallest objects can damage a spacecraft. Already they have dented the Space Shuttle and other spacecraft. In 1983 a speck of paint cracked the Space Shuttle's windshield.

4   The National Aeronautics and Space Administration (NASA) began to worry about space junk several decades ago. It watches anything at least 10 cm in diameter. There are more than 18,000 such objects, including about 850 working satellites. NASA believes that there are more than 100,000 pieces of junk 1–10 cm in diameter, and tens of millions smaller than that.

5   Low orbit space also has many satellites that no longer work. They stay in orbit for years, then fall into Earth's atmosphere and burn up. Now satellite owners try to move them out of the way. They send some into high orbit, where it is not crowded. They send others into Earth's atmosphere to burn up.

6   Satellites are big business. Ideally the owner uses the last bit of fuel to send a satellite into high orbit. If the company waits too long, the satellite runs out of fuel. Then it orbits as junk for about three years before it falls and burns up. If the company sends the satellite into high orbit too soon, it loses time when the satellite could be earning money.

Space Is Filling With Junk

7   Certain locations in space are especially crowded. Some satellites must keep the same location over Earth, so they travel at the same speed that Earth turns. Those locations are getting more crowded. A collision costs money and creates more debris. Only a few known collisions between two satellites have ever occurred, but the risk is growing.

8   In 2007 China created the most space junk ever. It used a missile to destroy an old weather satellite. That explosion created 2,300 pieces of debris larger than 4 cm in diameter, more than 35,000 pieces 1–4 cm in diameter, and a million pieces smaller than that. The international space community complained about the debris. Some nations complained that China just wanted to test its anti-satellite weapons.

9   In February 2008 the U.S. also shot down one of its own spy satellites. It would have fallen out of orbit in March. Most of it would have burnt up, but officials said that its rocket fuel could have landed and harmed people. Critics think that the U.S. really wanted to destroy secret photo equipment. China and Russia fear that the U.S. was just testing its anti-satellite weapons. No matter the reason, it caused more space junk.

10   Humans used to treat Earth's environment as dumping grounds for trash and pollution. Slowly they are learning to care for it. Now they also are learning that their actions affect space that once seemed so distant.

GET A CONTEXT CLUE

Directions: Below are sentences from "Space is Filling With Junk." First, read the sentence. Then, look back in the article and reread the paragraph in which the sentence is found. Circle the best answer to each question.

"Unfortunately, much of what *orbits* the Earth now is junk."

1. The word *orbit* means

    A. to burn
    B. to pollute
    C. to go around
    D. to rotate

"As a result of space exploration, space *debris* now circles the planet."

2. *Debris* is best defined as

    A. trash
    B. useful tools
    C. rocks
    D. building materials

"Low orbit space also has many *satellites* that no longer work."

3. The word *satellites* has to do with

    A. objects sent to space
    B. other places for meeting
    C. telephone lines
    D. small objects

"There are more than 18,000 such *objects,* including about 850 working satellites."

4. The word *object* means

    A. something that is flat
    B. something that is round
    C. something that is invisible
    D. something that can be seen or touched

"Certain *locations* in space are especially crowded."

5. The word *locations* means

    A. people
    B. types
    C. space ships
    D. places

"The *international* space community complained about the debris."

6. The word *international* means

    A. from one country
    B. a group of people trying to solve a problem
    C. from many countries
    D. Americans

WORD MAP

Directions: Follow the directions to map the word in the box below.

> **debris**

List two more words that mean the same.

junk

List two more examples of debris.

broken trees after a storm

List two more words that mean the opposite.

treasure

Draw a picture below to help you remember the meaning.

Write a definition IN YOUR OWN WORDS.

LOOK WHO'S TALKING

Directions: Below are sentences that relate to "Space Is Filling with Junk." Look back in the article and reread the paragraph in which you find the reference. Circle the best answer to each question.

1. In the fourth sentence of paragraph 3, the word *they* best refers to

   A. the junk

   B. nuts and bolts

   C. satellites

   D. the smallest objects

2. In the second sentence of paragraph 4, the word *it* refers to

   A. the objects

   B. the pieces

   C. NASA

   D. the space shuttle

3. In the third sentence of paragraph 5, the word *them* refers to

   A. the satellites

   B. the Earth

   C. the debris

   D. the owners

4. In paragraph 6, in the clause "it loses time when the satellite could be earning money," the word *it* refers to

   A. the satellite

   B. the debris

   C. the people

   D. the company

5. In the second sentence of paragraph 7, the word *they* refers to

   A. satellites that must keep the same location

   B. locations in space

   C. collisions between satellites

   D. locations that are especially crowded

6. In paragraph 9, the final sentence reads, "No matter the reason, it caused more space junk." The word *it* refers to

   A. the spy satellite

   B. the photo equipment

   C. shooting down the satellite

   D. the space station

HOW'S IT ORGANIZED?

This article is organized as a problem that needs solving.

Directions: Answer these questions in the spaces at the bottom.

1. What is the problem?

2. What is causing the problem?

3. Who has been worried about the problem for decades?

4. How did China increase the problem?

5. Why did the United States shoot down its own spy satellite?

6. What problems occur when satellites are shot down?

7. The last paragraph implies one possible solution to this problem.
   What is that solution?

Answers:

1.	
2.	
3.	
4.	
5.	
6.	
7.	

*On a separate sheet of paper write a summary of what your notes say about the problems with debris in outer space.

IS THAT A FACT?

Directions: Read the definitions of a fact and an inference below. Then read the paragraph that follows. At the bottom of the page, write an F on the blank if the sentence is a fact. Write an I if the sentence is an inference. Use the following definitions:

Fact—a statement that can be proven true from the paragraph

Inference—a guess as to what MIGHT be true, based on what you have read and what you already know about the subject

> In February 2008 the United States shot down a spy satellite. It had been in orbit since December of 2006 but had never functioned properly. The satellite would have fallen out of orbit in March. Most of it would have burnt up, but officials said that its one thousand pounds of rocket fuel could have landed in a populated area and harmed people. Critics suggest that the United States really wanted to destroy secret photo equipment. No matter the reason, it certainly caused more space junk.

_____ **1.** The United States shot down its own satellite.

_____ **2.** Shooting down the satellite created more space junk.

_____ **3.** Rocket fuel from the satellite could have caused damage on Earth.

_____ **4.** Debris from the satellite might not have hurt anyone.

_____ **5.** The satellite never functioned correctly.

MAKE A SPACE

Directions: Below are sentences that are missing punctuation and capitalization. First draw slash marks (/) between the words. Then rewrite each sentence in the space below it by filling in the missing punctuation and capitalization.

> Example:
>
> space / debris / is / any / object / in / orbit / that / no / longer / serves / a / useful / purpose
>
> Space debris is any object in orbit that no longer serves a useful purpose.

1. spacejunkpresentsadangertospacecraftandtohumansinthem

_____

_____

2. theystayinorbitforyearsbeforetheyfinallyfalltoearthsatmosphereandburnup

_____

_____

3. certainlocationsinspaceareespeciallycrowded

_____

_____

4. humansusedtotreatearthslandwaterandairasdumpinggroundsfortrashandpollution

_____

_____

TIME MY READ #2

Directions: With a partner, see how many words you can read correctly in 45 seconds. As you read, your partner will put an X through any word read incorrectly on his or her copy. When you are finished, trade your books or papers, and let your partner read while you keep score. Count the total number of words you read correctly. Write this score at the bottom of your page

debris dumping exploration satellites burnt travel engines distant	8
orbits explosion diameter atmosphere operators dented pieces fallen	16
fuel objects location missile functioned collision astronauts NASA	24
debris dumping exploration satellites burnt travel engines distant	32
orbits explosion diameter atmosphere operators dented pieces fallen	40
fuel objects location missile functioned collision astronauts NASA	48
debris dumping exploration satellites burnt travel engines distant	56
orbits explosion diameter atmosphere operators dented pieces fallen	64
fuel objects location missile functioned collision astronauts NASA	72
debris dumping exploration satellites burnt travel engines distant	80

Number of words read correctly _____

Is the score higher than it was in Time My Read #1?_____

Name _____ Date _____

WORD PARTS

Directions: Read the definitions below. Then draw a spaceship as it orbits on the left side of the orbital path. Show the spaceship shooting at space junk on the right side of the orbital path.

1. **orb**—(noun) a round object; a circle or ball

2. **orbit**—(noun) a path that circles around something else

3. **to orbit**—(verb) to move around something

4. **orbital**—(adjective) a word to describe the path of something moving around something else

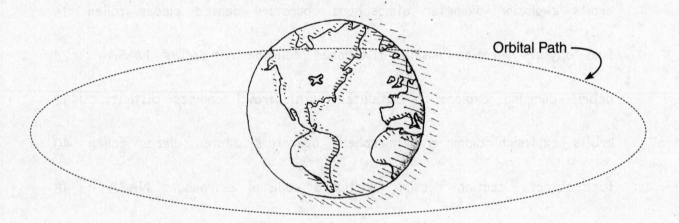

Orbital Path

Directions: The Latin root *loc* means "place." Read the sentences below. Using the clues in the sentences, write a definition on the back for each underlined word that begins with *loc*.

1. Space junk is not a <u>local</u> problem in America; it is a problem for every country in the world.

2. Space junk can fall on any <u>locality</u> on Earth.

3. Certain <u>locations</u> in space are very crowded with junk.

4. The space shuttle needs to <u>locate</u> space junk in its way.

SUMMARIZING ABCs

Directions: Now that you've read the article on debris in space, see how many words you can write about the topic in the boxes below.

A–C	D–F	G–I
J–L	**M–O**	**P–R**
S–T	**U–V**	**W–Z**

SENTENCE SUMMARIES

Directions: Below are four key words from the article "Space is Filling with Junk." Your job is to summarize, or restate, what you've learned in this article by using these four words in two sentences. Then, as a challenge, try to use all four words in one sentence to summarize the article.

Key Words

debris   satellite(s)

orbit   collision

Sentence Summaries:

1. _____

_____

2. _____

_____

Challenge Summary (all four words in one sentence!):

1. _____

_____

REACTION GUIDE

Directions: Now that you have read and studied information about "Space is Filling with Junk," reread the statements below, which you responded to before reading the article. Then think about how the author might respond to these statements. If you think the author would agree, put a checkmark on the line before the number. If you think the author would disagree, put an X on the line. Then below the statement, copy the words, phrases, or sentences from the article that provide evidence of the views stated by the author. Also note if there is no evidence to support the statement.

_____ **1.** Outer space is too big for us to worry about old satellites.

Evidence: _____

_____

_____

_____ **2.** If outer space is polluted, it can be cleaned up easily.

Evidence: _____

_____

_____

_____ **3.** Pollution in outer space is a problem for all countries.

Evidence: _____

_____

_____

TAKE A STAND

Directions: People often have differing feelings or opinions about an issue. When they discuss or argue their opposing views, they are taking part in a debate. A good persuasive argument is based on a claim that is supported by

Facts—statements that can be proven to be true

Statistics—numerical data gotten through research

Examples—instances that support an opinion

You and a partner are going to debate two of your other classmates. The topic you are going to debate is the following:

Pollution in outer space is a problem for all countries.

Decide with the other pair who will agree and who will disagree with this statement. Then answer these questions in order to win your debate.

1. What are your two strongest points to persuade the other side? (You can do Internet research to include facts, statistics, and examples.)

   A. _____

   B. _____

2. What might the other side say to argue against point A?

   _____

   _____

3. What might the other side say to argue against point B?

   _____

   _____

4. What will you say to prove the other side's arguments are wrong?

   _____

   _____

   _____

Name _____ Date _____

ASSESSMENT

Comprehension: Answer the questions about the following passage.

Space junk presents a danger to spacecraft and to humans in them. Most objects travel in a "low orbit" 500 to 1,200 miles above the Earth. They reach a speed of 22,300 miles per hour, so even the smallest bits of debris can damage a spacecraft. The space shuttle and other spacecraft have gotten dents from collisions. In 1993 a speck of paint cracked the space shuttle's windshield.

Certain locations in space are especially crowded. Some satellites must keep the same location over Earth, so they travel at the same speed as Earth turns. As more satellites go into space, those places are getting more crowded. Collisions cost money and create more debris. Although only three known collisions between two satellites have ever occurred, the risk is growing all the time.

1. Why should astronauts in spacecraft worry about space junk?

_____

_____

2. Why would a satellite travel at the same speed as the Earth?

_____

_____

3. Why don't scientists just blow up old satellites in outer space?

_____

_____

Fluency: The words in the following two sentences are all connected. The sentences are also missing punctuation and capitalization. Draw slash marks (/) between the words. Then rewrite each sentence by filling in the punctuation and capitalization.

1. certainlocationsinspaceareespeciallycrowded

_____

2. spacejunkpresentsadangertospacecraftandtohumansinthem

_____

_____

Fluency: Read the three sentences below. Imagine where you would pause within each sentence as you read it aloud. Draw a slash (/) mark between the phrases where you would pause. The first slash is done.

3. In February 2008 / the United States shot down a spy satellite.

4. As a result of space exploration space debris now circles the planet.

5. A collision costs money and creates more debris.

Vocabulary: Based on what you have learned in this lesson, match the following words with their definitions. Write the letter of the definition on the blank in front of the word it defines.

1. _____ debris   **A.** a round object; a ball

2. _____ orbit   **B.** to find where something is

3. _____ satellite   **C.** trash or junk left after a crash

4. _____ international   **D.** worked or operated

5. _____ location   **E.** to move around something

6. _____ orb   **F.** nearby, in the area

7. _____ locate   **G.** an object that orbits a planet

8. _____ fragile   **H.** involving several countries

9. _____ functioned   **I.** a place

10. _____ local   **J.** easily broken or ruined

Name _____ Date _____

ANTICIPATION GUIDE

Directions: Before you read the article "The World Focuses on Girls' Problems," read the statements below. If you agree with a statement, put a checkmark on the line next to it. If you disagree, put an X on the line.

_____ **1.** Girls are the most frequent victims of human rights violations.

_____ **2.** People in other lands have a right to treat girls in ways that are appropriate to their culture.

_____ **3.** Girls deserve the same educational opportunities as boys, no matter what their society believes.

Once you have responded to the statements above, write in the section below why you agree or disagree with each statement.

1. _____

_____

2. _____

_____

3. _____

_____

In the box below, draw a picture of what you think this article is about.

WORDSTORM

Directions: It's good to know more than just the dictionary definition of a word. Completing a wordstorm lets you write down information to help you understand what a word means, how it's related to other words, and how to use it in different ways.

What is the word or phrase?

developing nations

Here is the sentence from the text in which the phrase is used:

"Girls in some in developing nations remain largely under the control of men."

What are some other words or phrases that mean the same thing?

_____

What are three things you know about developing nations?

1. _____ 2. _____ 3. _____

Name three people other than teachers who would likely use this phrase.

1. _____ 2. _____ 3. _____

Draw a picture below that reminds you of the phrase *developing nations*.

Name _____ Date _____

LANGUAGE MINI-LESSON

Some verbs are easily confused with others. The following pairs of verbs have different meanings but are often confused for one another. With a partner, study the words below.

Lie and Lay: *Lie* means "to recline." *Lay* means "to put or place" something.

Present Tense	Past Tense	Past Participle
lie Sara *lies* down.	lay Sara *lay* down yesterday.	lain Sara *has lain* down.
lay Carlos *lays* a pen down.	laid Carlos *laid* down his pen.	laid Carlos *has laid* it down.

Rise and Raise: *Rise* means "to move up." *Raise* means "to lift something up."

Present Tense	Past Tense	Past Participle
rise The plane *rises*.	rose The plane *rose* yesterday.	risen The plane *has risen*.
raise Al *raises* his hand.	raised Al *raised* his hand.	raised Al *has raised* his hand.

Learn and Teach: *Learn* means "to gain knowledge or a skill." *Teach* means "to instruct."

Present Tense	Past Tense	Past Participle
learn Ted *learns* to ski.	learned Ted *learned* to ski.	learned Ted *has learned* to ski.
teach She *teaches* math.	taught She *taught* math once	taught She *has taught* math.

Directions: On a separate sheet of paper, fill out charts like the one above for the following sets of verbs: *sit/set* and *borrow/lend*. Check your answers in a dictionary.

ECHO READING

Directions: When you read, you should make breaks, and sometimes pauses, between groups of words. As your teacher reads each phrase, repeat aloud what is read and put a slash or line after that phrase. Then read the whole sentence aloud as a class. Do the first paragraph together as a class, and then do the second one on your own. The first sentence has been marked for you.

Girls / in some developing nations / remain largely under the control of men. / Rather than go to school, they work in the fields or care for siblings at home. In India and China, for example, families have abandoned hundreds of thousands of babies to orphanages, and 90 percent of them are girls. Some mothers even kill or refuse to feed a baby daughter soon after her birth.

Human trafficking is also a problem. This form of modern slavery has about 20 million victims, even in first-world countries. Criminals steal children or buy them from poor families. Boys often end up as laborers or soldiers. Girls also become laborers or victims of sex trafficking. They suffer sexual violence that causes depression and emotional problems.

What's Happening
IN THE WORLD?

BY LAWRENCE GABLE
© 2015 What's Happening Publications

SUBJECT: GLOBAL ISSUES

The World Focuses on Girls' Problems

1 **G**irls in much of the world face disadvantages. The United Nations (U.N.) recognizes that and has decided to pay special attention to girls' problems. It declared October 11, 2012 the first International Day of the Girl Child.

2 Many cultures place little value on girls. Girls in some developing nations remain largely under the control of men. Rather than go to school, they work in the fields or care for siblings at home. In India and China, for example, families have abandoned hundreds of thousands of babies to orphanages, and 90 percent of them are girls. Some mothers even kill or refuse to feed a baby daughter soon after her birth.

3 Human trafficking is also a problem. This form of modern slavery has about 20 million victims, even in first-world countries. Criminals steal children or buy them from poor families. Boys often end up as laborers or soldiers. Girls also become laborers or victims of sex trafficking. They suffer sexual violence that causes depression and emotional problems.

4 An event in Pakistan in October 2012 put girls' education in the news. The militants who controlled the region had closed many schools for girls. In 2009 an 11-year-old girl named Malala began speaking out against the ban on education. The militants warned her to be quiet and threatened her, so soon she had to flee.

5 One day Malala was in a small school bus. Taliban gunmen stopped the bus and shot her in the head. She suffered some brain damage, but she recovered in England. Many Pakistanis demonstrated in the streets to support her fight for education. In 2014 she won the Nobel Peace Prize.

6 Studies show how education helps girls. Educated girls earn higher incomes as adults. They bear fewer and healthier children, and are healthier themselves. About 75 million girls do not attend school and 250 million live in poverty. Education would change girls' lives.

7 In 2012 the first International Day of the Girl Child took place. Its focus was "Ending Child Marriage." In poor areas in more than fifty countries, parents sell millions of daughters as brides. This violates their human rights, of course. The girls are as young as six years old. Often the husbands are as old as their fathers.

8 The U.N. has studied the problem. Every year ten million girls have to become brides before their 18th birthdays. There are 200 million women in developing countries who are ages 20–24. About 70 million of them married before age 18, and 20 million of them had married before they turned 15.

9 Child marriage hurts girls. Certainly it robs them of their childhoods. It sends them to live away from family and friends. Their chances to go to school disappear, and they live a life of poverty. Many of the girls become the victims of violence from their husbands. Child marriage also often results in early and unwanted pregnancies. In developing countries problems from pregnancy are the leading cause of death for teenaged girls.

10 Every year the United Nations asks the nations of the world to change. They must protect girls from abuse and provide an education to girls. This will help girls to break out of poverty and live the safe, healthy lives that all people deserve.

QUICK READ/DRAW AND WRITE

Directions: First Reading—As you do your first reading of the article, your teacher will time you for one minute. When time is called, write the number of the paragraph where you stopped. **Paragraph # _____**

In the box below, draw a picture summarizing what you read.

Second Reading—As you do your second reading of the article, your teacher will time you for one minute. When time is called, write the number of the paragraph where you stopped. **Paragraph # _____**

Directions: Now continue reading the rest of the article. Below, write five important words that will help you remember the information from the article.

_____ _____ _____ _____ _____

CLOSE READING ANNOTATION

Third Reading—As you reread each paragraph in the article closely, answer the questions by annotating the text. Each numbered question corresponds to a paragraph in the article where the answer can be found. Write your brief answers in the space below each question.

1. What made the United Nations declare the International Day of the Girl?

_____

2. What is the author's purpose for writing paragraph 2?

_____

3. Why do you think the United Nations and others use the word *trafficking*?

_____

4/5. What was the author's purpose for writing paragraphs 4 and 5?

_____

6. According to the author, what are the benefits of a girl becoming educated?

_____

7. What dramatic evidence does the author give to show how child marriage violates young girls' rights?

_____

8. In paragraph 8, how does the author show how widespread child marriages are?

_____

9. What are the effects of child marriage?

_____

10. What is the author's purpose for writing paragraph 10?

_____

GRAMMAR GAMES

Directions: Reread the two paragraphs below. Words have been left out from the sentences. Think about the information from the article you have read and fill in words that make sense. The part of speech of each missing word is provided.

Many cultures place little value _____ girls. In developing
                                    (1. preposition)

nations _____ remain largely under the control of men. Rather
         (2. pronoun)

than go to school, they _____ in the fields or _____
                         (3. verb)   (4. verb)

for siblings at home. Families in India _____ China abandon
                                         (5. conjunction)

many girls to _____. Some mothers even refuse
               (6. plural noun)

to feed a baby daughter soon _____ her birth.
                              (7. preposition)

Human trafficking is also a _____. This form of modern
                             (8. noun)

slavery has about 20 million _____, even in first-world
                              (9. plural noun)

countries. Criminals _____ children or buy them from
                      (10. verb)

_____ families. _____ often end up as laborers or
 (11. adjective)   (12. plural noun)

soldiers. Girls also _____ laborers or victims of sex
                      (13. verb)

trafficking. _____ suffer sexual violence that often causes
              (14. pronoun)

depression _____ emotional problems.
            (15. conjunction)

© Houghton Mifflin Harcourt Publishing Company

HOW'S IT ORGANIZED?

This article is organized as a problem that needs solving.

Directions: Answer these questions in the spaces at the bottom.

1. What does the United Nations want to do to address girls' problems?

2. What examples does the author include to show that some cultures place little value on girls?

3. Why is human trafficking such a difficult problem?

4. After the attack on Malala, how did the people in Pakistan show they wanted to find a solution?

5. How might education solve the problems girls face?

6. Why is child marriage such a problem for young girls?

Answers:

1.	
2.	
3.	
4.	
5.	
6.	

The main idea of a selection reflects what the paragraphs or sentences are about. Put an X on the space next to the sentence that best states the main idea.

_____ **1.** Cultures have different ways of treating girls.

_____ **2.** Cultures that place little value on girls often abuse them.

_____ **3.** Without education, girls will always be at a disadvantage.

Explain why your choice is the best main or central idea.

_____

_____

IS THAT A FACT?

Directions: Read the definitions of a fact and an inference below. Then read the paragraphs that follow. At the bottom of the page, write an F on the blank if the sentence is a fact. Write an I if the sentence is an inference. Use the following definitions:

Fact—a statement that can be proven true from the paragraphs

Inference—a guess as to what MIGHT be true, based on what you have read and what you already know about the subject

---

The United Nations has studied the problem. Every year ten million girls have to become brides before their 18th birthdays. There are 200 million women in developing countries who are ages 20–24. About 70 million of them married before age 18, and 20 million of them had married before they turned 15.

Child marriage hurts girls. Certainly it robs them of their childhoods. It sends them to live away from family and friends. Their chances to go to school disappear, and they live a life of poverty. Many of the girls become the victims of violence from their husbands. Child marriage also often results in early and unwanted pregnancies.

_____ **1.** The United Nations cares about the abuse of girls.

_____ **2.** Most child marriages are not by the child's choice.

_____ **3.** Many child brides suffer violence from their husbands.

_____ **4.** Many of the girls in child marriages become pregnant.

_____ **5.** Victims of child marriage often have difficulty getting an education.

TIC-TAC-TOE SUMMARIZING

When you **summarize** in writing, you present all the key points the author is trying to make.

Directions: Write four sentences to summarize the article about girls' problems. To help you, there are nine words or phrases in the Tic-Tac-Toe graphic organizer below. To write a sentence, you must use three words or phrases in a row. The row can be horizontal (—), vertical (I), or diagonal (/).

disadvantage	girls	trafficking
education	culture	United Nations
victims	depression	child marriage

1. _____

_____

2. _____

_____

3. _____

_____

4. _____

_____

REACTION GUIDE

Directions: Now that you have read and studied information about "The World Focuses on Girls' Problems," reread the statements below, which you responded to before reading the article. Then think about how the author might respond to these statements. If you think the author would agree, put a checkmark on the line before the number. If you think the author would disagree, put an X on the line. Then below the statement, copy the words, phrases, or sentences from the article that provide evidence of the views stated by the author. Also note if there is no evidence in the article to support the statement.

_____ **1.** Girls are the most frequent victims of human rights violations.

Evidence: _____

_____

_____

_____ **2.** People in other lands have a right to treat girls in ways that are appropriate to their culture.

Evidence: _____

_____

_____

_____ **3.** Girls deserve the same educational opportunities as boys, no matter what their society believes.

Evidence: _____

_____

_____

TAKE A STAND

Directions: People often have differing feelings or opinions about an issue. When they discuss or argue their opposing views, they are taking part in a debate. A good persuasive argument is based on a claim that is supported by

Facts—statements that can be proven true

Statistics—numerical data gotten through research

Examples—instances that support an opinion

You and a partner are going to debate two of your other classmates. The topic you are going to debate is the following:

Other countries have a right to treat girls in ways that are appropriate to their culture.

Decide with the other pair who will agree and who will disagree with this statement. Then answer these questions in order to win your debate.

1. What are your two strongest points to persuade the other side? (You can do Internet research to include facts, statistics, and examples.)

   A. _____

   B. _____

2. What might the other side say to argue against point A?

   _____

   _____

3. What might the other side say to argue against point B?

   _____

   _____

4. What will you say to prove the other side's arguments are wrong?

   _____

   _____

   _____

WHAT'S THE COMBINATION?

Writing is more interesting when the writer joins, or combines, short sentences. Follow the directions below to learn different ways to combine two sentences.

What to do: You can join two sentences using the word *whose*. Use *whose* when a thing mentioned in the second sentence belongs to a person in the first sentence. In the example below, the pronoun *their* tells you that the *songs* in the second sentence belong to *the Beatles* in the first sentence, so replace *their* with *whose* in the combined sentence.

Example: *The Beatles* were a great band. *Their songs* made millions. New Sentence: The Beatles, whose songs made millions, were a great band. *Grammar Note:* Use commas (,) to separate the phrase with *whose* from the rest of the sentence.

Directions: Combine these sentences using the method above.

1. Girls have gotten the attention of the United Nations. Girls' lives are made miserable by child marriage.

_____

2. Pakistan puts girls at a disadvantage. Its culture gives women and girls little value.

_____

3. Malala was only eleven years old when she started writing for the BBC. Her blog was published anonymously.

_____

4. Malala won the Nobel Peace Prize in 2014. Malala's family is from Pakistan.

_____

5. The United Nations is asking countries to give girls equal rights. The United Nations' mission is to protect all people.

_____

ANALYZING A PROMPT

Directions: Read the writing prompt in the box below. Then follow the directions to learn how to analyze and answer it.

> You are a human rights advocate. You are going to deliver a speech to the U. N. General Assembly that will give information about the types of abuses some girls experience in many countries around the world. How will you describe some of the abuses and possible reasons for them? What evidence will you use from the article to persuade the General Assembly to take action to stop the abuse of girls around the world?

1. A writing prompt begins with some background information known as the **set up**. Underline the sentences that set up this assignment.

2. Use the following **R.A.F.T.** technique to finish analyzing the prompt.

Role: What are you supposed to be to answer it? A student? A politician?

Write what you are here: _____

Audience: To whom are you writing? A friend? A particular group?

Write who it is here: _____

Format: Check to see what type of writing you are doing. Is it an essay, a letter, a speech, a story, a description, an editorial, or a report?

Write what it is here: _____

Task: Another sentence in the prompt will tell you what you must do, or your "task." Question words like **why, how,** or **what** may tell the task.

If the question word is **why,** you will *give the reasons* that something is done.

If the question word is **how,** you will *explain the way* that something is done.

If the question word is **what,** you will *identify the thing* that is done.

Below, copy the sentence or question that describes your task.

_____

_____

ANALYZING ARGUMENTATIVE TEXTS

1. **Argumentative** articles are written to change someone's opinion. In the spaces below, name three groups besides students or teachers that might be interested in reading this article.

   a. _____ b. _____ c. _____

2. What main point or **precise claim** is the author making?

   _____

   _____

3. Give two reasons that provide **evidence** to support the author's claim.

   a. _____

   b. _____

4. **Domain-specific vocabulary** consists of words used in a specific subject, such as math, science, or social studies. Reread the article and list six domain-specific words used with this subject. After you select the words, write their definitions on the lines provided.

   a. _____ : _____

   b. _____ : _____

   c. _____ : _____

   d. _____ : _____

   e. _____ : _____

   f. _____ : _____

ASSESSMENT

1. Circle the letter of the conclusion that is **best** supported by evidence from the article.

    a. Many countries place little value on girls.

    b. Families in France and Pakistan abandon thousands of girls to orphanages.

    c. Many women worldwide are married before they are 18.

    d. Many children who are stolen are returned home.

2. Circle the letter of the sentence that **best** explains how paragraphs 4 and 5 are important to the development of the report on girls' problems.

    a. Paragraphs 4 and 5 explain that militants have no respect for girls.

    b. Paragraphs 4 and 5 put a human face on the treatment of girls worldwide.

    c. Paragraphs 4 and 5 prove that children can recover from brain damage.

    d. Paragraphs 4 and 5 show that people support girls' problems.

3. Circle the letter of the paragraph that best summarizes the information presented in the article.

    a. paragraph 1

    b. paragraph 2

    c. paragraph 7

    d. paragraph 9

    e. paragraph 10

4. Support the claim that child marriage is a major problem and that it hurts young girls. Below, cite three pieces of evidence from the article to support this claim.

    a. _____

    b. _____

    c. _____

5. A student is writing a report about the problem of child marriage. Read both sources and the directions that follow.

Source 1: www.helpinggirlsbefree.com—Child marriage for girls has negative effects on their lives well beyond adolescence. Girls who marry in their teens have health problems from getting pregnant too young and too often. These problems can lead to death during childbirth or from a sexually transmitted disease. If a girl gets pregnant in a poor country, there is little chance she will get an education. Because she cannot get an education, she cannot get a job that might free her from her marriage. In her marriage, there is a great chance she will suffer beatings and sexual abuse. She will also not have the freedom to leave her locality, and those in her village may isolate her, leaving her alone and depressed.

Source 2: www.childrenwhomarry.com—Worldwide, about 14 million girls under the age of 18 are married. In poorer countries, about one in seven girls are married before they turn fifteen. Most of these girls are forced into marriage without their consent. Girls this young are not physically ready to become wives and mothers. Many die in childbirth or become infected with HIV/AIDS. Many are physically or sexually abused. Girls this young are also not emotionally ready to handle motherhood or marriage. Often, because of the abuse, child brides experience great depression which may lead to suicide.

The student took notes about the information in the sources. Circle the letter of the note that correctly paraphrases, or restates, the information in **both** sources.

> **a.** Millions of girls experience child marriage.
>
> **b.** Child brides can die during childbirth or from disease.
>
> **c.** Child brides do not get an education and cannot get jobs.
>
> **d.** Children who are married too young are not physically or emotionally ready for motherhood and may become depressed.

Name _____ Date _____

ANTICIPATION GUIDE

Directions: Before you read the article "Global Zero Launches Its Campaign," read the statements below. If you agree with a statement, put a checkmark on the line next to it. If you disagree, put an X on the line.

_____ **1.** We don't have to worry about countries using nuclear weapons.

_____ **2.** We should stop countries from creating nuclear weapons.

_____ **3.** Nuclear weapons never should have been invented.

Once you have responded to the statements above, write in the section below why you agree or disagree with each statement.

1. _____

_____

2. _____

_____

3. _____

_____

In the box below, draw a picture of what you think this article is about.

WORDSTORM

Directions: It's good to know more than just the dictionary definition of a word. Completing a wordstorm lets you write down information to help you understand what a word means, how it's related to other words, and how to use it in different ways.

What is the word?

campaign

Here is the sentence from the text in which the word is used:

"In December 2008 a new campaign to eliminate nuclear weapons began in Paris."

What are some other words or phrases that mean the same thing?

_____

What are three things people might do during a campaign?

1. _____ 2. _____ 3. _____

Name three people other than teachers who would likely use this word.

1. _____ 2. _____ 3. _____

Draw a picture below that reminds you of the word *campaign*.

TIME MY READ #1

Directions: With a partner, see how many words you can read correctly in 45 seconds. As you read, your partner will put an X through any word read incorrectly on his or her copy. When you are finished, trade your books or papers, and let your partner read while you keep score. Count the total number of words you read correctly. Write this score at the bottom of your page.

nuclear catastrophe campaign destructive worldwide terrorists scientists technology	8
launching declaration reducing crisis solution inspections globally unstable	16
international program responding nations eliminating dream Nobel system	24
nuclear catastrophe campaign destructive worldwide terrorists scientists technology	32
launching declaration reducing crisis solution inspections globally unstable	40
international program responding nations eliminating dream Nobel system	48
nuclear catastrophe campaign destructive worldwide terrorists scientists technology	56
launching declaration reducing crisis solution inspections globally unstable	64
international program responding nations eliminating dream Nobel system	72
nuclear catastrophe campaign destructive worldwide terrorists scientists technology	80

Number of words read correctly _____

ECHO READING

Directions: When you read, you should make breaks, and sometimes pauses, between groups of words. As your teacher reads each phrase, repeat aloud what is read and put a slash or line after that phrase. Then read the whole sentence aloud as a class. Do the first paragraph together as a class, and then do the second one on your own. The first sentence has been marked for you.

There are / 27,000 / nuclear weapons / worldwide. / The U.S. and Russia own 96 percent of them. However, people fear that unstable small countries and terrorist groups could get them too. That is why there is such interest now in eliminating nuclear weapons.

It took 18 months to establish Global Zero. Finally, more than 100 people met in Paris in December 2008. Among them were scientists, winners of the Nobel Peace Prize, and former and current world leaders.

Those people in Paris wrote and signed a simple declaration. Its opening line states: "We believe that to protect our children, our grandchildren and our civilization from the threat of nuclear catastrophe, we must eliminate all nuclear weapons globally."

What's Happening

IN THE WORLD?

BY LAWRENCE GABLE
© 2014 What's Happening Publications

SUBJECT: GLOBAL ISSUES

1 **GLOBAL ZERO LAUNCHES ITS CAMPAIGN** Humans developed nuclear weapons more than 60 years ago. The United States dropped two nuclear bombs on Japan at the end of World War II, and the world has lived in fear of them ever since. In December 2008 a new campaign to eliminate nuclear weapons began in Paris. It calls itself Global Zero.

2 The U.S., the United Kingdom and Canada developed the first nuclear bombs. After seven years they had made the world's most destructive weapon. The two bombs that fell on Japan in 1945 killed or injured more than 200,000 people. Those are the only two times that any country has used nuclear weapons.

3 Now other countries have nuclear weapons too. China, Russia, France and Britain got them after the U.S. In 1970 those five nations agreed not to spread the technology to other countries. However, India, Pakistan and North Korea have developed weapons, and Israel almost certainly has nearly a hundred. Iran may be developing them too.

4 There are 16,000 nuclear weapons worldwide. The U.S. and Russia own 96 percent of them. However, people fear that unstable small countries and terrorist groups could get them too. That is why there is such interest in eliminating nuclear weapons.

5 It took 18 months to establish Global Zero. Finally more than 100 people met in Paris in December 2008. Among them were scientists, winners of the Nobel Peace Prize, and former and current world leaders.

6 Those people in Paris wrote and signed a simple declaration. Its opening line states: "We believe that to protect our children, our grandchildren and our civilization from the threat of nuclear catastrophe, we must eliminate all nuclear weapons globally."

7 Global Zero also launched a global public campaign. At its Web site individuals can sign that same declaration. Many thousands of people from all over the world have signed it. They also have organized local campaigns and groups on Internet sites like Facebook.

8 The U.S. and Russia are important to the campaign. Former President Carter and the former Soviet leader Mikhail Gorbachev have signed the declaration. In addition, Russia's President Vladimir Putin and Barack Obama have called for the elimination of all nuclear weapons. Global Zero sent delegations to meet with leaders in Moscow and Washington, D.C.

9 Global Zero has outlined three steps. First, it wants Russia and the U.S. to cut the number of weapons they have. Second, it wants the other countries to join Russia and the U.S. in slowly reducing their weapons to zero. Third, it wants a system for managing nuclear fuel from power plants and preventing the development of nuclear weapons. Reaching zero could take until 2035.

10 Getting to zero weapons is only part of the solution. The other part is staying at zero. Countries will have to believe that no country could develop a new program or restart an old one. Beyond that, there must be a plan for responding to a crisis.

11 Nations agree that the dangers have increased. Eliminating nuclear weapons used to be a wild dream, but now it could happen. Global Zero held an international conference in 2010 for 500 leaders. The campaign hopes to convince people that living with nuclear weapons is simply no way to live.

GET A CONTEXT CLUE

Directions: Below are sentences from "Global Zero Launches Its Campaign." First, read the sentence. Then, look back in the article and reread the paragraph in which the sentence is found. Circle the best answer to each question.

"In December 2008 a new *campaign* to eliminate nuclear weapons began in Paris."

1. The word *campaign* means

   A. a charge
   B. a movement
   C. an idea
   D. politics

"It took 18 months to *establish* Global Zero."

2. The word *establish* means

   A. to get rid of
   B. to create
   C. to discuss
   D. to clean up

"Those people in Paris wrote and signed a simple *declaration*."

3. The word *declaration* means

   A. a signed statement
   B. a law
   C. a speech
   D. a vote

"Global Zero also launched a *global* public campaign."

4. The word *global* has to do with

   A. something that affects the entire world
   B. something that is spread around
   C. something that is newsworthy
   D. something that is isolated

"Global Zero sent *delegations* to meet with leaders in Moscow and Washington, D.C."

5. The word *delegations* means

   A. armies
   B. missiles
   C. representatives
   D. students

"Getting to zero weapons is only part of the *solution*."

6. The word *solution* means

   A. the answer
   B. a body of fluid
   C. organizations
   D. raising questions

WORD CHOICE

Directions: The sentences below contain blanks for missing words. Three answer choices are listed after each blank. Read the sentence past the blank and choose the correct word. Write it in the blank.

It took 18 months to establish Global Zero. Finally more than 100

people _____ (*meeting, met, meet*) in Paris that December. Among

them _____ (*is, were, was*) scientists, winners of the Nobel Peace

Prize, and former and current world _____ (*leading, lead, leaders*).

They _____ (*are, won't, were*) instrumental in _____ (*bringing,*

bring, brought) the others together.

Those people in Paris _____ (*written, writing, wrote*) and

_____ (*sign, signed, signing*) a simple declaration. Global Zero also

_____ (*launch, launched, launching*) a global public campaign.

At its Web site, individuals from all over the world _____ (*can,*

could, can't) sign that same declaration. Many thousands of people

from all over the world have _____ (*signed, signature, sign*) it.

The U.S. and Russia _____ (*is, are, aren't*) critical to the

campaign's success. After its launch in Paris, Global Zero _____

(*sending, sent, send*) delegations to meet with leaders of the

other countries.

LOOK WHO'S TALKING

Directions: Below are sentences that relate to "Global Zero Launches Its Campaign."
Look back in the article and reread the paragraph in which you find the reference. Circle
the best answer to each question.

1. **In the second sentence of paragraph 2, the word *they* refers to**

   A. the U.S. and the United Kingdom
   B. the U.S., the United Kingdom, and Canada
   C. the U.S. and Canada
   D. the U.S., Canada, and Japan

2. **In the second sentence of paragraph 3, the word *them* refers to**

   A. the Japanese
   B. nuclear weapons
   C. nations
   D. terrorist groups

3. **In the last sentence of paragraph 5, the word *them* refers to**

   A. the U.S. and Russia
   B. current world leaders
   C. the citizens of Paris
   D. the people who established Global Zero

4. **In the third sentence of paragraph 7, the word *it* refers to**

   A. the declaration
   B. the campaign
   C. the Internet
   D. Facebook

5. **In paragraph 9 the word *it* refers all three times to**

   A. the weapons
   B. Global Zero
   C. the system
   D. the outline

6. **In the second sentence of paragraph 11, the word *it* refers to**

   A. a wild dream
   B. Global Zero
   C. eliminating nuclear weapons
   D. an international conference

NOTE MAKING

Directions: Read the boldfaced key words on the left side of the chart below. Then add notes that answer the question in parentheses under the key word.

Global Zero (What is Global Zero?)	
nuclear weapons (Who has nuclear weapons?)	
Global Zero members (Who are the members of Global Zero?)	
three steps (What three steps has Global Zero outlined?)	
increased danger (Why is there increased danger?)	

*On a separate sheet of paper, write a summary of what your notes say about the problems with the control of nuclear weapons.

IS THAT A FACT?

Directions: Read the definitions of a fact and an inference below. Then read the paragraph that follows. At the bottom of the page, write an F on the blank if the sentence is a fact. Write an I if the sentence is an inference. Use the following definitions:

Fact—a statement that can be proven true from the paragraph

Inference—a guess as to what MIGHT be true, based on what you have read and what you already know about the subject

Global Zero is recommending three steps toward its goal. First, it wants Russia and the United States to make big cuts in the number of weapons they have. Second, it wants other countries with nuclear weapons to join Russia and the United States in slowly reducing their weapons to zero. Third, it wants to establish an international system for managing nuclear fuel from power plants and preventing the development of nuclear weapons. Reaching zero could take until 2035.

_____ **1.** Global Zero does not trust countries to manage nuclear weapons on their own.

_____ **2.** Global Zero members know they have a difficult time ahead.

_____ **3.** Most countries are not eager to let go of their nuclear weapons.

_____ **4.** Russia and the United States have the most nuclear weapons.

_____ **5.** It is going to take many years to accomplish these goals.

MAKE A SPACE

Directions: Below are sentences that are missing punctuation and capitalization. First draw slash marks (/) between the words. Then rewrite each sentence in the space below it by filling in the missing punctuation and capitalization.

Example:

now / a / number / of / countries / possess / nuclear / weapons

Now a number of countries possess nuclear weapons.

---

1. ittookeighteenmonthstoestablishglobalzero

_____

_____

2. gettingzeroweaponsisonlypartofthesolution

_____

_____

3. nationsagreedthatthedangershaveincreased

_____

_____

4. peoplefeelthatsmallunstablecountriesandterroristscouldgetthemtoo

_____

_____

TIME MY READ #2

Directions: With a partner, see how many words you can read correctly in 45 seconds. As you read, your partner will put an X through any word read incorrectly on his or her copy. When you are finished, trade your books or papers, and let your partner read while you keep score. Count the total number of words you read correctly. Write this score at the bottom of your page.

nuclear catastrophe campaign destructive worldwide terrorists scientists technology	8
launching declaration reducing crisis solution inspections globally unstable	16
international program responding nations eliminating dream Nobel system	24
nuclear catastrophe campaign destructive worldwide terrorists scientists technology	32
launching declaration reducing crisis solution inspections globally unstable	40
international program responding nations eliminating dream Nobel system	48
nuclear catastrophe campaign destructive worldwide terrorists scientists technology	56
launching declaration reducing crisis solution inspections globally unstable	64
international program responding nations eliminating dream Nobel system	72
nuclear catastrophe campaign destructive worldwide terrorists scientists technology	80

Number of words read correctly _____

Is the score higher than it was in Time My Read #1? _____

WORD PARTS

Directions: A **base word** is a word that can stand alone. A **prefix** is a word part added to the beginning of a base word. For example, in the word **interoffice,** *office* is the base word and *inter-* is the prefix added at the beginning. The prefix *inter-* means "among" or "between." *Interoffice* describes something sent or happening between different offices. On the lines below, write a definition for each word. Try not to use the base word in the definition. If you don't know the base word, look it up in a dictionary or ask a partner.

1. interstate— _____

2. interplay— _____

3. international— _____

4. interracial— _____

5. interlock— _____

6. interview— _____

7. intersection— _____

8. intermingle— _____

9. intertwine— _____

10. interface— _____

11. interact— _____

12. interchange— _____

13. interstellar— _____

14. interfaith— _____

15. intercollegiate— _____

GLOBAL ZERO WORD PUZZLE

Directions: Complete the crossword puzzle.

Word List

GLOBAL
DECLARATION
INTERFAITH
SOLUTION
INTERACT
INTERNATIONAL
INTERSECTION
INTERSTATE
INTERVIEW
CAMPAIGN

Across

2. an answer to something
4. the entire world
7. a movement to make something happen
8. to work together
9. to ask someone about his or her life
10. between or among many countries

Down

1. a strong, signed statement
3. among different religions
5. between two or more states
6. a place where roads meet

WRITING FRAME

Directions: Use your knowledge and information from the article to complete the writing frame below.

Humans developed nuclear weapons a little more than sixty years

ago. The United States ended World War II by

_____ _____ . In December 2008,

a new campaign was launched by _____ . The purpose of

the campaign is to _____

_____ .

The first nuclear weapons were developed by the United States,

_____ and _____ . Now a number

of other countries possess them, including _____,

_____, and _____ .

It took 18 months to establish Global Zero. At the first meeting

in Paris, people signed a _____ that said we must

eliminate _____ . Global Zero recommends

these three steps toward its goal:

1. _____

2. _____

3. _____

Reaching zero could take _____ .

REACTION GUIDE

Directions: Now that you have read and studied information about "Global Zero Launches Its Campaign," reread the statements below, which you responded to before reading the article. Then think about how the author might respond to these statements. If you think the author would agree, put a checkmark on the line before the number. If you think the author would disagree, put an X on the line. Then below the statement, copy the words, phrases, or sentences from the article that provide evidence of the views stated by the author. Also note if there is no evidence to support the statement.

_____ **1.** We don't have to worry about countries using nuclear weapons.

Evidence: _____

_____

_____

_____ **2.** We should stop countries from creating nuclear weapons.

Evidence: _____

_____

_____

_____ **3.** Nuclear weapons never should have been invented.

Evidence: _____

_____

_____

Name _____ Date _____

TAKE A STAND

Directions: People often have differing feelings or opinions about an issue. When they discuss or argue their opposing views, they are taking part in a debate. A good persuasive argument is based on a claim that is supported by

Facts—statements that can be proven true

Statistics—numerical data gotten through research

Examples—instances that support an opinion

You and a partner are going to debate two of your other classmates. The topic you are going to debate is the following:

We should stop countries from creating their first nuclear weapons.

Decide with the other pair who will agree and who will disagree with this statement. Then answer these questions in order to win your debate.

1. What are your two strongest points to persuade the other side? (You can do Internet research to include facts, statistics, and examples.)

A. _____

B. _____

2. What might the other side say to argue against point A?

_____

_____

3. What might the other side say to argue against point B?

_____

_____

4. What will you say to prove the other side's arguments are wrong?

_____

_____

_____

Name _____ Date _____

ASSESSMENT

Comprehension: Answer the questions about the following passage.

It took 18 months to establish Global Zero. Finally more than 100 people met in Paris in December. The meeting included scientists, winners of the Nobel Peace Prize, and former and current world leaders. In Paris they wrote and signed a simple declaration. Global Zero is also launching a global public campaign. At its Web site individuals from all over the world can sign that same declaration. In fact, many thousands of people from 85 different countries had signed it. The campaign hopes to eliminate the development of nuclear weapons.

1. Why is the nuclear weapons debate so important?

_____

_____

2. What might happen if the international community doesn't control the development of nuclear weapons?

_____

_____

3. What do you think is the author's purpose in writing this article?

_____

_____

Fluency: The words in the following two sentences are all connected. The sentences are also missing punctuation and capitalization. Draw slash marks (/) between the words. Then rewrite each sentence by filling in the punctuation and capitalization.

1. peoplerealizethatgettingtozeroweaponsisonlypartofthesolution

_____

ASSESSMENT

**2. humansdevelopednuclearweaponsoversixtyyearsagoandnowmany
countrieshavethem**

_____

Fluency: Read the three sentences below. Imagine where you would pause within each sentence as you read it aloud. Draw a slash (/) mark between the phrases where you would pause. The first slash is done.

3. Getting zero weapons / is only part / of the solution.

4. Nations agree that the dangers of nuclear weapons have increased.

5. However, terrorists and small unstable countries might get them.

Vocabulary: Based on what you have learned in this lesson, match the following words with their definitions. Write the letter of the definition on the blank in front of the word it defines.

1. _____ interfaith   **A.** an answer to something

2. _____ solution   **B.** between two or more states

3. _____ declaration   **C.** a strong, signed statement

4. _____ interact   **D.** disaster or total failure

5. _____ interview   **E.** a movement to make something happen

6. _____ campaign   **F.** among different religions

7. _____ intersection   **G.** to communicate or work together

8. _____ catastrophe   **H.** to ask someone about his or her life

9. _____ global   **I.** a place where roads meet

10. _____ interstate   **J.** involving the entire world

Name _____ Date _____

ANTICIPATION GUIDE

Directions: Before you read the article "South Africa Fights Back Against Poachers," read the statements below. If you agree with a statement, put a checkmark on the line next to it. If you disagree, put an X on the line.

_____ **1.** Some wild animals have a hard time surviving because of humans.

_____ **2.** Hunting animals in order to make medicines should be illegal.

_____ **3.** Sometimes endangered species of animals are going to die off.

Once you have responded to the statements above, write in the section below why you agree or disagree with each statement.

1. _____

_____

2. _____

_____

3. _____

_____

In the box below, draw a picture of what you think this article is about.

PREDICTING ABCs

Directions: The article you are going to read is about poachers who kill rhinos for their horns. See how many boxes you can fill in below with words relating to this topic. For example, put the word *hunter* in the G–I box. Try to put at least one word in every box, and then try to write a word for every letter.

A–C	D–F	G–I
J–L	**M–O**	**P–R**
S–T	**U–V**	**W–Z**

LANGUAGE MINI-LESSON

An **adjective** is a word that describes a noun or pronoun. Adjectives answer the questions *what kind, which one, how many,* or *how much.*

The most common adjectives are called **articles.** These are the words *a, an,* and *the. A* is used before a word beginning with a consonant sound. For example: a tent or a school. *An* is used before a word beginning with a vowel *(a, i, e, o, u).* For example: *an* apple or *an* ocean. The third article is the word *the,* which is used to point out a particular person, place, or thing. Note how the articles are used in the sentence below.

The circus kept **an** elephant in **a** tent.

Many adjectives are formed from common nouns. For example, the noun *wind* adds a *-y* and becomes an adjective in the phrase "a *windy* day," where it describes the word *day.*

Adjectives can also be formed from proper nouns. For example, the noun *America* becomes an adjective to describe the word *car* in the phrase "an *American* car."

Directions: Rewrite the words below as adjectives. Use a dictionary if needed.

1. hunger _____ **2.** Africa _____ **3.** crime _____

4. India _____ **5.** medicine _____ **6.** danger _____

Pronouns can also be used as adjectives in two ways. The first way is to point out a particular noun. These pronouns are called **demonstrative pronouns.** The four demonstrative pronouns are *this, that, these,* and *those.* For example: **this** ball

The second way pronouns can be used as adjectives is to show ownership. These pronouns are called **possessive pronouns.** The seven possessive pronouns are *my, our, your, her, his, its,* and *their.* For example: **her** skirt

Directions: Underline the adjectives in the following sentences.

1. The Javan rhino lives in Indonesia, but the Indian rhino lives in India and Nepal.

2. Africa's white rhino is the largest, and its long front horn can be five feet long.

3. Some hunters are poor Africans who sell the horns to professional poachers.

4. Poachers kill white rhinos with their guns and use chain saws to take their horns.

5. The government sends special police units and army patrols to catch poachers.

ECHO READING

Directions: When you read, you should make breaks, and sometimes pauses, between groups of words. As your teacher reads each phrase, repeat aloud what is read and put a slash or line after that phrase. Then read the whole sentence aloud as a class. Do the first paragraph together as a class, and then do the second one on your own. The first sentence has been marked for you.

About 70% of the world's rhinoceros / live in South Africa. / They live in protected reserves and parks. Even so, poachers are killing hundreds of them for their horns. The government is trying to protect the rhinos, and in November it got help in court. A judge sent a poacher from Thailand to prison for 40 years. That is the longest sentence that a poacher in South Africa ever has received.

There are five species of rhino in the world. Each is threatened with extinction because of loss of habitat and poaching. The Javan rhino lives in Indonesia, but only several dozen remain. Only a couple of hundred Sumatran rhinos are still alive in Borneo and Sumatra. There are only 2,000 Indian rhinos left in northern India and Nepal.

What's Happening
IN THE WORLD?

BY LAWRENCE GABLE
© *2014 What's Happening Publications*

1   About 70% of the world's rhinoceros live in South Africa. They live in protected reserves and parks. Even so, poachers are killing hundreds of them for their horns. The government is trying to protect the rhinos, and in 2012 it got help in court. A judge sent a poacher from Thailand to prison for 40 years. That was the longest sentence that a poacher in South Africa ever had received.

South Africa Fights Back Against Poachers

2   There are five species of rhino in the world. Each is threatened with extinction because of loss of habitat and poaching. The Javan rhino lives in Indonesia, but only several dozen remain. Only a couple of hundred Sumatran rhinos are still alive in Borneo and Sumatra. There are only 3,000 Indian rhinos left in northern India and Nepal.

3   Two species live in Africa. Only a hundred years ago there were 100,000 black rhinos, but now there are only 5,000. The longer of its two horns grows to two feet long. The rhino itself stands six feet tall, 13 feet long, and weighs 3,500 pounds.

4   Africa's white rhino is the largest of the five species. It is six feet tall too, but it weighs twice as much as a black rhino. Its long front horn can grow to five feet long. Most of the 20,000 white rhinos live in South Africa.

5   Rhino populations have grown. Reserves and parks in Africa care for the animals, and some zoos around the world do too. However, recent poaching is lowering populations again. In 2007 poachers killed only 13 rhinos. By 2010 the number had risen to 333 rhinos though, and in 2013 the number grew to just over 1,000 rhinos.

6   International law has banned trade in rhino horn since 1977. However, the market for rhino horn has grown in recent years. The demand for it is high in Asia, especially in Vietnam. People use it as medicine, even though it has no medicinal value. This has led directly to the huge increase in poaching.

7   There are different kinds of poachers. Some are poor, hungry Africans who do it to stay alive. They usually track rhinos on foot and shoot them. Then they use an axe to remove the horns. They sell the horns to professional poachers for little profit. The professionals belong to criminal organizations that smuggle the horns across borders. The final price in Vietnam reaches $30,000 a pound.

8   The professional poachers can afford modern equipment. They travel by helicopter. Poachers shoot the rhinos with high-powered guns or with tranquilizer guns. Then they use chain saws to cut into the head and remove the horns. The animals that are not already dead bleed to death. Their reason for killing rhinos is to get rich.

9   Catching poachers is hard. It is impossible to guard the huge game reserves and parks closely. Professional poachers carry guns, so catching them is dangerous, even deadly work. South Africa's national parks have anti-poaching units. The government also sends special police units and army patrols to catch poachers. In 2013 they caught and arrested 343 people.

10   In 2012 South African courts finally began handing out long sentences. One South African got an eight-year sentence. Later that year two foreign poachers got 29 years. Then its sentence of 40 years sent the strongest message yet. Rhinos are a national treasure, and the government intends to protect them.

QUICK READ/DRAW AND WRITE

Directions: First Reading—As you do your first reading of the article, your teacher will time you for one minute. When time is called, write the number of the paragraph where you stopped. **Paragraph # _____**

In the box below, draw a picture summarizing what you read.

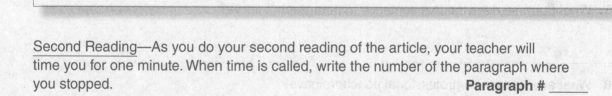

Second Reading—As you do your second reading of the article, your teacher will time you for one minute. When time is called, write the number of the paragraph where you stopped. **Paragraph # _____**

Directions: Now continue reading the rest of the article. Below, write five important words that will help you remember the information from the article.

_____ _____ _____ _____ _____

CLOSE READING ANNOTATION

Third Reading—As you reread each paragraph in the article closely, answer the questions by annotating the text. Each numbered question corresponds to a paragraph in the article where the answer can be found. Write your brief answers in the space below each question.

1. What is the author's purpose for writing the first paragraph?

_____

2/3. How does the author show you the shrinking number of rhinos worldwide?

_____

4. What information does the author give you about the white rhino?

_____

5. How have the reserves and parks helped the rhino populations?

_____

6. What makes the rhino horn so popular in Asia?

_____

7. What purpose does the last sentence in paragraph 7 serve?

_____

8. What advantages do professional poachers have?

_____

9. How is the first sentence in paragraph 9 supported by the other sentences in the paragraph?

_____

10. What conclusion does the author want to leave you with in paragraph 10?

_____

GRAMMAR GAMES

Directions: Reread the two paragraphs below. Words have been left out from the sentences. Think about the information from the article you have read and fill in words that make sense. The part of speech of each missing word is provided.

There are five species of rhino _____ the world. Each is
                                    (1. preposition)

_____ with extinction because of loss of habitat and poaching.
(2. verb)

The Javan _____ lives in Indonesia, _____ only
          (3. noun)   (4. conjunction)

several dozen remain. Only a couple of hundred Sumatran rhinos are

_____ alive in Borneo and Sumatra. There are only 2,000
(5. adverb)

Indian rhinos left in northern _____ and Nepal.
                               (6. proper noun)

Africa's white rhino is the largest of the _____ species.
                                            (7. adjective)

_____ is six feet tall too, but it _____ twice as much
(8. pronoun)   (9. verb)

as a black rhino. Its long front horn can _____ to five feet long.
                                           (10. verb)

Most of the 20,000 white rhinos live in South _____ .
                                               (11. proper noun)

International law has _____ trade in rhino horn since
                     (12. verb)

1977. However, the market for rhino horn has _____
                                              (13. verb)

in recent years.

CLOSE READING STRUCTURE

Directions: Understanding the structure of a text is important for two reasons. First, understanding the structure of a selection can help you remember the main idea and important details. Second, most academic writing you will encounter uses text structures to organize ideas.

1. Writers often include a statement in the **introduction** that catches the reader's attention. Then, the writer tells what the article will be about. On the space provided, copy the last sentence of the introduction to the article.

_____

_____

_____

2. On the space below, copy the sentences that best states what the author's **claim, main idea,** or **thesis** is for this article.

_____

_____

_____

3. On the space below, copy the sentence that shows where the author introduces another **opinion,** or **opposing claim,** about poachers.

_____

_____

4. Near the end of an article, the writer often restates the main idea and summarizes the evidence. This is called the **conclusion.** On the space below, write the sentence that best shows where the conclusion to the article begins.

_____

_____

_____

IS THAT A FACT?

Directions: Read the definitions of a fact and an inference below. Then read the paragraph that follows. At the bottom of the page, write an F on the blank if the sentence is a fact. Write an I if the sentence is an inference. Use the following definitions:

Fact—a statement that can be proven true from the paragraph

Inference—a guess as to what MIGHT be true, based on what you have read and what you already know about the subject

> The professional poachers can afford modern equipment. They travel by helicopter. Poachers shoot the rhinos with high-powered guns or with tranquilizer guns. Then they use chain saws to cut into the head and remove the horns. The animals that are not already dead simply bleed to death. Their reason for killing rhinos is to get rich. Catching poachers is dangerous because they have powerful weapons, and it is impossible to guard the huge game reserves and parks closely.

_____ **1.** Professional poachers are well organized.

_____ **2.** Though poachers don't always kill rhinos, they usually cause them to die.

_____ **3.** Professional poachers don't care about the lives of rhinos.

_____ **4.** The reserves can't always protect rhinos from poachers.

_____ **5.** Poachers have dangerous weapons.

_____ **6.** The reserves are too large to effectively guard.

SUMMARIZING ABCs

Directions: Now that you've read the article on the poaching of rhinos, see how many words you can write about this topic in the boxes below.

A–C	D–F	G–I
J–L	**M–O**	**P–R**
S–T	**U–V**	**W–Z**

REACTION GUIDE

Directions: Now that you have read and studied information about "South Africa Fights Back Against Poachers," reread the statements below, which you responded to before reading the article. Then think about how the author might respond to these statements. If you think the author would agree, put a checkmark on the line before the number. If you think the author would disagree, put an X on the line. Then below the statement, copy the words, phrases, or sentences from the article that provide evidence of the views stated by the author. Also note if there is no evidence to support the statement.

_____ **1.** Some wild animals have a hard time surviving because of humans.

Evidence: _____

_____

_____

_____ **2.** Hunting animals in order to make medicines should be illegal.

Evidence: _____

_____

_____

_____ **3.** Sometimes endangered species of animals are going to die off.

Evidence: _____

_____

_____

SENTENCE TRANSITIONS

An informational essay answers questions and provides information. Writers use transitional phrases to link ideas. Some transitional words and phrases include *to show, to prove, because, to explain, to verify, due to, instead of, furthermore, as a result,* and *in order to*.

Directions: Complete the following sentences using the phrases given.

Example: A poacher was sentenced to forty years in jail. A poacher was sentenced to forty years in jail *in order to send a message to other poachers who are killing rhinos.*

1. There are many types of rhinos, *such as*

_____

2. Rhinos are counted in India and Nepal *to verify*

_____

3. The government now has anti-poaching units *as a result*

_____

4. International law has banned trade in rhino horns *because*

_____

5. Criminals sell horns illegally and get rich *due to*

_____

Name _____ Date _____

PICKING UP PUNCTUATION

Commas can be used in a number of ways. The following are a few of them:

1. Use a comma with **introductory words and phrases.** For example: Even so, poachers are killing hundreds of rhinos for their horns.

2. Use commas with **interjections** such as *oh, well,* and *hey.* For example: Hey, that black rhino is in my living room!

3. Use a comma with **appositives.** An appositive is a noun, pronoun, or phrase that gives additional information about a noun or pronoun next to it. Use commas if the appositive is not vital to the meaning of the sentence. Example 1: The white rhino, the largest of the five species, weighs twice as much as the black rhino. (With or without the appositive, the white rhino weighs twice as much as the black rhino.) Example 2: The white rhino in my bedroom weighs twice as much as the black rhino. (Another white rhino might not weigh twice as much as the black rhino, so the appositive is vital to the meaning of the sentence.)

4. Finally, remember to put commas before ***and, but, or,* or *nor* when combining two sentences into one.** For example: The white rhino is six feet tall, and it weighs 3,500 pounds. If you combine the subjects when you join the sentences, do not use a comma. For example: The white rhino is six feet tall and weighs 3,500 pounds.

Directions: Use commas to punctuate the paragraph below.

International law has banned trade in rhino horn since 1977. However the market for rhino horn often used as medicine in Asia is growing. The demand for it is high especially in Vietnam. People use it as medicine even though it has no medicinal value. By 2010 the number of rhino deaths had risen to 333 and in 2012 the number reached 570. There are different kinds of poachers. Many are poor hungry Africans who do it to stay alive.

ANALYZING A PROMPT

Directions: Read the writing prompt in the box below. Then follow the directions to learn how to analyze and answer it.

> You have become an active member of Save the Rhinos, a conservation group. The group has asked you to write a travel brochure that explains why rhinos need more protection. They want to give the brochure to tourists visiting African and Asian animal preserves. Remember, these tourists know little about these animals. What information can you use from the article to educate tourists about the dangers that rhinos face and to help them realize that poaching is wrong?

1. A writing prompt begins with some background information known as the **set up.** Underline the sentences that set up this assignment.

2. Use the following **R.A.F.T.** technique to finish analyzing the prompt.

Role: What are you supposed to be to answer it? A student? A politician?

Write what you are here: _____

Audience: To whom are you writing? A friend? A particular group?

Write who it is here: _____

Format: Check to see what type of writing you are doing. Is it an essay, a letter, a speech, a story, a description, an editorial, or a report?

Write what it is here: _____

Task: Another sentence in the prompt will tell you what you must do, or your "task." Question words like **why, how,** or **what** may tell the task.

If the question word is **why,** you will *give the reasons* that something is done.

If the question word is **how,** you will *explain the way* that something is done.

If the question word is **what,** you will *identify the thing* that is done.

Below, copy the sentence or question that describes your task.

_____

_____

WHAT'S YOUR POINT?

When writing an essay it is important to have a strong **claim.** The **claim,** or **thesis statement,** states the main point the writer wants to get across. Once the thesis is introduced, the body of the essay should support that thesis with key points that provide evidence.

The article "South Africa Fights Back Against Poachers" presents information about the dangers wild rhinos face from illegal poaching. The article discusses how rhinos are hunted and killed for their horns and how professional criminals are part of the problem. Countries are attempting to make laws stronger and sentences longer to discourage poaching, which is causing rhino populations to diminish.

Directions: Which of these sentences provides the best **claim** for an essay on this topic? Circle the letter of your choice.

a. The rhinoceros is a vital source of income to many people in Asia.

b. There needs to be more international control over the problem of poaching rhinos in Africa and Asia.

c. Asian demand is creating a huge population decrease in different rhinoceros species.

In the space below, explain what is weak or wrong about the other two statements.

1. _____

_____

_____

2. _____

_____

_____

ASSESSMENT

1. The author claims that the world's rhinoceros population is growing smaller. Cite three pieces of evidence from the article to support this claim.

a. _____

b. _____

c. _____

2. Circle the letter of the paragraph in which the author explains why rhino horn is worth money.

   a. paragraph 1

   b. paragraph 6

   c. paragraph 7

   d. paragraph 9

3. Circle the letter of the paragraph that best summarizes the information in this article.

   a. paragraph 1

   b. paragraph 6

   c. paragraph 9

   d. paragraph 10

4. Which of the following sentences **best** supports the conclusion that South Africa wants to punish the rhino poachers they catch?

   a. Catching poachers is hard.

   b. South Africa's national parks have anti-poaching units.

   c. The government sends in special police units and army patrols.

   d. In 2012 South African courts finally began handing out long prison sentences.

5. A student is writing an editorial to convince people to donate to anti-poaching organizations that try to protect rhinoceros. Read the draft of the introduction below and the directions that follow.

Imagine that you are walking through some woods and you find a deer slowly bleeding to death because someone has cut off its antlers with a chain saw. How would you feel about this poor suffering animal? In Africa, finding a rhinoceros bleeding to death after having its horn savagely cut away is not uncommon, and the practice is not easy to stop. The poachers who do this are well-equipped.

The student took these notes from reliable sources:

— Most rhino horn is sent to Vietnam.

— Professional poachers can earn as much as $30,000 a pound for horns.

— Many poachers carry high-powered guns and night-vision binoculars.

— There are five species of rhinos in the world.

— Some poachers travel over huge areas in helicopters.

— Some poor Africans poach rhino horn to stay alive.

— Many poachers belong to criminal organizations that can easily smuggle horns.

Directions: Using information from the student's notes, write **one** paragraph developing the idea that is presented in the last sentence of the article's introduction.

Name _____ Date _____

ANTICIPATION GUIDE

Directions: Before you read the article "Somalia's Problems Lead to Piracy," read the statements below. If you agree with a statement, put a checkmark on the line next to it. If you disagree, put an X on the line.

_____ **1.** Countries ought to be able to protect their coastal waters, even if it means causing harm to other people.

_____ **2.** Stealing is always wrong under any circumstances.

_____ **3.** People can do anything to survive if their government fails.

Once you have responded to the statements above, write in the section below why you agree or disagree with each statement.

1. _____

_____

2. _____

_____

3. _____

_____

In the box below, draw a picture of what you think this article is about.

PREDICTING ABCs

Directions: The article you are going to read is about pirates. See how many boxes you can fill in below with words relating to this topic. For example, put the word *ship* in the S–T box. Try to put at least one word in every box, and then try to write a word for every letter.

A–C	D–F	G–I
J–L	**M–O**	**P–R**
S–T	**U–V**	**W–Z**

TIME MY READ #1

Directions: With a partner, see how many words you can read correctly in 45 seconds. As you read, your partner will put an X through any word read incorrectly on his or her copy. When you are finished, trade your books or papers, and let your partner read while you keep score. Count the total number of words you read correctly. Write this score at the bottom of your page.

piracy aid starving international fishing foreign ransom demanding	8
companies delivery undependable cargo tactics aboard captured attacks	16
effort hijacking operate restore members satellite vast coastal	24
piracy aid starving international fishing foreign ransom demanding	32
companies delivery undependable cargo tactics aboard captured attacks	40
effort hijacking operate restore members satellite vast coastal	48
piracy aid starving international fishing foreign ransom demanding	56
companies delivery undependable cargo tactics aboard captured attacks	64
effort hijacking operate restore members satellite vast coastal	72
piracy aid starving international fishing foreign ransom demanding	80

Number of words read correctly _____

ECHO READING

Directions: When you read, you should make breaks, and sometimes pauses, between groups of words. As your teacher reads each phrase, repeat aloud what is read and put a slash or line after that phrase. Then read the whole sentence aloud as a class. Do the first paragraph together as a class, and then do the second one on your own. The first sentence has been marked for you.

In the 1990s / Somali fishermen / formed their own "coast guards" / to stop foreign fishing. / They used guns to chase away foreign fishing boats. Then they started boarding the vessels and demanding "fees." Finally, their piracy really began when they seized the vessels and demanded a ransom from the companies that owned them.

Somalia's location puts the pirates in perfect position. The country is shaped like the number 7, and its coastline stretches almost 2,000 miles. To the north lies the Gulf of Aden. At the Horn of Africa, the coastline turns south along the Indian Ocean. Every year 16,000 cargo ships sail the Gulf of Aden as they enter or leave the Red Sea. At the top of the Red Sea lies the Suez Canal, which allows ships to take a shorter route to the Mediterranean Sea.

What's Happening
IN THE WORLD?

BY LAWRENCE GABLE
© 2014 What's Happening Publications

SUBJECT: GLOBAL ISSUES

Somalia's Problems Lead to Piracy

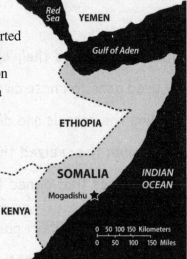

1   For thousands of years pirates have threatened ships at sea. Ancient Greek and Roman writings tell of them. The Vikings attacked European ships in the Middle Ages, and several centuries ago pirates like Blackbeard sailed the Caribbean. In the 1990s pirates started attacking again off Somalia's coast.

2   This piracy really started on land. In 1991 warlords in Somalia overthrew the central government. A civil war began and the fighting continues today. Hundreds of thousands of people have died, and 3.2 million Somalis are starving. The United Nations (U.N.) sent food by land, but warlords attacked the trucks. It never reached most Somalis, so the U.N. started sending the food by sea.

3   Somalia's fishing industry failed at the same time. International law gives countries control of their coastal waters. However, Somalia no longer had a government to protect its waters, so other countries sent ships across the Indian Ocean to catch tuna and shark there.

4   In the 1990s Somali fishermen formed their own "coast guards" to stop foreign fishing. They used guns to chase them away. Then they started boarding the vessels and demanding "fees." Their piracy really began when they held the vessels and demanded a ransom from the ships' owners.

5   In those same years they also began hijacking the U.N.'s food ships. Some shipping companies refused to make those trips. As a result, the delivery of food became undependable and Somalis suffered.

6   Somalia's location puts the pirates in perfect position. The country is shaped like the number "7." Its northern coastline stretches along the Gulf of Aden, then south along the Indian Ocean. Every year 16,000 cargo ships sail the Gulf of Aden, which connects to the Red Sea and the Suez Canal. The canal opens a shorter route between Europe and the Far East.

7   Somali pirates use modern equipment. They have large ships with satellite systems that locate their targets. Then they attack in small, fast boats that carry heavy machine guns and grenades. At night they race up to a ship, climb its sides and capture the crew. During the day they surround a ship, go aboard and demand a ransom.

8   In 2008 Somali pirates attacked more than 100 ships. They included container, cargo and cruise ships. They collected $100 million in ransom payments. At the end of the year they still held 18 of them and 300 crew members. The number of attacks rose in 2009.

In November 2008 pirates hijacked a supertanker far out in the Indian Ocean. Until then most attacks had taken place in the Gulf of Aden. It was the largest ship ever captured. They held it for several months, when they received a $3 million ransom.

9   That hijacking led to an international response. At least a dozen warships from different countries began to patrol the waters off Somalia. They aid vessels under attack and fight pirates. Although they had some success, they cannot control the million square miles of ocean where the pirates operate.

10   Piracy off Somalia does not just put ships' crews at risk. It also interrupts trade. Someday it may cause ships to sail around the southern tip of Africa instead. The biggest losers, though, are the Somali people. They are suffering and dying, and hoping for a government that will bring order to their lives.

GET A CONTEXT CLUE

Directions: Below are sentences from "Somalia's Problems Lead to Piracy." First, read the sentence. Then, look back in the article and reread the paragraph in which the sentence is found. Circle the best answer to each question.

"In 1991 warlords in Somalia *overthrew* the central government."

1. The word *overthrew* means

    A. to get rid of; to conquer
    B. to utilize
    C. to increase
    D. to stop

"Then they started *boarding* vessels and demanding fees."

2. The word *boarding* means

    A. coming onto another ship
    B. buying something
    C. towing a ship
    D. responding to something

"Somalia's *location* puts the pirates in perfect position."

3. The word *location* means

    A. government
    B. boats
    C. attitude
    D. place

"The canal opens a shorter *route* between Europe and the Far East."

4. The word *route* means

    A. course or way
    B. person
    C. ship
    D. time

"During the day they surround a ship, go aboard and demand a *ransom*."

5. The word *ransom* means

    A. food or a meal
    B. money for something stolen
    C. release for a prisoner
    D. a celebration

"Although they had some success, they cannot control the million square miles of ocean where the pirates *operate*."

6. The word *operate* means

    A. to go to school
    B. to perform surgery
    C. to commit their crimes
    D. to vacation

WORD CHOICE

Directions: The sentences below contain blanks for missing words. Three answer choices are listed after each blank. Read the sentence past the blank and choose the correct word. Write it in the blank.

Pirates have operated on many oceans for many years. But recently a new piracy problem has _____ (*developing, developed, developed*) off the waters of Somalia. The country of Somalia _____ (*lies, lays, laying*) in a perfect position because of its vantage point on the _____ (*continent, country, continental*) of Africa. When _____ (*their, they're, there*) fishing industry failed, the Somalis _____ (*formed, forming, formation*) their own "coast guard" and started _____ (*chase, chasing, chased*) foreign fishermen away. Then they started _____ (*seize, sized, seizing*) other countries' vessels and _____ (*demand, demanding, demands*) that the owners pay a ransom.

Also in 1991 they _____ (*began, begin, begun*) to seize United Nations ships containing food. This action _____ (*prevented, prevention, prevents*) the country of Somalia from getting food to its starving people. The pirates use modern technology such as _____ (*satellite, starlights, satellites*) to locate ships that they attack. At night they _____ (*racing, raced, race*) up to the ships in small boats and capture the crew.

LOOK WHO'S TALKING

Directions: Below are sentences that relate to "Somalia's Problems Lead to Piracy." Look back in the article and reread the paragraph in which you find the reference. Circle the best answer to each question.

1. In the last sentence of paragraph 2, the word *it* best refers to

    A. the piracy
    B. the food from the United Nations
    C. the trucks
    D. the United Nations

2. In the last sentence of paragraph 3, the word *its* refers to

    A. the fishing industry
    B. the pirates
    C. the country of Somalia
    D. the United Nations

3. In paragraph 4, the word *their* refers both times to

    A. the fishermen
    B. the Somali government
    C. the fishing industry
    D. the people of Somalia

4. In the second sentence of paragraph 8, the word *they* refers to

    A. the ships that were attacked
    B. the pirates who attacked
    C. the people
    D. the hostages

5. In the third sentence of paragraph 9, the word *they* refers to

    A. the supertanker
    B. the Indian Ocean
    C. the ransom
    D. the warships

6. In the last sentence of paragraph 10, the words *they* and *their* refer to

    A. the Somali people
    B. the pirates
    C. the ships
    D. the people held for ransom

HOW'S IT ORGANIZED?

This article is organized as a problem that needs solving.

Directions: Answer these questions in the spaces at the bottom.

1. What is the problem?

2. Why did this problem off Somalia's coast begin?

3. Why did Somalia's fishermen form "coast guards"?

4. How does this problem affect other countries?

5. Who is trying to solve the problem?

6. What results might come, or have come, from these solutions?

7. What problem does the international response to piracy still face?

Answers:

1.	
2.	
3.	
4.	
5.	
6.	
7.	

IS THAT A FACT?

Directions: Read the definitions of a fact and an inference below. Then read the paragraph that follows. At the bottom of the page, write an F on the blank if the sentence is a fact. Write an I if the sentence is an inference. Use the following definitions:

Fact—a statement that can be proven true from the paragraph

Inference—a guess as to what MIGHT be true, based on what you have read and what you already know about the subject

The hijacking of a Saudi supertanker led to an international effort against piracy off Africa's coast. At least a dozen warships from different countries began to patrol the waters off Somalia. They have international authority to come to the aid of vessels under attack and to fight pirates. Quickly they sank some boats and captured pirates, but they cannot control the millions of square miles of ocean where pirates operate.

_____ **1.** Before the large Saudi tanker was hijacked, most countries handled the problem on their own.

_____ **2.** Different countries are using warships to patrol the waters off the Somali coast.

_____ **3.** Pirates operate in too large an area for warships to prevent all attacks.

_____ **4.** Combating piracy can lead to violence.

_____ **5.** Stopping the piracy from Somalia will take some time.

_____ **6.** The Somali government cannot control the pirates that come from their country.

MAKE A SPACE

Directions: Below are sentences that are missing punctuation and capitalization. First draw slash marks (/) between the words. Then rewrite each sentence in the space below it by filling in the missing punctuation and capitalization.

Example:

in / the / 1990s / Somali / fishermen / formed / their / own / coast / guards / to / stop / foreign / fishing

In the 1990s Somali fishermen formed their own "coast guards" to stop foreign fishing.

1. theysailouttoseainlargeshipsthattheyhavecaptured

_____

_____

2. internationallawgivescountriescontroloftheircoastalwaters

_____

_____

3. nowatleastadozenwarshipspatrolthewatersoffsomalia

_____

_____

4. somaliasfishingindustryfailedatthesametime

_____

_____

TIME MY READ #2

Directions: With a partner, see how many words you can read correctly in 45 seconds. As you read, your partner will put an X through any word read incorrectly on his or her copy. When you are finished, trade your books or papers, and let your partner read while you keep score. Count the total number of words you read correctly. Write this score at the bottom of your page.

piracy aid starving international fishing foreign ransom demanding	8
companies delivery undependable cargo tactics aboard captured attacks	16
effort hijacking operate restore members satellite vast coastal	24
piracy aid starving international fishing foreign ransom demanding	32
companies delivery undependable cargo tactics aboard captured attacks	40
effort hijacking operate restore members satellite vast coastal	48
piracy aid starving international fishing foreign ransom demanding	56
companies delivery undependable cargo tactics aboard captured attacks	64
effort hijacking operate restore members satellite vast coastal	72
piracy aid starving international fishing foreign ransom demanding	80

Number of words read correctly _____

Is the score higher than it was in Time My Read #1?_____

WORD PARTS

Directions: The Latin word *civis* means "citizen." Read the definitions below. Then, in the boxes, draw a picture of what each word means.

1. **citizen**—(noun) a resident of a country who can vote and is protected by that country's government and armed forces

2. **civilian**—(noun) a person who is not in the military

3. **civil**—(adjective) polite; behaving in a proper or well-mannered way

citizen	civilian	civil

Directions: The Latin word *navis* means "ship." Read the sentences below. Using the clues in the sentences, write a definition for each underlined word that begins with *nav-*.

1. The harbor was filled with warships from the enemy's <u>navy</u>, so the people of the city were scared.

2. When my father drives the car on trips, my mom acts as the <u>navigator</u>, looking at the map to tell him where to turn.

3. The sailor put on his <u>naval</u> uniform when he was ready to go on board the ship for a voyage.

4. The captain of the large supertanker was a good sailor because he could <u>navigate</u> the ship under the low bridge and not hit anything.

Name _____ Date _____

SUMMARIZING ABCs

Directions: Now that you've read the article on Somalia's pirates, see how many words you can write about this topic in the boxes below.

A–C	D–F	G–I
J–L	M–O	P–R
S–T	U–V	W–Z

SENTENCE SUMMARIES

Directions: Below are four key words or phrases from the article "Somalia's Problems Lead to Piracy." Your job is to summarize, or restate, what you've learned in this article by using these four words or phrases in two sentences. Then, as a challenge, try to use all four words or phrases in one sentence to summarize the article.

Key Words or Phrases

ransom   Somalia's civil war

piracy   international effort

Sentence Summaries:

1. _____

_____

2. _____

_____

Challenge Summary (all four words or phrases in one sentence!):

1. _____

_____

REACTION GUIDE

Directions: Now that you have read and studied information about "Somalia's Problems Lead to Piracy," reread the statements below, which you responded to before reading the article. Then think about how the author might respond to these statements. If you think the author would agree, put a checkmark on the line before the number. If you think the author would disagree, put an X on the line. Then below the statement, copy the words, phrases, or sentences from the article that provide evidence of the views stated by the author. Also note if there is no evidence to support the statement.

_____ **1.** Countries ought to be able to protect their coastal waters, even if it means causing harm to other people.

Evidence: _____

_____

_____

_____ **2.** Stealing is always wrong under any circumstances.

Evidence: _____

_____

_____

_____ **3.** People can do anything to survive if their government fails.

Evidence: _____

_____

_____

TAKE A STAND

Directions: People often have differing feelings or opinions about an issue. When they discuss or argue their opposing views, they are taking part in a debate. A good persuasive argument is based on a claim that is supported by

Facts—statements that can be proven true

Statistics—numerical data gotten through research

Examples—instances that support an opinion

You and a partner are going to debate two of your other classmates. The topic you are going to debate is the following:

Stealing is always wrong under any circumstances.

Decide with the other pair who will agree and who will disagree with this statement. Then answer these questions in order to win your debate.

1. What are your two strongest points to persuade the other side? (You can do Internet research to include facts, statistics, and examples.)

    A. _____

    B. _____

2. What might the other side say to argue against point A?

    _____

    _____

3. What might the other side say to argue against point B?

    _____

    _____

4. What will you say to prove the other side's arguments are wrong?

    _____

    _____

    _____

ASSESSMENT

Comprehension: Answer the questions about the following passage.

The piracy off Somalia's coast really started on land. In 1991 warlords in Somalia overthrew the central government. A civil war began and the fighting continues today. Hundreds of thousands of people have died, and 3.2 million Somalis are starving. The United Nations (U.N.) sent food by land, but warlords attacked the trucks. It never reached most Somalis, so the U.N. started sending the food by sea.

Somalia's fishing industry failed at the same time. The country no longer had a government to protect its waters, so other countries sent ships across the Indian Ocean to catch tuna and shark there.

1. What are some of the reasons why piracy occurs in Somalia?

_____

_____

2. What was the author's purpose for writing about Somalia's pirates?

_____

_____

Fluency: The words in the following two sentences are all connected. The sentences are also missing punctuation and capitalization. Draw slash marks (/) between the words. Then rewrite each sentence by filling in the punctuation and capitalization.

1. somaliasfishingindustryfailedatthesametime

_____

2. finallytheirpiracyreallybeganwhentheyseizedthevesselsforaransom

_____

_____

Fluency: Read the three sentences below. Imagine where you would pause within each sentence as you read it aloud. Draw a slash (/) mark between the phrases where you would pause. The first slash is done.

3. The country/is shaped like a 7, and it has miles of coastline.

4. Every year 16,000 cargo ships sail the Gulf of Aden as they enter or leave the Red Sea.

5. In the 1990s Somali fishermen formed their own "coast guards" to stop foreign fishing.

Vocabulary: Based on what you have learned in this lesson, match the following words with their definitions. Write the letter of the definition on the blank in front of the word it defines.

1. _____ overthrew   **A.** behaving in a well-mannered way

2. _____ civilian   **B.** a place

3. _____ route   **C.** a country's ships and sailors

4. _____ navy   **D.** climbing onto a ship

5. _____ civil   **E.** a person who is not in the military

6. _____ navigator   **F.** course or way

7. _____ ransom   **G.** to direct a boat or other vehicle

8. _____ navigate   **H.** got rid of; ended

9. _____ boarding   **I.** money demanded for something stolen

10. _____ location   **J.** the person who directs a boat or other vehicle

Name _____ Date _____

ANTICIPATION GUIDE

Directions: Before you read the article "A Saudi Woman Makes Film History," read the statements below. If you agree with a statement, put a checkmark on the line next to it. If you disagree, put an X on the line.

_____ **1.** Films and movies are watched all over the world.

_____ **2.** Films about different cultures can sometimes be controversial.

_____ **3.** Girls deserve the same educational opportunities as boys, no matter what their society believes.

Once you have responded to the statements above, write in the section below why you agree or disagree with each statement.

1. _____

_____

2. _____

_____

3. _____

_____

In the box below, draw a picture of what you think this article is about.

WORDSTORM

Directions: It's good to know more than just the dictionary definition of a word. Completing a wordstorm lets you write down information to help you understand what a word means, how it's related to other words, and how to use it in different ways.

What is the word?

tradition

Here is the sentence from the text in which the word is used:

"Although laws do not prohibit her from riding a bike, it goes against tradition."

What are some other words or phrases that mean the same thing?

_____

What are three things you know about tradition?

1. _____ 2. _____ 3. _____

Name three people other than teachers who would likely use this word.

1. _____ 2. _____ 3. _____

Draw a picture below that reminds you of the word *tradition*.

LANGUAGE MINI-LESSON

An **adverb** is a word that answers the questions *how*, *when*, *where*, or *to what degree*. **Adverbs** give more information about verbs. For example: The dog barked **loudly**. (The adverb *loudly* gives more information about how the dog barked.)

Many adverbs are formed by adding *-ly* to an adjective (*near* becomes *nearly*). You can also form adverbs by dropping the *-e* at the end of an adjective and adding *-ly* (*gentle* becomes *gently*). Another way is to change a *-y* at the end of an adjective to *i* and add *-ly* (*lazy* becomes *lazily*).

Directions: Turn the following adjectives into adverbs.

1. complete _____   **3.** easy _____

2. playful _____   **4.** bare _____

Other forms of adverbs and adjectives are used to compare two or more things. When you are comparing two things you use the comparative form. When you are comparing more than two things, you use the superlative form. Study the chart below.

Adjectives and adverbs with one syllable.

Adjective	thin	thinner	thinnest
Adverb	fast	faster	fastest

Adjectives and adverbs with two syllables.

Adjective	awful	**more** awful	**most** awful
Adverb	calmly	**more** calmly	**most** calmly

Adjectives and adverbs with more than two syllables.

Adjective	beautiful	**more** beautiful	**most** beautiful
Adverb	gracefully	**more** gracefully	**most** gracefully

Directions: Fill in the missing forms of the words in the chart.

Adjective or Adverb	Comparative	Superlative
loyal		
		most historic
	more obediently	
high		

ECHO READING

Directions: When you read, you should make breaks, and sometimes pauses, between groups of words. As your teacher reads each phrase, repeat aloud what is read and put a slash or line after that phrase. Then read the whole sentence aloud as a class. Do the first paragraph together as a class, and then do the second one on your own. The first sentence has been marked for you.

In order to understand / the meaning of this new film, / it is important / to understand / Saudi culture. / The state religion is Islam. It controls cultural matters in the kingdom. For 250 years Saudi Arabia's rulers have enforced religious law. In return, religious leaders have supported the rulers. Religion guides the courts, education and public morality. It teaches that people must be loyal and obedient to the ruler, as long as he follows Islamic law. As a result, dissent in Saudi Arabia is unwelcome and change does not happen easily.

Men control Saudi culture. In public women must wear the "abaya" that covers them from head to toe. Women may not appear in public without a male relative. Men and women may not work together in public. Girls and women attend schools only with other girls. Women are not allowed to drive cars either.

© Houghton Mifflin Harcourt Publishing Company

What's Happening
IN THE WORLD?

BY LAWRENCE GABLE
© 2014 What's Happening Publications

SUBJECT: HUMAN RIGHTS and HISTORY

A Saudi Woman Makes Film History

1 The international film industry makes many films every year. In 2013 a new film from Saudi Arabia made a place in film history. "Wadjda" was the first feature-length motion picture ever filmed completely in that country. In addition, its director, Haifaa al-Mansour, was the first Saudi woman to make a full-length film.

2 In order to understand the meaning of that film, it is important to understand Saudi culture. The state religion is Islam. It controls cultural matters in the kingdom. For 250 years Saudi Arabia's rulers have enforced religious law. In return, religious leaders have supported the rulers.

3 Religion guides the courts, education and public morality. It teaches that people must be loyal and obedient to the ruler, as long as he follows Islamic law. As a result, dissent in Saudi Arabia is unwelcome and change does not happen easily.

4 Men control Saudi culture. In public women must wear the "abaya" that covers them from head to toe. Women may not appear in public without a male relative. Men and women may not work together in public. Girls and women attend schools only with other girls. Women are not allowed to drive cars either.

5 The film industry in Saudi Arabia barely exists. Until the early 1980s there were a few movie theaters. They showed foreign films, of course. However, the religious authorities closed all cinemas down because they felt that such films spread immorality. Saudi film directors have made only about a dozen films, always in other countries.

6 Ms. Mansour had no intention of being a pioneer in film. As a girl she watched films from the video store. She liked Jackie Chan movies, and liked seeing life in other countries. She attended college in Egypt and returned to Saudi Arabia for work. When she saw that the company would not promote her because she is a woman, she went to Australia to study film.

7 Her life changed after she made a few successful short films. Her hobby suddenly became her profession. She wrote "Wadjda," but needed the government's approval to make a film in Saudi Arabia. It approved her project partly because no law actually prohibited it.

8 The film's main character is an 11-year-old girl named Wadjda. She falls in love with a green bicycle. She dreams of buying it, and finds funny ways of earning money. Although laws do not prohibit her from riding a bike, it goes against tradition. She is not thinking about tradition though. She simply wants to ride a bike.

9 "Wadjda" first appeared in 2012. It won prizes at a few international film festivals. It is available to Saudi audiences on DVD, and there are plans to show it on television too. It even became the government's first entry ever in competition for an Academy Award.

10 Haifaa al-Mansour tried to make a happy film. She says that a bicycle and a little girl who will not give up her dream are playful on the surface. She knows, though, that Saudis are looking beneath the surface too. They are examining how women and girls live in Saudi Arabia, and perhaps even are considering changes. Ms. Mansour insists that changes are indeed coming for Saudi women. Her historic success as a filmmaker is surely proof of that.

QUICK READ/DRAW AND WRITE

Directions: First Reading—As you do your first reading of the article, your teacher will time you for one minute. When time is called, write the number of the paragraph where you stopped.   **Paragraph #** _____

In the box below, draw a picture summarizing what you read.

Second Reading—As you do your second reading of the article, your teacher will time you for one minute. When time is called, write the number of the paragraph where you stopped.   **Paragraph #** _____

Directions: Now continue reading the rest of the article. Below, write five important words that will help you remember the information from the article.

_____ _____ _____ _____ _____

CLOSE READING ANNOTATION

Third Reading—As you reread each paragraph in the article closely, answer the questions by annotating the text. Each numbered question corresponds to a paragraph in the article where the answer can be found. Write your brief answers in the space below each question.

1. What makes the film titled "Wadjda" so unique?

_____

2. What is the relationship between religious leaders and rulers in Saudi Arabia?

_____

3. What is meant by the word *dissent*?

_____

4. What is the author's purpose for writing paragraph 4?

_____

5. What is the meaning of the word *immorality*?

_____

6. For what reasons did Haifaa al-Mansour want to study film?

_____

7. Why did the government approve Mansour's film?

_____

8. What is the author's purpose for writing paragraph 8?

_____

9. How was the film recognized by the film community?

_____

10. How is Mansour's film about more than just a girl wanting to ride a bike?

_____

GRAMMAR GAMES

Directions: Reread the two paragraphs below. Words have been left out from the sentences. Think about the information from the article you have read and fill in words that make sense. The part of speech of each missing word is provided.

In order to understand the meaning of this new film, it is important

to _____ Saudi culture. The state religion is Islam.
    (1. verb)

_____ controls cultural matters in the kingdom. For 250 years
(2. pronoun)

Saudi Arabia's _____ have enforced religious laws. In return,
            (3. plural noun)

religious leaders _____ supported the rulers. Religion guides
            (4. helping verb)

the courts, education _____ public morality. It teaches that
            (5. conjunction)

people must be loyal and obedient to the _____, as long as he
                        (6. noun)

_____ Islamic law. As a result, dissent in Saudi _____
(7. verb)   (8. proper noun)

is unwelcome and change does not_____ easily.
                    (9. verb)

    Men control Saudi culture. In public women must _____
                                    (10. verb)

the "abaya" that covers them from head to _____. Women may
                        (11. noun)

not appear in public without a _____ relative. Men and women
                (12. adjective)

may not work together _____ public.
            (13. preposition)

Name _____ Date _____

HOW'S IT ORGANIZED?

This article is organized like a nonfiction narrative, such as the story of a real person's life.

Directions: Answer these questions in the spaces below.

1. How does the first paragraph grab the reader's interest?

2. How do the next four paragraphs establish the background for the story?

3. In paragraph 6, what part of Haifaa al-Mansour's life is discussed?

4. What conflict does Mansour have with the government?

5. How does the film reflect conflicts Mansour has faced?

6. The **resolution** is when the conflict is resolved or worked out. What is the final resolution of this nonfiction narrative?

Answers:

1.	
2.	
3.	
4.	
5.	
6.	

The main idea of a selection reflects what the paragraph or sentences are about. Put an X on the space next to the sentence that best states the main idea.

_____ 1. Women in Saudi Arabia don't have the same rights as men.

_____ 2. Despite restrictions on women in Saudi society, one woman took a risk with a film that began to change people's views.

_____ 3. Haifaa al-Mansour's film helped change how we see women in Saudi Arabia.

Explain why your choice is the best main or central idea.

_____

_____

IS THAT A FACT?

Directions: Read the definitions of a fact and an inference below. Then read the paragraph that follows. At the bottom of the page, write an F on the blank if the sentence is a fact. Write an I if the sentence is an inference. Use the following definitions:

Fact—a statement that can be proven true from the paragraph

Inference—a guess as to what MIGHT be true, based on what you have read and what you already know about the subject

---

The film's main character is an 11-year-old girl named Wadjda. She falls in love with a green bicycle. She dreams of buying it and finds funny ways of earning money. Although laws do not prohibit her from riding a bike, it goes against tradition. She is not thinking about tradition though. She simply wants to ride a bike.

The film, titled "Wadjda," first appeared in 2012. It won prizes at a few international film festivals. It is available to Saudi audiences on DVD, and there are plans to show it on television too. It even became the government's first entry ever in a competition for an Academy Award.

_____ **1.** The film "Wadjda" stars an 11-year-old girl.

_____ **2.** It is unusual for girls in Saudi Arabia to want to own and ride bikes.

_____ **3.** Wadjda was not afraid to go against her culture to fulfill her dream of riding a bike.

_____ **4.** In 2012 the film was very well received by Saudi audiences.

_____ **5.** The Saudi government ended up supporting the film.

_____ **6.** It was unusual for girls to find ways to earn money.

TIC-TAC-TOE SUMMARIZING

When you **summarize** in writing, you present all the key points the author is trying to make.

Directions: Write four sentences to summarize the article about Saudi women and film. To help you, there are nine words in the Tic-Tac-Toe graphic organizer below. To write a sentence, you must use three words in a row. The row can be horizontal (—), vertical (I), or diagonal (/).

film	culture	tradition
women	Saudi Arabia	religion
dissent	public	changes

1. _____

_____

2. _____

_____

3. _____

_____

4. _____

_____

REACTION GUIDE

Directions: Now that you have read and studied information about "A Saudi Woman Makes Film History," reread the statements below, which you responded to before reading the article. Then think about how the author might respond to these statements. If you think the author would agree, put a checkmark on the line before the number. If you think the author would disagree, put an X on the line. Then below the statement, copy the words, phrases, or sentences from the article that provide evidence of the views stated by the author. Also note if there is no evidence to support the statement.

_____ **1.** Films and movies are watched all over the world.

Evidence: _____

_____

_____

_____ **2.** Films about different cultures can sometimes be controversial.

Evidence: _____

_____

_____

_____ **3.** Girls deserve the same educational opportunities as boys, no matter what their society believes.

Evidence: _____

_____

_____

TAKE A STAND

Directions: People often have differing feelings or opinions about an issue. When they discuss or argue their opposing views, they are taking part in a debate. A good persuasive argument is based on a claim that is supported by

Facts—statements that can be proven true

Statistics—numerical data gotten through research

Examples—instances that support an opinion

You and a partner are going to debate two of your other classmates. The topic you are going to debate is the following:

Women are entitled to the same rights as men despite their country's culture.

Decide with the other pair who will agree and who will disagree with this statement. Then answer these questions in order to win your debate.

1. What are your two strongest points to persuade the other side? (You can do Internet research to include facts, statistics, and examples.)

A. _____

B. _____

2. What might the other side say to argue against point A?

_____

_____

3. What might the other side say to argue against point B?

_____

_____

4. What will you say to prove the other side's arguments are wrong?

_____

_____

_____

WHAT'S THE COMBINATION?

Writing is more interesting when the writer joins, or combines, short sentences. Follow the directions below to learn different ways to combine two sentences.

What to do: You can move a part of one sentence into another by using the word *that*. The **subject,** or thing the sentence is about, must be the same for both sentences, and the part you move must be important to understanding the entire thought. In the example below, it's important that the reader knows that the trucks are so loud that the person cannot sleep.

Example: The trucks *rumble down the highway*. The trucks keep me awake at night.

Combined sentence: The trucks *that rumble down the highway* keep me awake at night.

Directions: Combine these sentences using the method above.

1. Some films can be watched in Saudi Arabia. These films are foreign.

_____

2. The films were under tight control in Saudi Arabia. They were shown in cinemas.

_____

3. Cultures sometimes have rules. Some rules may seem to be unfair.

_____

4. Some traditions don't allow a woman to do things. Those traditions might keep her from achieving her goal.

_____

5. The film was about a girl who wanted a bicycle. The film became very popular in the country.

_____

© Houghton Mifflin Harcourt Publishing Company

Name _____ Date _____

ANALYZING A PROMPT

Directions: Read the writing assignment in the box below. Then follow the directions to learn how to analyze and answer it.

> You are a filmmaker and colleague of Haifaa al-Mansour. You are giving a speech to a Saudi government committee about the value of film, and you want to explain the benefits films can bring to a society. You do not want to show disrespect to your culture, tradition, or your religion. What examples of benefits will you use to persuade the committee to promote more filmmaking by women?

1. A writing prompt begins with some background information known as the **set up.** Underline the sentences that set up this assignment.

2. Use the following **R.A.F.T.** technique to finish analyzing the prompt.

Role: What are you supposed to be to answer it? A student? A politician?

Write what you are here: _____

Audience: To whom are you writing? A friend? A particular group?

Write who it is here: _____

Format: Check to see what type of writing you are doing. Is it an essay, a letter, a speech, a story, a description, an editorial, or a report?

Write what it is here: _____

Task: Another sentence in the prompt will tell you what you must do, or your "task." Question words like **why, how,** or **what** may tell the task.

If the question word is **why,** you will *give the reasons* that something is done.

If the question word is **how,** you will *explain the way* that something is done.

If the question word is **what,** you will *identify the thing* that is done.

Below, copy the sentence or question that describes your task.

_____

_____

ANALYZING INFORMATIONAL TEXT

1. Informational articles are written to provide data or descriptions that explain something. Below name three groups that might be interested in reading this article besides students and teachers.

a. _____ **b.** _____ **c.** _____

2. What main point is the author making in this article?

_____

_____

3. Give two of the most important facts you learned in this article.

a. _____

b. _____

4. **Domain-specific vocabulary** consists of words used in a specific subject such as math, science, or social studies. Reread the article and list six domain-specific words used with this subject. After you select the words, write their definitions on the lines provided

a. _____ : _____

b. _____ : _____

c. _____ : _____

d. _____ : _____

e. _____ : _____

f. _____ : _____

ASSESSMENT

1. Read the following excerpt from the article. Based on the words and sentences around the word *dissent*, circle the letter of what you think the word means.

Religion guides the courts, education and public morality. It teaches that people must be loyal and obedient to the ruler, as long as he follows Islamic law. As a result, **dissent** in Saudi Arabia is unwelcome and change does not happen easily.

a. criticism of a person in power

b. film making

c. modern clothing

d. obedience to the law

2. Circle the letter of the sentence that **best** explains how paragraph 4 is important to the development of the article "A Saudi Woman Makes Film History."

a. Paragraph 4 shows that men are mean to women.

b. Paragraph 4 shows that it's hard for women to work if they must wear the "abaya" that covers them from head to toe.

c. Paragraph 4 explains that women can't work together in public on a film project.

d. Paragraph 4 explains that men dominate Saudi culture, and it is very hard for a woman to be independent and successful.

3. Circle the letter of the paragraph that best summarizes the information presented in the article.

a. paragraph 1

b. paragraph 5

c. paragraph 8

d. paragraph 10

4. The author states that Haifaa al-Mansour knows women in Saudi Arabia see her film as something much deeper than just a movie about a girl riding a bicycle. Copy the sentences from the article where the author makes this statement.

_____

_____

_____

_____

_____

_____

5. A reporter has written a script of what an interview with Mansour might be like. Read the script and complete the task that follows.

Reporter: Ms. Mansour, you have done things not ordinarily done by women in Saudi Arabia. Where did you get the courage to be different?

Mansour: Well, as a student I attended college in Egypt. I had the opportunity to see women in different roles doing different things.

Reporter: But why did you choose film to make a statement about women?

Mansour: I watched lots of movies growing up, and I studied film in Australia.

Reporter: I see. Were you trying to go against 250 years of Islamic law?

Mansour: No, I just made a movie about a girl who wanted to ride a bicycle. Islamic law says a girl cannot ride a bicycle.

Reporter: Have you been surprised by the success of your film?

Mansour: Very surprised! But the Saudi government is very angry about it.

Copy the two sentences from the script that are not supported by the facts in the article.

a. _____

_____

b. _____

Name _____ Date _____

ANTICIPATION GUIDE

Directions: Before you read the article "Families of Missing Persons Get Help," read the statements below. If you agree with a statement, put a checkmark on the line next to it. If you disagree, put an X on the line.

_____ **1.** Many people other than soldiers are lost in wars.

_____ **2.** Losing a relative is sad, but it doesn't cause practical problems.

_____ **3.** Families of missing relatives have a hard time getting help.

Once you have responded to the statements above, write in the section below why you agree or disagree with each statement.

1. _____

_____

2. _____

_____

3. _____

_____

In the box below, draw a picture of what you think this article is about.

WORDSTORM

Directions: It's good to know more than just the dictionary definition of a word. Completing a wordstorm lets you write down information to help you understand what a word means, how it's related to other words, and how to use it in different ways.

What is the word?

<u>**prisoner**</u>

Here is the sentence from the text in which the word is used:

<u>*"They include soldiers who may have died or become prisoners."*</u>

What are some other words or phrases that mean the same thing?

_____

What are three problems that the families of prisoners might have?

1. _____ 2. _____ 3. _____

Name three people other than teachers who would likely use this word.

1. _____ 2. _____ 3. _____

Draw a picture below that reminds you of the word *prisoner*.

TIME MY READ #1

Directions: With a partner, see how many words you can read correctly in 45 seconds. As you read, your partner will put an X through any word read incorrectly on his or her copy. When you are finished, trade your books or papers, and let your partner read while you keep score. Count the total number of words you read correctly. Write this score at the bottom of your page.

relatives property flee agreement records remarrying exchange civilians	8
targets mortuaries scientists warfare prisoners separated victims villages	16
exact reunites inheritance practical mourned relatives thousands victims	24
relatives property flee agreement records remarrying exchange civilians	32
targets mortuaries scientists warfare prisoners separated victims villages	40
exact reunites inheritance practical mourned relatives thousands victims	48
relatives property flee agreement records remarrying exchange civilians	56
targets mortuaries scientists warfare prisoners separated victims villages	64
exact reunites inheritance practical mourned relatives thousands victims	72
relatives property flee agreement records remarrying exchange civilians	80

Number of words read correctly _____

ECHO READING

Directions: When you read, you should make breaks, and sometimes pauses, between groups of words. As your teacher reads each phrase, repeat aloud what is read and put a slash or line after that phrase. Then read the whole sentence aloud as a class. Do the first paragraph together as a class, and then do the second one on your own. The first sentence has been marked for you.

Since 1863 / the International Committee / of the Red Cross / (ICRC) / has helped victims of war /all over the world. / In fact, humanitarian law gives the ICRC the power to protect the dignity of the victims of war. That includes identifying missing persons.

The ICRC gathers all the information that it can about missing persons. It uses records from governments and from Red Cross workers who visit prisons, hospitals and mortuaries. When it identifies someone, it tries to reach the family. It sends information out through its own Web site, radio and printed messages. If it can, it contacts families directly. When things go well, it reunites families.

What's Happening

IN THE WORLD?

BY LAWRENCE GABLE
© 2014 *What's Happening Publications*

SUBJECT: GLOBAL ISSUES

Families of Missing Persons Get Help

1 When countries are at war, many soldiers and civilians go missing. This happened to hundreds of thousands of people during the Iran-Iraq War (1980–88). Many of their families still do not know what happened to their relatives. In 2008 Iran and Iraq signed an agreement to work with the Red Cross to find those missing persons.

2 Since 1863 the International Committee of the Red Cross (ICRC) has helped victims of war all over the world. In fact, humanitarian law gives the ICRC the power to protect the dignity of the victims of war. That includes identifying missing persons.

3 The ICRC works with countries to get information about missing persons. They include soldiers who may have died or become prisoners. They also include large numbers of civilians who have become targets in modern warfare. Civilians die in attacks on their towns and villages. Many flee to other places for safety, even to a neighboring country. Too often small children become separated from their families.

4 Identifying the dead takes time. Because of the many wars around the world, scientists have become more and more exact. They take DNA or blood samples from family members in order to help identify a body.

5 The ICRC gathers all the information that it can about missing persons. It uses records from governments and from Red Cross workers who visit prisons, hospitals and mortuaries. When it identifies someone, it tries to reach the family. It sends information out through its own Web site, radio and printed messages. If it can, it contacts families directly. When things go well, it reunites families.

6 Relatives suffer emotional pain when they do not know the fate of a loved one. They worry that the relative may be dead and lying in an unmarked grave. They also worry that the relative might be alive, but suffering horribly in a prison or hospital. In either case, they continue to hope that the relative will return.

7 Having a missing relative also affects practical parts of daily life. It delays the inheritance of land, property and money. It also prevents a spouse from remarrying and creating a new life. In some cultures the grown children cannot marry without the permission of a parent who is missing.

8 The ICRC played an active role during the Iran-Iraq war. In those eight years it visited almost 40,000 Iranian and 67,000 Iraqi prisoners of war. It helped many of them return home. However, Iran reports that at least 11,000 Iranians are still missing. At least 375,000 Iraqis are too, but the number could be closer to a million.

9 The agreement with the ICRC is helping families. Unfortunately, exact records of soldiers and civilians who are missing do not seem to exist. However, under the new agreement the ICRC is allowing Iran and Iraq collect and share information. It also is leading to the exchange and identification of bodies.

10 About a million people died in the Iran-Iraq war. The families of those who died mourned their loss, but their tragedy lies in the past. It is different for the families of the missing though, because their pain is still present. Finally the ICRC's work is bringing them information and an end to their wondering and suffering.

GET A CONTEXT CLUE

Directions: Below are sentences from "Families of Missing Persons Get Help." First, read the sentence. Then, look back in the article and reread the paragraph in which the sentence is found. Circle the best answer to each question.

"In 2008 Iraq and Iran signed an *agreement* to work with the Red Cross to find those missing persons."

1. The word *agreement* means

    A. contract
    B. law
    C. petition
    D. lease

"Because of the many wars around the world, scientists have become more and more *exact*."

2. The word *exact* means

    A. precise or correct
    B. patient
    C. relaxed
    D. worried or nervous

"When things go well, it *reunites* families."

3. The word *reunites* means

    A. reorganizes
    B. finds missing people
    C. brings together again
    D. respects family members

"They also worry that the relative might be alive, but suffering *horribly* in a prison or hospital."

4. The word *horribly* means

    A. unwillingly
    B. frequently
    C. terribly
    D. sadly

"It delays the *inheritance* of land, property and money."

5. The word *inheritance* means

    A. promotion or advancement
    B. farming
    C. possessions
    D. property passed at the owner's death

"The families of those who died *mourned* their loss, but their tragedy lies in the past."

6. The word *mourned* means

    A. talked about
    B. fought over
    C. felt sad about; grieved
    D. celebrated

Name _____ Date _____

WORD CHOICE

Directions: The sentences below contain blanks for missing words. Three answer choices are listed after each blank. Read the sentence past the blank and choose the correct word. Write it in the blank.

The ICRC works with countries to get information about _____ (*misses, missed, missing*) persons. They include soldiers who _____ (*might had, might have, might has*) died or _____ (*become, became, becoming*) prisoners. They also include large numbers of civilians who _____ (*have become, have became, have becoming*) targets in modern warfare. Civilians _____ (*die, death, dies*) in attacks on their towns and villages. Many _____ (*flight, flea, flee*) to other places for safety, even to a neighboring country. Too often small children _____ (*become, became, becoming*) separated from _____ (*there, their, they're*) families.

The _____ (*identify, identification, identity*) of the dead takes time. Because of the many wars around the world, scientists _____ (*have become, have became, have becoming*) more and more exact. They take DNA blood samples from family members in order to help _____ (*identify, identifying, identifies*) a body.

© Houghton Mifflin Harcourt Publishing Company

Lesson 23: Families of Missing Persons Get Help   **425**

LOOK WHO'S TALKING

Directions: Below are sentences that relate to "Families of Missing Persons Get Help."
Look back in the article and reread the paragraph in which you find the reference. Circle
the best answer to each question.

1. In the last sentence of the first
paragraph, the word *those* best
refers to

A. the soldiers in Iran
B. people in Iraq
C. the people in the Red Cross
D. missing soldiers and civilians

2. In paragraph 3, the word *they* refers
both times to

A. soldiers
B. civilians
C. missing persons
D. the Red Cross

3. In the last sentence of paragraph 4,
the word *they* refers to

A. the scientists
B. the soldiers
C. the ICRC
D. the civilians

4. In the first sentence of paragraph 6,
they refers to

A. the ICRC
B. the relatives
C. the scientists
D. the civilians

5. In paragraph 7 both references to *it*
are about

A. the relatives
B. having a missing relative
C. the civilians
D. the scientists

6. In paragraph 10, the word *them* in
the final sentence refers to

A. the prisoners
B. the missing civilians
C. the families of the missing
D. the ICRC

NOTE MAKING

Directions: Read the boldfaced key words on the left side of the chart below. Then add notes that answer the question in parentheses under the key word.

the ICRC (What is the ICRC?)	
Helping victims of war (How does the ICRC help victims of war?)	
Problems (What kinds of problems has the ICRC encountered?)	
Iran-Iraq War prisoners (How many prisoners did the ICRC visit?)	
New agreement (What is the new agreement?)	

*On a separate sheet of paper write a summary of what your notes say about the work of the ICRC.

IS THAT A FACT?

Directions: Read the definitions of a fact and an inference below. Then read the paragraph that follows. At the bottom of the page, write an F on the blank if the sentence is a fact. Write an I if the sentence is an inference. Use the following definitions:

Fact—a statement that can be proven true from the paragraph

Inference—a guess as to what MIGHT be true, based on what you have read and what you already know about the subject

---

The new agreement with the ICRC will help families. Unfortunately, exact records of soldiers and civilians who are missing do not seem to exist. However, under the new agreement the ICRC will help Iran and Iraq collect and share information. It will also help with the exchange of information and bodies. About a million people died in the Iran-Iraq War. The families of those who died mourned their loss. It is different for the families of the missing, though, because their pain is still present. The ICRC's work will bring them information and end their suffering.

_____ **1.** The ICRC has become more efficient in locating missing people.

_____ **2.** The ICRC has a high level of international support.

_____ **3.** Civilians are often casualties of war.

_____ **4.** The Iraq-Iran War killed about a million people, including soldiers.

_____ **5.** The ICRC seeks to help people in difficult times.

_____ **6.** Countries that once fought each other will share information after their war.

MAKE A SPACE

Directions: Below are sentences that are missing punctuation and capitalization. First draw slash marks (/) between the words. Then rewrite each sentence in the space below it, filling in the missing punctuation and capitalization.

> Example:
>
> the / new / agreement / with / the / icrc / will / help / families
>
> The new agreement with the ICRC will help families.

1. whencountriesareatwarmanysoldiersandciviliansgomissing

_____

_____

2. civilianshavebecometargetsinmodernwarfare

_____

_____

3. havingfamilymembersmissingaffectspracticalpartsofdailylife

_____

_____

4. theinternationalcommitteeoftheredcrosshashelpedvictimsofwarallovertheworld

_____

_____

TIME MY READ #2

Directions: With a partner, see how many words you can read correctly in 45 seconds. As you read, your partner will put an X through any word read incorrectly on his or her copy. When you are finished, trade your books or papers, and let your partner read while you keep score. Count the total number of words you read correctly. Write this score at the bottom of your page.

relatives property flee agreement records remarrying exchange civilians	8
targets mortuaries scientists warfare prisoners separated victims villages	16
exact reunites inheritance practical mourned relatives thousands victims	24
relatives property flee agreement records remarrying exchange civilians	32
targets mortuaries scientists warfare prisoners separated victims villages	40
exact reunites inheritance practical mourned relatives thousands victims	48
relatives property flee agreement records remarrying exchange civilians	56
targets mortuaries scientists warfare prisoners separated victims villages	64
exact reunites inheritance practical mourned relatives thousands victims	72
relatives property flee agreement records remarrying exchange civilians	80

Number of words read correctly _____

Is the score higher than it was in Time My Read #1? _____

Name _____ Date _____

WORD PARTS

Directions: A suffix is added to the end of a base word to change its part of speech. Suffixes do this in many ways. For example, the suffix **-an** can turn the root of a **noun** into an **adjective**. The noun *Mexico* becomes the adjective *Mexican*, describing someone from Mexico. The suffix **-an** and the suffix **-ian** can also describe one who is, practices, or works with the base word. For example, an *electrician* works with *electricity*. Write a definition of each word below. Look up the word in a dictionary or ask a partner if needed.

1. Iranian— _____

2. authoritarian— _____

3. Costa Rican— _____

4. barbarian— _____

5. musician— _____

6. beautician— _____

7. Republican— _____

8. optician— _____

9. partisan— _____

10. humanitarian— _____

Directions: Draw pictures to show the meanings of two of these words.

© Houghton Mifflin Harcourt Publishing Company

Lesson 23: Families of Missing Persons Get Help　　　　**431**

ICRC WORD PUZZLE

Directions: Complete the crossword puzzle.

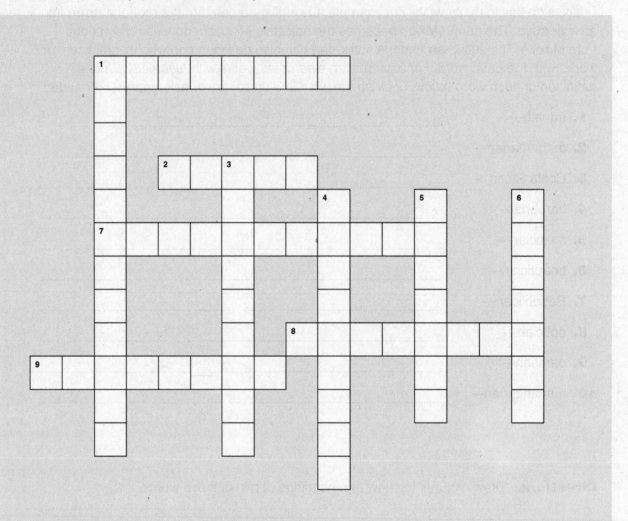

Word List

MOURNED
HUMANITARIAN
AGREEMENT
REUNITE
BARBARIAN
INHERITANCE
HORRIBLY
EXACT
PRISONER
PARTISAN

Across

1. terribly or badly
2. correct or precise
7. property passed at the owner's death
8. a strong supporter of a political party
9. a person kept against his or her wishes

Down

1. concerning the well-being of people
3. a contract
4. a savage or uncivilized person
5. to bring people back together
6. felt sad about; grieved

WRITING FRAME

Directions: Use your knowledge and information from the article to complete the writing frame below.

When countries are at war, many soldiers and civilians go missing. That happened to _____ during the Iran-Iraq War. Since 1863 the International Committee of the Red Cross (ICRC) has _____. The ICRC has worked with countries to _____. Civilians die in attacks on their towns, and the ICRC goes in after these tragedies and _____.

Identifying the dead takes a lot of time. Scientists have been able to _____. They can take blood samples of family members and _____. During the eight years of the Iraq-Iran War, the ICRC visited _____ and helped many of them _____.

REACTION GUIDE

Directions: Now that you have read and studied information about "Families of Missing Persons Get Help," reread the statements below, which you responded to before reading the article. Then think about how the author might respond to these statements. If you think the author would agree, put a checkmark on the line before the number. If you think the author would disagree, put an X on the line. Then below the statement, copy the words, phrases, or sentences from the article that provide evidence of the views stated by the author. Also note if there is no evidence to support the statement.

_____ **1.** Many people other than soldiers are lost in wars.

Evidence: _____

_____

_____

_____ **2.** Losing a relative is sad, but it doesn't cause practical problems.

Evidence: _____

_____

_____

_____ **3.** Families of missing relatives have a hard time getting help.

Evidence: _____

_____

_____

TAKE A STAND

Directions: People often have differing feelings or opinions about an issue. When they discuss or argue their opposing views, they are taking part in a debate. A good persuasive argument is based on a claim that is supported by

Facts—statements that can be proven to be true

Statistics—numerical data gotten through research

Examples—instances that support an opinion

You and a partner are going to debate two of your other classmates. The topic you are going to debate is the following:

It is okay to kill civilians during a war if it ends the conflict sooner.

Decide with the other pair who will agree and who will disagree with this statement. Then answer these questions in order to win your debate.

1. What are your two strongest points to persuade the other side? (You can do Internet research to include facts, statistics, and examples.)

   A. _____

   B. _____

2. What might the other side say to argue against point A?

   _____

   _____

3. What might the other side say to argue against point B?

   _____

   _____

4. What will you say to prove the other side's arguments are wrong?

   _____

   _____

ASSESSMENT

Comprehension: Answer the questions about the following passage.

The ICRC gathers all the information it can about missing persons. It uses records from governments and from Red Cross workers who visit hospitals and mortuaries. When it identifies someone, it tries to reach the family. Relatives suffer emotional pain when they don't know the fate of a loved one. They worry that the relative might be dead and lying in an unmarked grave. They also worry that a relative could be suffering horribly in a hospital or prison. The new agreement between Iraq and Iran will help the ICRC locate many more people.

1. How would you describe the work of the ICRC?

_____

_____

2. What is especially hard for relatives during warfare?

_____

_____

3. What was the author's purpose for writing about the ICRC?

_____

_____

Fluency: The words in the two sentences below are all connected. The sentences are also missing punctuation and capitalization. Draw slash marks (/) between the words. Then rewrite each sentence by filling in the punctuation and capitalization.

1. manyfamiliesstilldonotknowwhathappenedtotheirrelatives

_____

2. havingamissingrelativealsoaffectspracticalpartsofdailylife

_____

_____

Fluency: Read the three sentences below. Imagine where you would pause within each sentence as you read it aloud. Draw a slash (/) mark between the phrases where you would pause. The first slash is done.

3. It delays/the inheritance of land, property, and money.

4. If it can, it contacts families directly and reunites family members.

5. Relatives suffer emotional pain when they don't know the fate of a loved one.

Vocabulary: Based on what you have learned in this lesson, match the following words with their definitions. Write the letter of the definition on the blank in front of the word it defines.

1. _____ mourned   **A.** precise or correct

2. _____ agreement   **B.** a person kept against his or her wishes

3. _____ humanitarian   **C.** a strong supporter of an idea or political party

4. _____ exact   **D.** to bring people back together

5. _____ partisan   **E.** felt sad about; grieved

6. _____ horribly   **F.** property passed at the owner's death

7. _____ barbarian   **G.** a contract

8. _____ inheritance   **H.** terribly or badly

9. _____ reunite   **I.** a savage or uncivilized person

10. _____ prisoner   **J.** concerning the well-being of people

Name _____ Date _____

ANTICIPATION GUIDE

Directions: Before you read the article "'How Big Was It?,'" read the statements below. If you agree with a statement, put a checkmark on the line next to it. If you disagree, put an X on the line.

_____ **1.** Earthquakes have killed 320,000 people in one year.

_____ **2.** Measuring earthquakes helps city planners determine the extent of the damage.

_____ **3.** Science can now offer detailed information about earthquakes by measuring them.

Once you have responded to the statements above, write in the section below why you agree or disagree with each statement.

1. _____

_____

2. _____

_____

3. _____

_____

In the box below, draw a picture of what you think this article is about.

PREDICTING ABCs

Directions: The article you are going to read is about how earthquakes are measured. See how many boxes you can fill in below with words relating to this topic. For example, put the word *shaking* in the S–T box. Try to put at least one word in every box, and then try to write a word for every letter.

A–C	D–F	G–I

J–L	M–O	P–R

S–T	U–V	W–Z

LANGUAGE MINI-LESSON

A **preposition** shows the relationship between a noun or pronoun and another noun or pronoun in the sentence. For example, in the sentence below, the preposition *on* shows the relationship between the bird and the roof.

The bird with beautiful blue feathers is **on** our roof.

Prepositions are usually part of a group of words called a **prepositional phrase.** The prepositional phrase in the sentence above is *on our roof.* Here are some common prepositions.

above	about	across	after	against	along	around
as	at	before	behind	below	beside	between
by	down	during	except	for	from	in
inside	into	like	near	of	off	on
out	over	to	under	until	up	with

There are two kinds of prepositional phrases. An **adjective phrase** gives more information about a noun or pronoun. In the sentence above, *on our roof* gives more information about the noun *bird*.

An **adverb phrase** gives more information about a verb, an adjective, or an adverb. It answers the questions *where, when, how, why,* or *to what degree.* For example, in the sentence below, the prepositional phrase *into the kitchen* tells where the boy ran.

The boy ran **into the kitchen.**

Directions: Underline the prepositional phrases in each sentence below. Then write in the blank whether they act as an **adjective** or **adverb.**

1. In 2010 earthquakes killed 320,000 people around the world. _____

2. The seismometer records the intensity of movement. _____

3. Older seismographs had an arm with a needle. _____

4. Much damage can happen during an earthquake. _____

5. Concern around the world is mounting about quakes. _____

ECHO READING

Directions: When you read, you should make breaks, and sometimes pauses, between groups of words. As your teacher reads each phrase, repeat aloud what is read and put a slash or line after that phrase. Then read the whole sentence aloud as a class. Do the first paragraph together as a class, and then do the second one on your own. The first sentence has been marked for you.

By the late 1800s / seismologists had made / two instruments / to help their studies. / One was the seismometer, which feels movements and records when they occur. The other was the seismograph. It records the intensity and duration of movements onto a piece of paper. When the earthquake struck San Francisco in 1906, seismographs recorded information from it.

In 1931 two American seismologists improved a scale for measuring the intensity of earthquakes. Intensity refers to the effect they have on people, buildings and the landscape. The scale, called the Mercalli Intensity Scale, assigns values in Roman numerals. Level I means that very few people felt the quake at all. Level XII means that the area suffered total damage.

BY LAWRENCE GABLE
© *2014 What's Happening Publications*

SUBJECT: **GLOBAL ISSUES**

"How Big Was It?"

1 In 2010 earthquakes killed 320,000 people worldwide. In 2011 an earthquake in Japan caused a tsunami and led to a nuclear disaster. Every year there are about a dozen major earthquakes in the world. Whenever one strikes, the first question is, "How big was it?" Seismologists provide the answer.

2 People always have tried to understand earthquakes. Ancient civilizations often believed that their gods were angry. About 2,000 years ago the Chinese developed the first instruments to detect movement in the ground.

3 The science of seismology developed in the 18th century. An American, John Winthrop, was the founder of seismology. He tried to find scientific causes for earthquakes, not religious ones. Soon it became common for people to write down information about quakes. That included when they struck, how long they shook, and descriptions of the shaking.

4 By the late 1800s seismologists had made two instruments to help their studies. One was the seismometer, which feels movements and records when they occur. The other was the seismograph. It records the intensity and duration of movements onto a piece of paper. When the earthquake struck San Francisco in 1906, seismographs recorded information from it.

5 In 1931 two American seismologists improved a scale for measuring the intensity of earthquakes. Intensity refers to the effect they have on people, buildings and the landscape. The scale, called the Mercalli Intensity Scale, assigns values in Roman numerals. Level I means that very few people felt the quake at all. Level XII means that the area suffered total damage.

6 The Mercalli Scale depends completely on eyewitnesses. As a result, the Mercalli level for the same earthquake changes from place to place. Even so, city planners still use Mercalli levels because they tell where earthquake damage is worst.

7 In 1935 another American, Charles Richter, developed another scale. His idea was actually to measure the amount of shaking. For much of the 20th century his scale was the standard measurement of an earthquake's power.

8 Richter's scale used readings from seismographs. Seismographs are now digital, but older ones had an arm with a needle that drew a line on paper. As the waves from an earthquake shook the arm, the needle drew jagged lines along the paper. When an earthquake moved the arm .001 of a millimeter, Richter called that magnitude "1.0." When it moved .01 of a millimeter, he called it "2.0." One whole number on the scale represented ten times more movement.

9 By the late 1970s seismologists had a better scale for measuring large quakes. They call it "moment magnitude." This considers more things about Earth's plates that moved and caused the shaking. Its calculations include the length of the plates that slipped, the distance one plate moved compared to the other, and how rigid the rock in the area is. Moment magnitude measures the total energy that the earthquake released, not just the energy and movement at the surface.

10 Modern seismographs can detect strong earthquakes from anywhere in the world. Seismologists can offer a lot of detailed information quickly. Now when people ask how strong a quake was, the answer they get is better than ever.

QUICK READ/DRAW AND WRITE

Directions: <u>First Reading</u>—As you do your first reading of the article, your teacher will time you for one minute. When time is called, write the number of the paragraph where you stopped. **Paragraph #** _____

In the box below, draw a picture summarizing what you read.

<u>Second Reading</u>—As you do your second reading of the article, your teacher will time you for one minute. When time is called, write the number of the paragraph where you stopped. **Paragraph #** _____

Directions: Now continue reading the rest of the article. Below, write five important words that will help you remember the information from the article.

_____ _____ _____ _____ _____

© Houghton Mifflin Harcourt Publishing Company

CLOSE READING ANNOTATION

Third Reading—As you reread each paragraph in the article closely, answer the questions by annotating the text. Each numbered question corresponds to a paragraph in the article where the answer can be found. Write your brief answers in the space below each question.

1. How does the writer grab your attention in the first paragraph?

_____

2. How did ancient civilizations explain earthquakes?

_____

3. What was the big change in thinking about earthquakes in the 18th century?

_____

4. What is the author's purpose for writing paragraph 4?

_____

5. What is the Mercalli Intensity Scale?

_____

6. What is a possible disadvantage of the Mercalli Intensity Scale?

_____

7. What is the purpose of the last sentence in paragraph 7?

_____

8. What is so important about the last sentence in paragraph 8?

_____

9. What is different about the measurement of "moment magnitude"?

_____

10. What is the purpose of the last paragraph?

_____

GRAMMAR GAMES

Directions: Reread the two paragraphs below. Words have been left out from the sentences. Think about the information from the article you have read and fill in words that make sense. The part of speech of each missing word is provided.

People have always _____ to understand earthquakes.
(1. verb)

Ancient civilizations _____ believed that their gods were angry.
(2. adverb)

About 2,000 years ago the Chinese developed the first instruments

to detect _____ in the ground.
(3. noun)

The science of seismology developed in the 18th _____.
(4. noun)

An American, John Winthrop, was the founder of _____.
(5. noun)

He tried to find _____ causes for earthquakes, not religious
(6. adjective)

ones. Soon it became common for people to _____ down
(7. verb)

information about quakes. That _____ when they struck, how long
(8. verb)

they shook, and descriptions _____ the shaking.
(9. preposition)

By the late 1800s seismologists had _____ two instruments
(10. verb)

to help their studies. One was _____ seismometer, which feels
(11. article)

movements and records when _____ occur.
(12. pronoun)

CLOSE READING STRUCTURE

Directions: Understanding the structure of a text is important for two reasons. First, understanding the structure of a selection can help you remember the main idea and important details. Second, most academic writing you will encounter uses text structures to organize ideas.

1. Writers often include a statement in the **introduction** that catches the reader's attention. Then, the writer tells what the article will be about. On the space provided, copy the last sentence of the introduction to this article.

_____

_____

2. On the space below, copy the sentence that best states what the author's **claim, main idea,** or **thesis** is for this article.

_____

_____

3. On the space below, copy the sentence that shows where the author provides **evidence** to support the claim.

_____

_____

4. Near the end of an article, the writer often restates the claim and summarizes the evidence. This is called the **conclusion.** On the space below, copy the sentence that best shows where the conclusion **begins.**

_____

_____

IS THAT A FACT?

Directions: Read the definitions of a fact and an inference below. Then read the paragraph that follows. At the bottom of the page, write an F on the blank if the sentence is a fact. Write an I if the sentence is an inference. Use the following definitions:

<u>Fact</u>—a statement that can be proven true from the paragraph

<u>Inference</u>—a guess as to what MIGHT be true, based on what you have read and what you already know about the subject

> By the late 1970s seismologists had a better scale for measuring large quakes. They call it "moment magnitude." This considers more things about Earth's plates that moved and caused the shaking. Its calculations include the length of the plates that slipped, the distance one plate moved compared to the other, and how rigid the rock in the area is. Moment magnitude measures the total energy that the earthquake released, not just the energy and movement at the surface. Modern seismographs can detect strong earthquakes from anywhere in the world.

_____ **1.** Scientists have been trying to figure out how to measure earthquakes for many years.

_____ **2.** The reference to plates slipping is about huge slabs of rock.

_____ **3.** Moment magnitude is one of the best measurements of earthquakes.

_____ **4.** One calculation of magnitude is the distance that a plate slips.

_____ **5.** Moment magnitude measures the total energy released by the quake.

_____ **6.** We can now detect earthquakes from any place they occur.

SUMMARIZING ABCs

Directions: Now that you've read the article on seismology, see how many words about measuring earthquakes you can write in the boxes below.

A–C	D–F	G–I
J–L	**M–O**	**P–R**
S–T	**U–V**	**W–Z**

REACTION GUIDE

Directions: Now that you have read and studied information about "How Big Was It?," reread the statements below, which you responded to before reading the article. Then think about how the author might respond to these statements. If you think the author would agree, put a checkmark on the line before the number. If you think the author would disagree, put an X on the line. Then below the statement, copy the words, phrases, or sentences from the article that provide evidence of the views stated by the author. Also note if there is no evidence to support the statement.

_____ **1.** Earthquakes have killed 320,000 people in one year.

Evidence: _____

_____

_____

_____ **2.** Measuring earthquakes helps city planners determine the extent of the damage.

Evidence: _____

_____

_____

_____ **3.** Science can now offer detailed information about earthquakes by measuring them.

Evidence: _____

_____

_____

SENTENCE TRANSITIONS

An informational essay answers questions and provides information. Writers use transitional phrases to link ideas. Some transitional words and phrases include *to show, to prove, because, to explain, to verify, due to, instead of, furthermore, as a result,* and *in order to*.

Directions: Complete the following sentences using the phrases given.

Example: Scientists use moment magnitude to measure earthquakes. Scientists use moment magnitude to measure earthquakes *as a result of new scientific developments*.

1. After an earthquake, ancient civilizations used religion *in order to*

_____

2. John Winthrop tried to use science instead of religion *to explain*

_____

3. In the late 1800s there were two instruments used *to show*

_____

4. The Mercalli Scale was used *to explain*

_____

5. The term "moment magnitude" refers to the distance that plates moved *instead of*

_____

PICKING UP PUNCTUATION

Quotation Marks (" ") are used for a number of reasons in writing. Read the rules below to learn how to use them.

1. Use quotation marks to show when a person is speaking. Place the marks at the beginning and end of the words spoken. For example: "Many people did not survive the San Francisco 1906 earthquake," said our teacher.

2. Use commas to set off the quote from the speaker. Always place the commas before the quotation marks. For example: "Yesterday's earthquake," said the scientist, "measured 2.5 on the Richter Scale."

3. If a quote is a question or exclamation, place the question mark or exclamation point inside the quotation marks at the end. For example: "Why do earthquakes happen?" asked the student. "Wow, that was scary!" yelled the child.

4. If you, and not the speaker, are asking the question, place the question mark outside the quotation marks. For example: Did the scientist say, "The earthquake was small"?

5. Periods always go inside the quotation marks. For example: My teacher said, "John Winthrop was the founder of seismology."

6. When you talk about a word or phrase as being a word or phrase, set it within quotation marks. For example: "Moment magnitude" is the name of the new scale for measuring earthquakes.

Directions: Place the correct punctuation in the sentences below.

1. The news reporter said There was a strong earthquake in Japan

2. Why can't we tell asked the student when an earthquake is going to happen

3. One method for measuring earthquakes is called the Richter Scale

4. Why did the news reporter say The damage is more serious than expected

5. Hey that earthquake was scary yelled the little boy

ANALYZING A PROMPT

Directions: Read the writing prompt in the box below. Then follow the directions to learn how to analyze and answer it.

> You are a seismologist who is preparing an essay for other seismologists on the advantages of using moment magnitude to measure earthquakes. But some seismologists want to stick with the older methods because they've been in use longer. In your argument you will explain how using moment magnitude is more effective than the older methods. You will read your argument aloud to the group. What will you say to support your view that the other methods are not as effective?

1. A writing prompt begins with some background information known as the **set up.** Underline the sentences that set up this assignment.

2. Use the following **R.A.F.T.** technique to finish analyzing the prompt.

Role: What are you supposed to be to answer it? A student? A politician?

Write what you are here: _____

Audience: To whom are you writing? A friend? A particular group?

Write who it is here: _____

Format: Check to see what type of writing you are doing. Is it an essay, a letter, a speech, a story, a description, an editorial, or a report?

Write what it is here: _____

Task: Another sentence in the prompt will tell you what you must do, or your "task." Question words like **why, how,** or **what** may tell the task.

If the question word is **why,** you will *give the reasons* that something is done.

If the question word is **how,** you will *explain the way* that something is done.

If the question word is **what,** you will *identify the thing* that is done.

Below, copy the sentence or question that describes your task.

_____

_____

WHAT'S YOUR POINT?

When writing an essay it is important to have a strong claim. The **claim**, or **thesis statement**, states the main point the writer wants to get across. Once the **thesis** is introduced, the body of the essay should support that thesis with key points that provide **evidence**.

The article "'How Big Was It?'" explains how our understanding of earthquakes and our methods of measuring them have advanced over the last two thousand years. Ancient civilizations believed earthquakes were caused by angry gods. John Winthrop, the founder of seismology, was the first to try to find scientific causes for earthquakes. Since his time, instruments such as seismometers and seismographs have been developed to record earthquakes, and methods such as the Mercalli Intensity Scale, the Richter scale, and moment magnitude have been developed to measure their effects.

Directions: Which of these sentences provides the best **claim** for an essay on this topic? Circle the letter of your choice.

a. Earthquakes are some of nature's deadliest disasters and have killed hundreds of thousands of people over the years.

b. The development of instruments to measure earthquakes has allowed people to know much more about the causes and sizes of these natural disasters.

c. People who think that earthquakes are caused by religion are out of date, because science gives us a better explanation.

In the space below, explain what is weak or wrong about the other two statements.

1. _____

_____

_____

2. _____

_____

_____

ASSESSMENT

1. This question has two parts. First, answer **Part A.** Then, answer **Part B.**

Part A: Circle the letter of the sentence that best states the author's main purpose in writing "'How Big Was It?'"

   a. The author wants people to realize that ancient people were ignorant to think gods caused earthquakes because they were angry.

   b. The author wants to inform the reader of how the science of seismology grew and became more accurate over time.

   c. The author wants people to know that the size of an earthquake depends on the instruments used to measure it.

   d. The author wants to inform the reader about how we measure earthquakes today.

Part B: Circle the letters of the sentences that support your answer to **Part A.**

   a. By the late 1800s seismologists had made two instruments to help their studies.

   b. Every year there are about a dozen major earthquakes in the world.

   c. In 1931 two American seismologists improved a scale for measuring the intensity of earthquakes.

   d. By the late 1970s seismologists had a better scale for measuring large quakes.

   e. Moment magnitude measures the total energy the earthquake released.

2. Circle the letters of the two paragraphs that explain why it is important to have people describe what they experienced during an earthquake.

   a. paragraph 3

   b. paragraph 5

   c. paragraph 6

   d. paragraph 7

   e. paragraph 10

3. The article is written in chronological order, which means the events are presented in the order in which they happened. Cite three pieces of evidence from the article that show it is written in chronological order.

a. _____

b. _____

c. _____

4. A student is writing an informative report about seismology for the school newspaper. Read the following paragraph from the student's report and complete the task that follows.

Mankind has been trying to understand the power of earthquakes for thousands of years. In ancient days, people often thought natural events such as tornadoes, lightning, and earthquakes occurred because they had done something to anger the gods. People today don't often think about ancient gods. The Chinese developed instruments over 2,000 years ago to detect ground movement. In the 1700s, John Winthrop tried to find scientific causes for earthquakes. By the late 1800s, seismologists had invented two instruments, the seismometer and the seismograph, to help measure an earthquake's power. It made sense to give the instruments similar names. The seismograph was used to measure the huge earthquake in San Francisco in 1906.

Below, copy the two sentences that do not support the underlined sentence and should be removed from this paragraph.

a. _____

_____

b. _____

_____

Global Issues

Quarterly Performance Assessment

Sharks Find Themselves in Danger

What's Happening
IN THE WORLD?

BY LAWRENCE GABLE
© *2014 What's Happening Publications*

Sharks Find Themselves in Danger

1 Sharks swim in all of the world's seas. They are at the top of the food chain, so they have no natural predators. Humans have been killing too many of them though. Now a few places are taking steps to stop it.

2 When populations of large animals fall, it is hard for them to recover. They grow slowly and take longer than small animals to reproduce. Larger sharks take 15–20 years. Even though they live a long time, they produce few young.

3 For millions of years only two things caused their early deaths. One was illness, and the other was larger sharks. Most female sharks bear their young in shallow waters where large sharks cannot swim easily. Most species of sharks are small, and they also seek protection there.

4 Recently various human activities have hurt sharks. Real estate development has caused the loss of shallow coastal environments. In addition, sewers and rivers carry pollution from cities and chemicals from farmland into the water. Sharks no longer have the good nursery grounds that they need.

5 Commercial fishing also harms shark populations. Fishermen who fish for swordfish and tuna use "longlines." Their main line can be 50 miles long. It has many hundreds of short lines and hooks that hang from it. Every year tens of millions of sharks also go for the bait and die accidentally.

6 Finning is yet another danger to sharks. Fishermen catch sharks and cut their fins off. Then they throw the bleeding animals back into the ocean. Of course a shark without fins cannot swim, so it sinks to the bottom and slowly dies. Scientists figure that 73 million sharks die this way each year. Fishermen use finning in order to supply enough fins for a Chinese delicacy, shark fin soup.

7 Shark fin soup is a dish for special occasions among wealthy Chinese. Fine restaurants serve it, and it is on the menu at banquets and weddings. It is a symbol of wealth, and in the last twenty years many millions more people have been able to afford it. The Chinese mainland, Hong Kong and Taiwan eat 95 percent of the world's shark fins.

8 Only a few nations have laws against finning. In general, the laws prohibit fishermen from bringing fins into port without their being attached to the bodies. In April 2011 Chile passed such a law. Even in China there have been ads in which the NBA star Yao Ming and the actor Jackie Chan refuse to eat shark fin soup. In Thailand and Singapore awareness campaigns already may have reduced the demand for shark fins by 25 percent.

9 Shark fins bring high profits. Fishermen sell them for hundreds of dollars per pound. Restaurants often sell a bowl of shark fin soup for $100. In July 2011 Hawaii became the first state in the U.S. to ban the possession and sale of shark fins. Since then another eight states have passed similar laws. They believe that if the buying stops, the killing will too.

10 Shark fins still appear in many restaurants, but statistics show that laws against finning are helping. Worldwide fishermen kill about 100 million sharks every year. Although sharks populations remain in great danger, the world seems to be paying real attention to them.

QUARTERLY PERFORMANCE ASSESSMENT

1. This question has two parts. First, answer **Part A.** Then, answer **Part B.**

Part A: What is the author's main purpose for writing "Sharks Find Themselves in Danger"?

  a. The author wants people to stop buying and eating shark fin soup.

  b. The author wants readers to know that using "longlines" may cause sharks to disappear.

  c. The author wants readers to know how human actions are killing off the shark population, and that those actions should be stopped.

  d. The author wants readers to understand all the reasons sharks die.

Part B: Circle the letter of the sentence from the text that supports your answer to **Part A.**

  a. Recently various human activities have hurt sharks.

  b. Fishermen use finning in order to supply enough fins for a Chinese delicacy, shark fin soup.

  c. When populations of large animals fall, it is hard for them to recover.

  d. Shark populations are in great danger, but finally the world seems to be paying attention.

2. The author is trying to persuade readers to help stop the killing of the world's sharks. To persuade someone, writers often appeal to a reader's emotions by using strong images. Circle the letter of the paragraph in the article that uses vivid descriptions to appeal to the readers' emotions.

  a. paragraph 3

  b. paragraph 5

  c. paragraph 6

  d. paragraph 8

3. Support the claim that countries are beginning to try to save the world's shark population. On the lines below, cite three pieces of evidence from the article to support this claim.

a. _____

b. _____

c. _____

4. A student is writing an editorial for a newspaper to convince people that they should boycott a local restaurant for serving shark fin soup. Read the paragraphs from the draft of the student's letter and complete the task that follows.

Most everyone loves seafood, but people often don't realize that what they eat can affect the world's environment. For example, one of our local restaurants serves shark fin soup, but I doubt those that order it know the damage it causes.

Shark fin soup is a Chinese delicacy, but the way sharks are killed to make it is horrible. I certainly don't know the recipe, but you must use the fins of sharks. When some fishermen catch a shark, they cut off its fin while it's still alive. This obviously hurts the shark. They then throw the bleeding shark back into the ocean. Since the shark is unable to swim without its fins, it sinks to the bottom and slowly dies. The fins are then sold to restaurants to make the soup. We lose over 73 million sharks a year by killing them in this horrible way.

Below, copy the sentence that should be removed from the second paragraph because it does not support the underlined sentence.

_____

_____

Sports, Arts, and Self-Expression

Unit

4

Name _____ Date _____

ANTICIPATION GUIDE

Directions: Before you read the article "The NFL Recognizes Brain Damage to Players," read the statements below. If you agree with a statement, put a checkmark on the line next to it. If you disagree, put an X on the line.

_____ **1.** Only professional athletes are at risk for concussions.

_____ **2.** The National Football League can't be responsible for a player's medical problems.

_____ **3.** An athlete should stay quiet about a teammate's injuries.

Once you have responded to the statements above, write in the section below why you agree or disagree with each statement.

1. _____

_____

2. _____

_____

3. _____

_____

In the box below, draw a picture of what you think this article is about.

WORDSTORM

Directions: It's good to know more than just the dictionary definition of a word. Completing a wordstorm lets you write down information to help you understand what a word means, how it's related to other words, and how to use it in different ways.

What is the word?

concussion

Here is the sentence from the text in which the word is used:

"Pro football players have been getting concussions for a long time."

What are some other words or phrases that mean the same thing?

_____

What are three ways people might get a concussion?

1. _____ 2. _____ 3. _____

Name three people other than teachers who would likely use this word.

1. _____ 2. _____ 3. _____

Draw a picture below that reminds you of the word *concussion*.

TIME MY READ #1

Directions: With a partner, see how many words you can read correctly in 45 seconds. As you read, your partner will put an X through any word read incorrectly on his or her copy. When you are finished, trade your books or papers, and let your partner read while you keep score. Count the total number of words you read correctly. Write this score at the bottom of your page.

concussions symptoms fluid consciousness league slurred sensitive researchers	8
permanent examinations trauma agreement suicide mental repeated former	16
serious dementia disease settlement retired athletes sacrificed approved	24
concussions symptoms fluid consciousness league slurred sensitive researchers	32
permanent examinations trauma agreement suicide mental repeated former	40
serious dementia disease settlement retired athletes sacrificed approved	48
concussions symptoms fluid consciousness league slurred sensitive researchers	56
permanent examinations trauma agreement suicide mental repeated former	64
serious dementia disease settlement retired athletes sacrificed approved	72
concussions symptoms fluid consciousness league slurred sensitive researchers	80

Number of words read correctly _____

ECHO READING

Directions: When you read, you should make breaks, and sometimes pauses, between groups of words. As your teacher reads each phrase, repeat aloud what is read and put a slash or line after that phrase. Then read the whole sentence aloud as a class. Do the first paragraph together as a class, and then do the second one on your own. The first sentence has been marked for you.

Concussions in sports / do not happen / only in football. / They can occur whenever an athlete receives a direct blow to the upper body, especially the head, neck, or chest. Fluid surrounds and protects the brain, but some blows shake the brain or cause it to strike the skull. That trauma leads to temporary damage to the brain.

In recent years researchers have learned a lot about concussions. Now they know that 60 percent of teenage athletes will get a concussion. Concussions in teenagers take longer to heal than they do in adults. Researchers also believe that far too many concussions go untreated. Athletes and coaches have not recognized the symptoms or understood the danger.

What's Happening
IN THE USA?

BY LAWRENCE GABLE
2015 What's Happening Publications

SUBJECT: SPORTS, ARTS and SELF-EXPRESSION

The NFL Recognizes Brain Damage to Players

1 Pro football players have been getting concussions for a long time. In recent years the National Football League (NFL) has begun to address the problem. It understands that these brain injuries can affect players long after their careers are over. In April 2015 the league settled a lawsuit by agreeing to pay money for their medical care.

2 Concussions in sports do not happen only in football. They can occur whenever an athlete receives a direct blow to the upper body, especially the head, neck or chest. Fluid surrounds and protects the brain, but some blows shake the brain or cause it to strike the skull. That trauma leads to temporary damage in the brain.

3 Symptoms of most concussions are hard to notice. They can last from just a few minutes to several weeks. Most often the athletes do not lose consciousness. They may be confused, have difficulty concentrating, and lose memory.

4 Brain trauma can have obvious symptoms too. They include headache, dizziness, vomiting, slurred speech and double vision. People can become sensitive to light and unable to sleep. As time passes, depression often sets in.

5 In recent years researchers have learned a lot about concussions. Now they know that 60 percent of teenage athletes will get a concussion. Concussions in teenagers take longer to heal than they do in adults. Researchers also believe that far too many concussions go untreated. Athletes and coaches have not recognized the symptoms or understood the danger.

6 Researchers also know that anyone who has had a concussion is at high risk of getting another one. In fact, that athlete is at least four times more likely to get a concussion than other athletes. Too often athletes do not want to report a concussion to coaches or doctors. However, there is a terrible risk. A second concussion before the first one has healed often does permanent damage.

7 Many pro football players suffer brain trauma multiple times. Then after they retire the long-term symptoms appear. Their brains do not work well, and depression and dementia follow. In recent years a number of former players even have committed suicide. Examinations show that they had CTE. This disease comes from repeated trauma, and it ruins the brain.

8 The lawsuit against the NFL represented 5,000 former players. Its goal was to force the NFL to pay for medical care. The money will cover not only retired players who already have permanent brain damage. It is also for players who will have it in the future.

9 The NFL and the former players first came to an agreement in August 2013. The league agreed to pay $765 million over the next twenty years. Players with serious disease get up to $5 million. Families of brain-damaged players who have committed suicide may get $4 million. Players with dementia can get $3 million. Smaller amounts will go to players with lesser mental problems.

10 A judge had to approve that settlement, but she refused. She wanted the NFL to provide more money for retired players who have, or will have, brain damage. When the NFL increased the total amount of money, the judge approved. The NFL admits that football is causing permanent damage. Now, after years in court, the league is finally sending money to players who sacrificed their health for the sport.

Name _____ Date _____

GET A CONTEXT CLUE

Directions: Below are sentences from "The NFL Recognizes Brain Damage to Players." First, read the sentence. Then, look back in the article and reread the paragraph in which the sentence is found. Circle the best answer to each question.

"That *trauma* leads to temporary damage in the brain."

1. The word *trauma* means

   A. blood
   B. injury
   C. scratch
   D. skull

"People can *become sensitive* to light and unable to sleep."

2. The phrase *become sensitive* means

   A. to lie
   B. to talk
   C. to react
   D. to have feelings

"Athletes and coaches have not recognized the *symptoms* or understood the danger."

3. The word *symptoms* means

   A. signals
   B. dreams
   C. goals
   D. ideas

"Many pro football players suffer brain trauma *multiple* times."

4. The word *multiple* means

   A. hardly any
   B. occasional
   C. one
   D. many

"Their brains do not work well, and depression and dementia *follow*."

5. The word *follow* means

   A. to heal
   B. to eventually happen
   C. to fade away
   D. to stop

"A judge had to approve that *settlement*, but she refused."

6. The word *settlement* means

   A. argument
   B. colony
   C. agreement
   D. community

WORD CHOICE

Directions: The sentences below contain blanks for missing words. Three answer choices are listed after each blank. Read the sentence past the blank and choose the correct word. Write it in the blank.

Concussions in sports don't happen only in football. They can

_____ (*occur, occurrence, occurred*) whenever an athlete

_____ (*receive, receives, received*) a direct blow to the upper

body, _____ (*special, especial, especially*) the head, neck or chest.

Fluid _____ (*surrounds, surround, surrounded*) and _____

(*protects, protect, protected*) the brain, but some blows _____

(*shook, shakes, shake*) the brain or _____ (*cause, caused, causes*)

it to _____ (*struck, stroke, strike*) the skull. That trauma

_____ (*leads, lead, led*) to temporary damage in the brain.

The NFL and the former players first _____ (*come, came, coming*)

to an agreement in August 2013. The league _____ (*agreed, agrees,*

agree) to pay $765 million over the next twenty years. Players with a

serious _____ (*diseases, disease, diseased*) get up to $5 million.

Families of _____ (*brain-damage, brain-damaged,*

brain-damaging) players who have committed suicide may get $4 million.

Smaller amounts will go to players with _____ (*less, lesser, least*)

mental problems.

LOOK WHO'S TALKING

Directions: Below are sentences that relate to "The NFL Recognizes Brain Damage to Players." Look back in the article and reread the paragraph in which you find the reference. Circle the best answer to each question.

1. In the third sentence of paragraph 1, the word *their* best refers to

    A. the NFL
    B. the brain
    C. the retired players
    D. the cells

2. In the second sentence of paragraph 2, the word *they* refers to

    A. the brain
    B. the concussions
    C. the person
    D. the players

3. In the second sentence of paragraph 5, the word *they* refers to

    A. the players
    B. the NFL
    C. the researchers
    D. the league

4. In the third sentence of paragraph 7, the word *their* refers to

    A. the brain experts
    B. the retired players
    C. the coaches
    D. the NFL

5. In the second sentence of paragraph 8, the word *its* refers to

    A. the league
    B. the players
    C. the retired players
    D. the lawsuit

6. In the last sentence of paragraph 10, the word *their* refers to

    A. the former players
    B. the NFL
    C. the coaches
    D. the doctors

NOTE MAKING

Directions: Read the bold-faced key words on the left side of the chart below. Then add notes that answer the question in parentheses under the key word.

concussion
(What is it?)

effects on brain
(What are they?)

researchers
(What do they say?)

retired players
(What do they want?)

agreement
(What is it?)

*On a separate sheet of paper write a summary of what your notes say about how the NFL handled the issue of concussions.

© Houghton Mifflin Harcourt Publishing Company

IS THAT A FACT?

Directions: Read the definitions of a fact and an inference below. Then read the paragraph that follows. At the bottom of the page, write an F on the blank if the sentence is a fact. Write an I if the sentence is an inference. Use the following definitions:

Fact—a statement that can be proven true from the paragraph

Inference—a guess as to what MIGHT be true, based on what you have read and what you already know about the subject

> In recent years researchers have learned a lot about concussions. Now they know that 60 percent of teenaged athletes will get a concussion. Concussions in teenagers take longer to heal than they do in adults. Researchers also believe that far too many concussions go untreated. Athletes and coaches have not recognized the symptoms or understood the danger. Researchers also know that anyone who has had a concussion is at high risk of getting another one. In fact, that athlete is at least four times more likely to get a concussion than other athletes.

_____ **1.** Researchers are more knowledgeable about concussions than they once were.

_____ **2.** Teenage athletes get the most concussions.

_____ **3.** Coaches don't seem to be too concerned about concussions.

_____ **4.** A player who has had a concussion is likely to get another.

_____ **5.** Teenager's brains are not as developed as those of adults and that affects the ability of the brain to heal from a concussion.

_____ **6.** Researchers are more aggressive today in studying concussions than they were in the past.

MAKE A SPACE

Directions: Below are sentences that are missing punctuation and capitalization. First draw slash marks (/) between the words. Then rewrite each sentence in the space below it by filling in the missing punctuation and capitalization.

Example:

lots / of / sports / involve / contact / but / football / players / suffer / repeated /

blows / to / the / head

Lots of sports involve contact, but football players suffer repeated blows to the head.

1. concussionsinsportsdonothappenonlyinfootball

_____

_____

2. mostoftentheathletesdonotloseconsciousness

_____

_____

3. toooftenathletesdonotwanttoreportaconcussiontocoachesordoctors

_____

_____

4. whenthenflincreasedtheamountofmoneythejudgeapprovedthesettlement

_____

_____

TIME MY READ #2

Directions: With a partner, see how many words you can read correctly in 45 seconds. As you read, your partner will put an X through any word read incorrectly on his or her copy. When you are finished, trade your books or papers, and let your partner read while you keep score. Count the total number of words you read correctly. Write this score at the bottom of your page.

concussions symptoms fluid consciousness league slurred sensitive researchers	8
permanent examinations trauma agreement suicide mental repeated former	16
serious dementia disease settlement retired athletes sacrificed approved	24
concussions symptoms fluid consciousness league slurred sensitive researchers	32
permanent examinations trauma agreement suicide mental repeated former	40
serious dementia disease settlement retired athletes sacrificed approved	48
concussions symptoms fluid consciousness league slurred sensitive researchers	56
permanent examinations trauma agreement suicide mental repeated former	64
serious dementia disease settlement retired athletes sacrificed approved	72
concussions symptoms fluid consciousness league slurred sensitive researchers	80

Number of words read correctly _____

Is the score higher than it was in Time My Read #1?_____

WORD PARTS

Directions: A **base word** is a word that can stand alone. A **prefix** is a word part added to the beginning of a base word. For example, in the word **misspeak, speak** is the base word and **mis-** is the prefix. The prefix **mis-** means "wrong" or "wrongly." *Misspeak* means to say something wrong or incorrectly. Write a definition for each word below. Do not use the base word in the definition. If you don't know the base word, such as *deed* in *misdeed,* look it up in a dictionary or ask a partner.

1. misunderstand—_____

2. misplace—_____

3. mistrust—_____

4. misjudge—_____

5. misfire—_____

6. misbehave—_____

7. mishandle—_____

8. misuse—_____

9. mistaken—_____

10. misinform—_____

11. misfit—_____

12. mismanage—_____

13. mistrial—_____

14. mislead—_____

15. misdeed—_____

BRAIN DISEASE WORD PUZZLE

Directions: Complete the crossword puzzle.

Word List

SETTLEMENT
CONCUSSION
CONSCIOUSNESS
SYMPTOM
SENSITIVE
PERMANENT
SERIOUS
TRAUMA
OBVIOUS
MULTIPLE

Across

1. something easily seen or noticed
6. something that is bad or severe
7. a signal from the body of an illness
8. an injury to the brain from a hard hit on the head
10. the state of being awake or aware of one's surroundings

Down

2. easily affected by something
3. a very bad injury caused by force
4. an agreement between parties in a lawsuit
5. not able to be changed
9. more than once; many times

WRITING FRAME

Directions: Use your knowledge and information from the article to complete the writing frame below.

Concussions in sports do not happen only in football. They can occur _____ to the upper body. Symptoms of most concussions are _____ _____.

Many players suffer brain trauma multiple times. After they retire they _____ _____. In recent years a number of former players have even _____.

The NFL and former players came to an agreement in _____. A judge _____. She wanted the NFL _____. When the NFL increased _____. Now the league is finally _____. The league agreed to pay _____.

REACTION GUIDE

Directions: Now that you have read and studied information about "The NFL Recognizes Brain Damage to Players," reread the statements below, which you responded to before reading the article. Then think about how the author might respond to these statements. If you think the author would agree, put a checkmark on the line before the number. If you think the author would disagree, put an X on the line. Then below the statement, copy the words, phrases, or sentences from the article that provide evidence of the views stated by the author. Also note if there is no evidence to support the statement.

_____ **1.** Only professional athletes are at risk for concussions.

Evidence: _____

_____

_____

_____ **2.** The National Football League can't be responsible for a player's medical problems.

Evidence: _____

_____

_____

_____ **3.** An athlete should stay quiet about a teammate's injuries.

Evidence: _____

_____

_____

TAKE A STAND

Directions: People often have differing feelings, or opinions, about an issue. When they discuss or argue their opposing views, they are taking part in a debate. A good persuasive argument is based on a claim that is supported by

Facts—statements that can be proven true

Statistics—numerical data gotten through research

Examples—instances that support an opinion

You and a partner are going to debate two of your other classmates. The topic you are going to debate is the following:

An athlete should stay quiet about a teammate's injuries.

Decide with the other pair who will agree and who will disagree with this statement. Then answer these questions in order to win your debate.

1. What are your two strongest points to persuade the other side? (You can do Internet research to include facts, statistics, and examples.)

A. _____

B. _____

2. What might the other side say to argue against point A?

_____

_____

3. What might the other side say to argue against point B?

_____

_____

4. What will you say to prove the other side's arguments are wrong?

_____

_____

_____

ASSESSMENT

Comprehension: Answer the questions about the following passage.

Many pro football players suffer brain trauma multiple times. Then after they retire the long-term symptoms appear. Their brains do not work well, and depression and dementia follow. In recent years a number of former players even have committed suicide. Examinations show that they had CTE. This disease comes from repeated trauma, and it ruins the brain.

The lawsuit against the NFL represented 5,000 former players. Its goal was to force the NFL to pay for medical care. The money will cover not only retired players who already have permanent brain damage. It is also for players who will have it in the future.

1. What long-term problems do concussions cause?

_____

_____

2. What was the author's purpose for writing about concussions?

_____

_____

Fluency: The words in the following two sentences are all connected. The sentences are also missing punctuation and capitalization. Draw slash (/) marks between the words. Then rewrite each sentence by filling in the punctuation and capitalization.

1. symptomsofmostconcussionsarehardtonotice

_____

2. theleagueisfinallysendingmoneytoplayerswhosacrificedtheirhealth

_____

Fluency: Read the three sentences below. Imagine where you would pause within each sentence as you read it aloud. Draw a slash (/) mark between the phrases where you would pause. The first slash is done.

3. Concussions in sports / do not only happen in football.

4. Once a player has gotten a concussion, his chances of getting another are increased.

5. Brain trauma can have obvious symptoms too.

Vocabulary: Based on what you have learned in this lesson, match the following words with their definitions. Write the letter of the definition on the blank in front of the word it defines.

1. _____ settlement   **A.** a very bad injury caused by force

2. _____ concussion   **B.** not able to be changed

3. _____ consciousness   **C.** more than once; many times

4. _____ symptom   **D.** an agreement between parties in a lawsuit

5. _____ sensitive   **E.** the state of being awake and aware of one's surroundings

6. _____ permanent   **F.** something that is very bad or severe

7. _____ serious   **G.** something easily seen or noticed

8. _____ trauma   **H.** easily affected by something

9. _____ obvious   **I.** a signal from the body of an illness

10. _____ multiple   **J.** an injury to the brain caused by a hard hit

Name _____ Date _____

ANTICIPATION GUIDE

Directions: Before you read the article "Americans Love Their Marathons," read the statements below. If you agree with a statement, put a checkmark on the line next to it. If you disagree, put an X on the line.

_____ **1.** Marathons are popular running events.

_____ **2.** Competitive running is popular all over the world.

_____ **3.** Only qualified athletes should be eligible to run marathons.

Once you have responded to the statements above, write in the section below why you agree or disagree with each statement.

1. _____

_____

2. _____

_____

3. _____

_____

In the box below, draw a picture of what you think this article is about.

WORDSTORM

Directions: It's good to know more than just the dictionary definition of a word. Completing a wordstorm lets you write down information to help you understand what a word means, how it's related to other words, and how to use it in different ways.

What is the word?

marathon

Here is the sentence from the text in which the word is used:

"When the modern Olympics began in 1896, they had a marathon."

What are some other words or phrases that mean the same thing?

_____

What are three things you know about marathons?

1. _____ 2. _____ 3. _____

Name three people other than teachers who would likely use this word.

1. _____ 2. _____ 3. _____

Draw a picture below that reminds you of the word *marathon*.

Name _____ Date _____

LANGUAGE MINI-LESSON

Sometimes a sentence has two or more subjects. When a sentence has more than one subject, they are called a **compound subject.** If the two or more subjects are joined by the word *and*, you usually use a plural verb in the sentence.

Example 1: David **is** (singular) at the store.

Example 2: David and Maria (compound subject) **are** (plural) here.

Sometimes a compound subject that is joined by *and* is thought of as one thing. In this case, use a singular verb.

Example: Spaghetti and meatballs (one thing) **is** my favorite food.

Directions: Circle the correct form of the verb in the sentences below.

1. Professional and amateur athletes [*is, are*] allowed to run in a marathon.

2. An ancient Greek runner [*was, were*] the first marathon runner.

3. The first American marathon [*was, were*] in Boston.

4. The well-known dish of fish and chips [*is, are*] served in London, site of a popular marathon.

5. At first, women [*was, were*] not allowed to run in a marathon.

6. The first Olympic marathon [*was, were*] in 1896.

7. Today the top 15 male and female Boston finishers [*is, are*] given money.

8. Raising money for charity [*is, are*] one reason some people run.

9. Most marathon runners [*is, are*] recreational athletes.

10. There [*is, are*] more than one thousand marathons in America.

ECHO READING

Directions: When you read, you should make breaks, and sometimes pauses, between groups of words. As your teacher reads each phrase, repeat aloud what is read and put a slash or line after that phrase. Then read the whole sentence aloud as a class. Do the first paragraph together as a class, and then do the second one on your own. The first sentence has been marked for you.

An Olympic marathon victory / in 1908 / created even more interest. / An American won the race in London that summer. His victory began a sort of "marathon mania." Within a year New York City, for example, had five marathons for amateur runners. Other marathons in New York followed quickly. The running boom in the U.S. really began in the 1970s, thanks to an Olympic marathon victory in 1972 by Frank Shorter.

It took some time for marathons to have a standard distance. Legend says that the Greek messenger ran 25 miles. The first Olympic marathon in 1896 went 24.8 miles. Finally in 1921 the distance became 26 miles, 385 yards.

What's Happening
IN THE USA?

BY LAWRENCE GABLE
© 2015 What's Happening Publications

SUBJECT: SPORTS, ARTS and SELF-EXPRESSION

Americans Love Their Marathons

1 America was shocked by the bombings at the Boston Marathon on April 15, 2013. That marathon is the oldest and most famous of all marathons in the U.S. It began in 1897, and now there are hundreds of them. They are joyous events in communities all around the country.

2 The marathon's origin lies in the Olympic Games. It honors a long run by a messenger in ancient Greece during a war. When the modern Olympics began in 1896, they had a marathon. It has become tradition that the men's marathon is the final event of the entire Summer Olympic Games. The runners finish in the Olympic Stadium.

3 The 1896 Olympic marathon created immediate interest in the U.S. A year later the Boston Marathon began. It is now the world's oldest annual marathon.

4 An Olympic marathon victory in 1908 created even more interest. An American won the race in London that summer. His victory began a sort of "marathon mania." Within a year New York City, for example, had five marathons for amateur runners. Other marathons in New York followed quickly. The running boom in the U.S. really began in the 1970s, thanks to an Olympic marathon victory in 1972 by Frank Shorter.

5 It took some time for marathons to have a standard distance. Legend says that the Greek messenger ran 25 miles. The first Olympic marathon in 1896 went 24.8 miles. Finally in 1921 the distance became 26 miles, 385 yards.

6 The Boston Marathon is always held on the third Monday in April. Only 15 runners participated in the first race in 1897. Entering the race used to be free, and the winners received an olive wreath. Now about 30,000 runners from 90 countries start the race. The entry fee is about $175 for U.S. residents and $225 for nonresidents.

The top 15 finishers in the men's and women's divisions win a cash prize. The first-place man and woman both receive about $150,000.

MARATHON FINISH LINE

7 The New York City Marathon is the world's largest. When it began in November 1970, only 127 runners ran. Since 2009 more than 40,000 runners have finished the race each year. The route takes runners all through the city and across four bridges. Getting into it is hard. Of course the marathon accepts the world-class runners. Beyond them though, more than 105,000 people from all over the world send in applications. A lottery selects the other runners.

8 For many years men said that women were not strong enough to run marathons. In 1972 the Boston Marathon finally became the first major race to allow women. However, there was one woman who had run in Boston before that. In 1967 Kathrine Switzer registered for the race as "K.V. Switzer," so officials were unaware that she was a woman. She finished the race just fine.

9 Most marathon runners are recreational athletes who are not trying to win the race. Instead they want the sense of accomplishment that comes from finishing such a long race. Many people support each other by running in groups or on teams. Many also earn money for charity by asking friends to support their run.

10 Marathons are becoming more and more popular. Since 2001 participation almost has doubled. Now more than 500,000 runners finish a marathon every year. Clearly Americans have made marathons part of the culture, and nothing is going to stop them from running.

QUICK READ/DRAW AND WRITE

Directions: First Reading—As you do your first reading of the article, your teacher will time you for one minute. When time is called, write the number of the paragraph where you stopped. **Paragraph # _____**

In the box below, draw a picture summarizing what you read.

Second Reading—As you do your second reading of the article, your teacher will time you for one minute. When time is called, write the number of the paragraph where you stopped. **Paragraph # _____**

Directions: Now continue reading the rest of the article. Below, write five important words that will help you remember the information from the article.

_____   _____   _____   _____   _____

CLOSE READING ANNOTATION

Third Reading—As you reread each paragraph in the article closely, answer the questions by annotating the text. Each numbered question corresponds to a paragraph in the article where the answer can be found. Write your brief answers in the space below each question.

1. Why is the Boston Marathon significant to the history of running?

_____

2. What is the author's purpose for writing paragraph 2?

_____

3. Why do you think the author chose the word *immediate* in the first sentence of this paragraph?

_____

4. What does the author mean by "marathon mania"?

_____

5. In which previous paragraph does the author introduce readers to the legend of the Greek messenger?

_____

6. What is the author's purpose for writing paragraph 6?

_____

7. What does the term *world-class* mean in paragraph 7?

_____

8. Why do you think the author ended paragraph 8 with the sentence, "She finished the race just fine"?

_____

9. What are some reasons recreational athletes run marathons?

_____

10. What might the author be referring to with the phrase, "and nothing is going to stop them from running"?

_____

GRAMMAR GAMES

Directions: Reread the two paragraphs below. Words have been left out from the sentences. Think about the information from the article you have read and fill in words that make sense. The part of speech of each missing word is provided.

The New York City Marathon is the _____ largest.
                                                    (1. possessive adjective)

When _____ began in November 1970, only 127 runners
           (2. pronoun)

_____ . Since 2009 more than 40,000 _____ have
     (3. verb)   (4. plural noun)

finished the race each year. The _____ takes runners all
                                                    (5. noun)

through the city and _____ four bridges. Getting into
                                    (6. preposition)

_____ is hard. Of course the marathon _____ the
     (7. pronoun)   (8. verb)

world-class runners. Beyond them though, more than 105,000 people

_____ all over the world _____ in applications. A
(9. preposition)   (10. verb)

lottery selects the other _____ .
                                     (11. plural noun)

For many years _____ said that women were not
                        (12. collective noun)

strong enough to run marathons. In 1967, Kathrine Switzer _____
                                                                              (13. verb)

for the race as "K. V. Switzer," so officials were unaware that she was a

_____ . She finished _____ race just fine.
     (14. noun)   (15. article)

© Houghton Mifflin Harcourt Publishing Company

HOW'S IT ORGANIZED?

This article is organized in chronological order, or in the time order that things happened.

Directions: Answer these questions in the spaces at the bottom.

1. What is the Boston Marathon?

2. Why does the author mention ancient Greece in the first sentence of paragraph 2?

3. What time period is covered in paragraph 3?

4. How does the author introduce the 20th century?

5. In which paragraph does the author first discuss the 21st century?

6. For what reason does paragraph 8 go back to the 1960s and 1970s?

7. What time period is the author talking about in the last paragraph?

Answers:

1.	
2.	
3.	
4.	
5.	
6.	
7.	

The main idea reflects what an article is about. Put an X on the line next to the sentence that best states the main idea of this article, and write a reason for your choice below.

_____ **1.** Marathons have a rich history and have increased greatly in popularity.

_____ **2.** Runners who participate in marathons are strong and competitive.

_____ **3.** Women are strong enough to run marathons and should be included.

Explain why your choice is the best main or central idea.

_____

_____

_____

IS THAT A FACT?

Directions: Read the definitions of a fact and an inference below. Then read the paragraph that follows. At the bottom of the page, write an F on the blank if the sentence is a fact. Write an I if the sentence is an inference. Use the following definitions:

Fact—a statement that can be proven true from the paragraph

Inference—a guess as to what MIGHT be true, based on what you have read and what you already know about the subject

---

For many years men said that women were not strong enough to run marathons. In 1972 the Boston Marathon finally became the first major race to allow women. However, there was one woman who had run in Boston before that. In 1967 Kathrine Switzer registered for the race as "K.V. Switzer," so officials were unaware that she was a woman. She finished the race just fine.

Most marathon runners are recreational athletes who are not trying to win the race. Instead they want the sense of accomplishment that comes from finishing such a long race. Many people support each other by running in groups or on teams. Many also earn money for charity by asking friends to support their run.

_____ **1.** People underestimated women's ability to finish a marathon.

_____ **2.** The Boston Marathon was the first race to allow women.

_____ **3.** Kathrine Switzer was clever to enroll with just her initials.

_____ **4.** People who run the marathon are happy just to say that they finished the race.

_____ **5.** The Boston Marathon is a good vehicle for people to do charitable things.

_____ **6.** People who run the race tend to help and support each other.

TIC-TAC-TOE SUMMARIZING

When you **summarize** in writing, you present all the key points the author is trying to make.

Directions: Write four sentences to summarize the article about marathons. To help you, there are nine words or phrases in the Tic-Tac-Toe graphic organizer below. To write a sentence, you must use three words or phrases in a row. The row can be horizontal (—), vertical (I), or diagonal (/).

Olympics	marathon mania	New York City Marathon
women	marathon	recreational athletes
Boston Marathon	public	race

1. _____

   _____

2. _____

   _____

3. _____

   _____

4. _____

   _____

REACTION GUIDE

Directions: Now that you have read and studied information about "Americans Love Their Marathons," reread the statements below, which you responded to before reading the article. Then think about how the author might respond to these statements. If you think the author would agree, put a checkmark on the line before the number. If you think the author would disagree, put an X on the line. Then below the statement, copy the words, phrases, or sentences from the article that provide evidence of the views stated by the author. Also note if there is no evidence to support the statement.

_____ **1.** Marathons are popular running events.

Evidence: _____

_____

_____

_____ **2.** Competitive running is popular all over the world.

Evidence: _____

_____

_____

_____ **3.** Only qualified athletes should be eligible to run marathons.

Evidence: _____

_____

_____

TAKE A STAND

Directions: People often have differing feelings or opinions about an issue. When they discuss or argue their opposing views, they are taking part in a debate. A good persuasive argument is based on a claim that is supported by

Facts—statements that can be proven true

Statistics—numerical data gotten through research

Examples—instances that support an opinion

You and a partner are going to debate two of your other classmates. The topic you are going to debate is the following:

The only people that should be eligible to run marathons are qualified athletes.

Decide with the other pair who will agree and who will disagree with this statement. Then answer these questions in order to win your debate.

1. What are your two strongest points to persuade the other side? (You can do Internet research to include facts, statistics, and examples.)

A. _____

B. _____

2. What might the other side say to argue against point A?

_____

_____

3. What might the other side say to argue against point B?

_____

_____

4. What will you say to prove the other side's arguments are wrong?

_____

_____

_____

WHAT'S THE COMBINATION?

Writing is more interesting when the writer joins, or combines, short sentences. Follow the directions below to learn different ways to combine two sentences.

What to do: You can sometimes join two sentences about the same topic by taking an adjective from one and using it as an adverb to modify an adjective or verb in the other. In the sentences below, find the adjective in the second sentence, and then use it as an adverb in the first sentence. In these examples you do that by adding –*y* or –*ly* to the adjective.

Example: The hurricane wind is blowing. The wind is very strong.

New sentence: The hurricane wind is blowing strongly.

Directions: Combine these sentences using the method above.

1. The race was competitive. The competition was very intense.

_____

2. The distance of a marathon is long. The length is incredible.

_____

3. The New York and Boston Marathons are popular. Their popularity is immense.

_____

4. Many marathon runners run for recreation. They are glad to run for recreation.

_____

5. Kathrine Switzer registered for the Boston Maraton as "K.V. Switzer." Registering without using her first name was clever.

_____

6. The exhausted runner dragged herself across the finish line. She was weak.

_____

ANALYZING A PROMPT

Directions: Read the writing prompt in the box below. Then follow the directions to learn how to analyze and answer it.

> After the bombing at the Boston Marathon, city officials want to cancel future marathons due to safety concerns. You are a runner who decides to write a newspaper editorial that describes the importance of the marathon in American culture and history. What information in the article can help you make your case? How is the rich history of the marathon important for the city of Boston and for the world as well?

1. A writing prompt begins with some background information known as the **set up.** Underline the sentence that sets up this assignment.

2. Use the following **R.A.F.T.** technique to finish analyzing the prompt.

Role: What are you supposed to be to answer it? A student? A politician?

Write what you are here: _____

Audience: To whom are you writing? A friend? A particular group?

Write who it is here: _____

Format: Check to see what type of writing you are doing. Is it an essay, a letter, a speech, a story, a description, an editorial, or a report?

Write what it is here: _____

Task: Another sentence in the prompt will tell you what you must do, or your "task." Question words like **why, how,** or **what** may tell the task.

If the question word is **why,** you will *give the reasons* that something is done.

If the question word is **how,** you will *explain the way* that something is done.

If the question word is **what,** you will *identify the thing* that is done.

Below, copy the sentence or question that describes your task.

_____

_____

ANALYZING INFORMATIONAL TEXT

1. Informational articles are written to provide data or descriptions that explain something. Below name three groups that might be interested in reading this article besides students and teachers.

a. _____ **b.** _____ **c.** _____

2. What main point is the author making in this article?

_____

_____

3. Give two of the most important facts you learned in this article.

a. _____

b. _____

4. **Domain-specific vocabulary** consists of words used in a specific subject such as math, science, or social studies. Reread the article and list six domain-specific words used with this subject. After you select the words, write their definitions on the lines provided.

a. _____ : _____

b. _____ : _____

c. _____ : _____

d. _____ : _____

e. _____ : _____

f. _____ : _____

ASSESSMENT

1. This question has two parts. First, answer Part A. Then, answer Part B.

Part A: Circle the letter of the sentence that best states the author's main purpose for writing "Americans Love Their Marathons."

a. The author wants to inform the reader of the growth in popularity of marathon racing in America.

b. The author wants to inform the reader about the Boston Marathon bombing in 2013.

c. The author wants the reader to know the origins of famous marathons.

d. The author wants to inform the reader that many people now run in marathons.

Part B: Circle the letters of the sentences that support your answer to **Part A.**

a. The 1896 Olympic marathon created immediate interest in the United States.

b. The running boom in the United States really began in the 1970s, thanks to an Olympic marathon victory in 1972 by Frank Shorter.

c. An Olympic marathon victory in 1908 created even more interest in the sport in the United States.

d. America was shocked by the bombings in Boston on April 15, 2013.

e. In 1972 the Boston Marathon became the first major race to allow women to enter.

2. Circle the letter of the paragraph that best summarizes what the article is about.

a. paragraph 1

b. paragraph 3

c. paragraph 4

d. paragraph 6

e. paragraph 10

3. This article is organized using chronological order, or a structure that follows the order in which things happened over time. In paragraphs 5, 6, and 8 in the article, the author goes back to an earlier time. Explain below what the author's purpose was for going out of chronological order in each paragraph.

Paragraph 5: _____

_____

Paragraph 6: _____

_____

Paragraph 8: _____

_____

4. A student is writing an informative article about the history of the marathon for a sports magazine. Read the paragraphs from a draft of the student's article and complete the task that follows.

The beginnings of the marathon go back to early Greece. Legend says that after the Greeks had won a great battle, a soldier ran 25 miles to tell the city that they had won. After proclaiming victory, he dropped dead. Greece honored him by creating the marathon race in the early Olympics.

Marathons have become huge over the years. Only 15 runners participated in the first Boston Marathon in 1897. Now over 30,000 people run in the Boston Marathon. New York City has the largest marathon in the world with over 40,000 runners.

The writer needs a better transition sentence between the two paragraphs above. Circle the letter of the sentence below that best connects the information in the underlined sentences above.

a. It takes a lot of practice and determination to train for a marathon.

b. People still feel honored to race in a marathon, and their numbers are growing.

c. Clearly Americans have made marathons part of their culture.

d. More than 105,000 people apply to run in the New York City Marathon.

Name _____ Date _____ 499

ANTICIPATION GUIDE

Directions: Before you read the article "Doping Damages Even the Best," read the statements below. If you agree with a statement, put a checkmark on the line next to it. If you disagree, put an X on the line.

_____ **1.** Athletes have used drugs to help themselves for many years.

_____ **2.** Drugs to improve performance are not that harmful.

_____ **3.** Athletes who used steroids should lose any awards they won.

Once you have responded to the statements above, write in the section below why you agree or disagree with each statement.

1. _____

_____

2. _____

_____

3. _____

_____

In the box below, draw a picture of what you think this article is about.

PREDICTING ABCs

Directions: The article you are going to read is about athletes using drugs to improve their performance. See how many boxes you can fill in below with words relating to this topic. For example, put the word *muscle* in the M–O box. Put at least one word in every box, and then try to write a word for every letter.

A–C	D–F	G–I
J–L	M–O	P–R
S–T	U–V	W–Z

Name _____ Date _____

Directions: With a partner, see how many words you can read correctly in 45 seconds. As you read, your partner will put an X through any word read incorrectly on his or her copy. When you are finished, trade your books or papers, and let your partner read while you keep score. Count the total number of words you read correctly. Write this score at the bottom of your page.

stimulant serious health athletes amphetamines fatigue testing energy	8
cyclist investigators positive steroids stimulates accuses medals officials	16
admitted production thickens artificial increase supplied raided world-class	24
stimulant serious health athletes amphetamines fatigue testing energy	32
cyclist investigators positive steroids stimulates accuses medals officials	40
admitted production thickens artificial increase supplied raided world-class	48
stimulant serious health athletes amphetamines fatigue testing energy	56
cyclist investigators positive steroids stimulates accuses medals officials	64
admitted production thickens artificial increase supplied raided world-class	72
stimulant serious health athletes amphetamines fatigue testing energy	80

Number of words read correctly _____

ECHO READING

Directions: When you read, you should make breaks, and sometimes pauses, between groups of words. As your teacher reads each phrase, repeat aloud what is read and put a slash or line after that phrase. Then read the whole sentence aloud as a class. Do the first paragraph together as a class, and then do the second one on your own. The first sentence has been marked for you.

Athletes constantly want / to improve / their performances. / Usually they do it through long hours of training and practice. However, many of them have improved through drugs, too. Now doping, the use of artificial stimulants, has become a problem for some of America's most famous athletes.

Doping includes serious health risks. Since some athletes are unwilling to take those risks, they find themselves unable to compete at the same level. International organizations that govern tennis, cycling, soccer, and the Olympic Games have banned it. America's pro sports leagues have banned it, too.

For many years athletes used things to ease pain and get energy. They used alcohol, caffeine, and stimulants called amphetamines. Amphetamines, though, caused the deaths of some athletes.

BY LAWRENCE GABLE
© 2014 What's Happening Publications

SUBJECT: SPORTS, ARTS and SELF-EXPRESSION

Doping Damages Even the Best

1   **A**thletes always want to improve. Usually they do it through long hours of training. However, many of them have used drugs too. Now doping, the use of artificial stimulants, has become problem for some of America's best athletes.

2   Doping includes serious health risks. Since some athletes are unwilling to take those risks, they cannot compete at the same level. International organizations for tennis, cycling, soccer and the Olympic Games have banned drugs, and America's pro sports leagues have too.

3   For many years athletes used things to ease pain or get energy. They used alcohol, caffeine and stimulants called amphetamines, which increase energy. In 1967 amphetamines caused the death of a cyclist during the Tour de France. Soon after that the Tour began testing riders for drugs.

4   Other forms of doping followed. In the 1970s athletes started taking steroids. Doctors use them to stimulate the growth of cells and bone. They make athletes larger and stronger, but they also present health risks. They cause mood swings and acne, as well as high blood pressure and heart damage.

5   Then in the 1980s a hormone called EPO became popular. It helps people with cancers and kidney diseases because it stimulates the production of red blood cells. In athletes it increases energy, but it thickens the blood and can lead to heart attacks.

6   Doping has made headlines in American sports. The track star Marion Jones always denied having used steroids. Then in 2007 she admitted that she had, in fact, used them. She also expressed her shame for having cheated in competitions and having lied to federal investigators. Ms. Jones ended up in prison for six months. The sport took away the titles that she had won since 2000, including five Olympic medals. The steroids that she took had come from a laboratory called Balco.

7   The investigation of Balco started with Ms. Jones's former coach. In 2003 he sent a sample of a steroid from Balco to the U.S. Anti-Doping Agency. Investigators then raided the lab and found that it had sent steroids to athletes.

8   The investigation also led some athletes to testify before a grand jury. One was Ms. Jones. Another was the baseball player Barry Bonds, who swore that he never had knowingly used steroids. However, the government said that investigators had found a positive test for steroids when they raided the Balco lab. The government accused him of having lied too, and a jury convicted him of obstruction of justice in 2011.

9   Two world-class American cyclists also have had problems. Floyd Landis won the Tour de France in 2006, but he tested positive for doping. Officials took his title away and banned him from racing for two years. Lance Armstrong won the Tour de France seven times. In 2012 he also lost those titles, and he received a lifetime ban. In 2013 he finally admitted to his doping.

10   In 2007 a new American cycling team took a strong stand against doping. Team Slipstream's anti-doping program tested its riders 1,200 times in its first season. The team wanted to win races, but not at the cost of its riders' health. It also hoped to gain fans who believe in fair competition.

11   Doping is certainly a health issue. Athletes of all ages should not have to take harmful drugs in order to compete. It is also a character issue, since it is cheating. Doping charges have damaged the reputations of terrific athletes. In the end, athletes may decide that anything they achieve while doping feels shameful after all.

GET A CONTEXT CLUE

Directions: Below are sentences from "Doping Damages Even the Best." First, read the sentence. Then, look back in the article and reread the paragraph in which the sentence is found. Circle the best answer to each question.

"Now doping, the use of artificial *stimulants,* has become a problem for some of America's best athletes."

1. The word *stimulant* means

   A. something that increases energy
   B. something that makes one sleepy
   C. something that brings peace of mind
   D. something that fights disease

"Since some athletes are unwilling to take those *risks,* they can't compete at the same level."

2. The word *risks* means

   A. opportunities for fame
   B. awards
   C. challenges
   D. chances of injury

"Other forms of *doping* followed."

3. The word *doping* means

   A. being stupid
   B. lying
   C. using drugs
   D. cheating

"The investigation also led some athletes to *testify* before a grand jury."

4. The word *testify* means

   A. speak the truth in court
   B. lie
   C. take a test
   D. sit

"Two *world-class* American cyclists also have had problems."

5. The term *world-class* means

   A. good
   B. foreign
   C. student
   D. among the very best

"Doping is certainly a health *issue.*"

6. The word *issue* means

   A. disease
   B. matter of concern
   C. sport
   D. choice

WORD MAP

Directions: Follow the directions to map the word in the box below.

> **stimulant**

List two more words that
mean the same.

List two more things
that are stimulants.

List two more words that
mean the opposite.

> energy booster

> coffee

> depressant

Draw a picture below to help
you remember the meaning.

Write a definition
IN YOUR OWN WORDS.

LOOK WHO'S TALKING

Directions: Below are sentences that relate to "Doping Damages Even the Best." Look back in the article and reread the paragraph in which you find the reference. Circle the best answer to each question.

1. **In the second sentence of paragraph 2, the word *they* best refers to**

   A. the international organizations
   B. the athletes
   C. pro sports leagues
   D. the Olympics

2. **In the third sentence of paragraph 4, the word *them* refers to**

   A. the steroids
   B. the athletes
   C. the cyclists
   D. the stimulants

3. **In paragraph 5, the word *it* refers each time to**

   A. the cells
   B. the EPO hormone
   C. kidney disease
   D. cancer

4. **In the last sentence of paragraph 7, the word *it* refers to**

   A. the lab
   B. the agency
   C. the steroids
   D. the United States

5. **In the fourth sentence of paragraph 8, the word *they* refers to**

   A. the athletes
   B. the agency
   C. the investigators
   D. the lab

6. **In the last sentence of paragraph 10, *it* refers to**

   A. Team Slipstream
   B. the season
   C. riders' health
   D. the steroids

HOW'S IT ORGANIZED?

This article is organized in chronological order, or in the time order that things happened.

Directions: Answer these questions in the spaces at the bottom.

1. What started the stimulant controversy in 1967?

2. What stimulant did athletes begin using in the 1970s?

3. What were the risks of these new drugs?

4. What stimulants became popular in the 1980s?

5. How did the international organization for track react to Marion Jones's confession?

6. What did the U.S. Anti-Doping Agency learn in 2003?

7. Why did Floyd Landis lose his Tour de France title in 2006?

8. Finally, who has taken a stand against doping in cycling since 2007?

Answers:

1.	
2.	
3.	
4.	
5.	
6.	
7.	
8.	

*On a separate sheet of paper write a summary of what your notes say about the problems of doping in sports.

IS THAT A FACT?

Directions: Read the definitions of a fact and an inference below. Then read the paragraph that follows. At the bottom of the page, write an F on the blank if the sentence is a fact. Write an I if the sentence is an inference. Use the following definitions:

Fact—a statement that can be proven true from the paragraph

Inference—a guess as to what MIGHT be true, based on what you have read and what you already know about the subject

Doping includes serious health risks. Since some athletes are unwilling to take those risks, they cannot compete at the same level. International organizations for tennis, cycling, soccer and the Olympic Games have banned drugs, and America's pro sports leagues have too. Doping is certainly a health issue. Athletes of all ages should not have to take harmful drugs in order to compete. It is also a character issue since it is cheating. Doping charges have damaged the reputations of terrific athletes. In the end, athletes may decide that anything they achieve while doping feels shameful after all.

_____ **1.** Athletes are willing to risk their health in order to win.

_____ **2.** Athletes' reputations can be ruined if they are accused of using illegal drugs.

_____ **3.** Some athletes aren't ashamed of using doping to improve performance.

_____ **4.** The Olympics have made the use of drugs against the rules.

_____ **5.** Not all athletes are concerned about the health effects of doping.

MAKE A SPACE

Directions: Below are sentences that are missing punctuation and capitalization. First draw slash marks (/) between the words. Then rewrite each sentence in the space below it by filling in the missing punctuation and capitalization.

> Example:
>
> now / doping / is / making / headlines / in / american / sports
>
> Now doping is making headlines in American sports.

1. dopingortheuseofartificialstimulantshasbecomeaproblemforathletes

_____

_____

2. theamericancyclingteamhastakenastandagainstdoping

_____

_____

3. athletesofallagesshouldnothavetousedopingtocompete

_____

_____

4. inathletesitincreasesenergybutthickensthebloodandleadstoheartattacks

_____

_____

TIME MY READ #2

Directions: With a partner, see how many words you can read correctly in 45 seconds. As you read, your partner will put an X through any word read incorrectly on his or her copy. When you are finished, trade your books or papers, and let your partner read while you keep score. Count the total number of words you read correctly. Write this score at the bottom of your page.

stimulant serious health athletes amphetamines fatigue testing energy	8
cyclist investigators positive steroids stimulates accuses medals officials	16
admitted production thickens artificial increase supplied raided world-class	24
stimulant serious health athletes amphetamines fatigue testing energy	32
cyclist investigators positive steroids stimulates accuses medals officials	40
admitted production thickens artificial increase supplied raided world-class	48
stimulant serious health athletes amphetamines fatigue testing energy	56
cyclist investigators positive steroids stimulates accuses medals officials	64
admitted production thickens artificial increase supplied raided world-class	72
stimulant serious health athletes amphetamines fatigue testing energy	80

Number of words read correctly _____

Is the score higher than it was in Time My Read #1? _____

WORD PARTS

Directions: A **base word** is a word that can stand alone. A **prefix** is a word part added to the beginning of a base word. For example, in the word **antitheft, theft** is the base word and **anti-** is the prefix added to the beginning. The prefix **anti-** means "against" or "opposite of." *Antitheft* means something that stops people from stealing. Write a definition for each word below. Try not to use the base word in the definition. If you don't know the base word, look it up in a dictionary or ask a partner.

1. antiaircraft—_____

2. antifogging—_____

3. antisocial—_____

4. antilock—_____

5. antimissile—_____

6. antiforeigner—_____

7. antifreeze—_____

8. antibiotic—_____

9. antiwar—_____

10. antimilitary—_____

11. antifungal—_____

12. antiperspirant—_____

13. antiterrorist—_____

14. antiglare—_____

15. antiregulatory—_____

SUMMARIZING ABCs

Directions: Now that you've read the article on athletes using performance-enhancing drugs, see how many words you can write about this topic in the boxes below.

A–C	D–F	G–I
J–L	**M–O**	**P–R**
S–T	**U–V**	**W–Z**

SENTENCE SUMMARIES

Directions: Below are four key words from the article "Doping Damages Even the Best." Your job is to summarize, or restate, what you've learned in this article by using these four words in two sentences. Then, as a challenge, try to use all four words in one sentence to restate the article.

Key Words

stimulants   athletes

risks   investigations

Sentence Summaries:

1. _____

_____

2. _____

_____

Challenge Summary (All four words in one sentence!):

1. _____

_____

REACTION GUIDE

Directions: Now that you have read and studied information about "Doping Damages Even the Best," reread the statements below, which you responded to before reading the article. Think about how the author would respond to these statements. If you think the author would agree, put a checkmark on the line before the number. If you think the author would disagree, put an X on the line. Then, below the statement, copy the words, phrases, or sentences in the article that provide evidence of the views stated by the author. Also note if there is no evidence to support the statement.

_____ **1.** Athletes have used drugs to help themselves for many years.

Evidence: _____

_____

_____

_____ **2.** Drugs to improve performance are not that harmful.

Evidence: _____

_____

_____

_____ **3.** Athletes who used steroids should lose any awards they won.

Evidence: _____

_____

_____

Name _____ Date _____

TAKE A STAND

Directions: People often have differing feelings or opinions about an issue. When they discuss or argue their opposing views, they are taking part in a debate. A good persuasive argument is based on a claim that is supported by:

Facts—statements that can be proven to be true

Statistics—numerical data gotten through research

Examples—instances that support an opinion

You and a partner are going to debate two of your other classmates. The topic you are going to debate is the following:

Athletes who use steroids should lose any awards they have won.

Decide with the other pair who will agree and who will disagree with this statement. Then answer these questions in order to win your debate.

1. What are your two strongest points to persuade the other side? (You can do Internet research to include facts, statistics, and examples.)

   A. _____

   B. _____

2. What might the other side say to argue against point A?

   _____

   _____

3. What might the other side say to argue against point B?

   _____

   _____

4. What will you say to prove the other side's arguments are wrong?

   _____

   _____

   _____

Name _____ Date _____

Comprehension: Answer the questions about the following passage.

   Doping is certainly a health issue. Athletes of all ages should not have to take harmful drugs in order to compete. It is also a character issue, since it is cheating. Doping charges have damaged the reputations of terrific athletes. In the end, athletes may decide · that anything they achieve while doping feels shameful after all.

1. Why has doping become so tempting for athletes?

_____

_____

2. Why would people be concerned about an athlete's use of drugs?

_____

_____

3. For what purpose do you think the author wrote this article about doping?

_____

_____

Fluency: The words in the two sentences below are all connected. The sentences are also missing punctuation and capitalization. Draw slash marks (/) between the words. Then rewrite each sentence by filling in the punctuation and capitalization.

   1. inathletesitincreasesenergybutitthickensthebloodandcanleadtoheartattacks

_____

   2. floydlandisdeniedusingsteroidsandhasbeenbannedfromracing

_____

Name _____ Date _____

Fluency: Read the three sentences below. Imagine where you would pause within each sentence as you read it aloud. Draw a slash (/) mark between the phrases where you would pause. The first slash is done.

3. Since some athletes / are unwilling to take those risks, they can't compete at the same level.

4. Now the government says that it found a positive test for steroids.

5. The team wants to win races, but not at the cost of the riders' health.

Vocabulary: Based on what you have learned in this lesson, match the following words with their definitions. Write the letter of the correct definition on the blank in front of the word it defines.

1. _____ stimulant   **A.** used against planes

2. _____ antisocial   **B.** using drugs or steroids

3. _____ doping   **C.** among the best in the world

4. _____ antiforeigner   **D.** against someone from another country

5. _____ testify   **E.** danger

6. _____ antiperspirant   **F.** someone who likes to be alone

7. _____ issue   **G.** to speak the truth in court

8. _____ world-class   **H.** something that keeps one from sweating

9. _____ antiaircraft   **I.** something that increases energy

10. _____ risk   **J.** topic or subject

Name _____ Date _____

ANTICIPATION GUIDE

Directions: Before you read the article "Title IX Has Brought Changes for Women," read the statements below. If you agree with a statement, put a checkmark on the line next to it. If you disagree, put an X on the line.

_____ **1.** Equal rights for women is a fairly new idea.

_____ **2.** A lot of people think that women are not as qualified as men to do certain jobs.

_____ **3.** Women and girls are usually not interested in playing sports.

Once you have responded to the statements above, write in the section below why you agree or disagree with each statement.

1. _____

_____

2. _____

_____

3. _____

_____

In the box below, draw a picture of what you think this article is about.

PREDICTING ABCs

Directions: The article you are going to read is about Title IX, a law that gives women equal rights to those of men in education and sports. See how many boxes you can fill in below with words relating to this topic. For example, put the word *athletes* in the A–C box. Put at least one word in every box, and then try to write a word for every letter.

A–C	D–F	G–I
J–L	**M–O**	**P–R**
S–T	**U–V**	**W–Z**

LANGUAGE MINI-LESSON

Sometimes a sentence has two subjects. When a sentence has more than one subject, the subject is called a **compound subject**. If the compound subjects are joined by *and*, the verb should be plural. If the subjects are joined by the words *or* or *nor*, the verb should agree with the part closest to *or* or *nor*.

Example 1: Neither the dogs nor Tommy (1) **is** (singular) here**.**

Example 2: Louisa or her cousins (more than 1) **are** (plural) going to the store**.**

Directions: Circle the correct form of the verb in each sentence below.

1. Neither law schools nor medical schools [*was, were*] accepting women in the past.

2. A high school girl or one of her female friends [*was, were*] treated differently than boys before Title IX.

3. Neither a high school girl nor her female friends [*was, were*] getting equal treatment from schools.

4. Now, neither volleyball nor any other female sport [*is, are*] treated as inferior.

5. Before Title IX men's and women's locker rooms and training facilities [*was, were*] not of equal quality.

6. After Title IX men and women [*is, are*] treated equally.

7. Medical and law schools [*is, are*] accepting women.

8. Neither high school nor college girls [*is, are*] participating in unequal programs.

9. Girls and women [*is, are*] granted equal rights by Title IX.

10. Still, too few coaches or athletic directors [*is, are*] women.

ECHO READING

Directions: When you read, you should make breaks, and sometimes pauses, between groups of words. As your teacher reads each phrase, repeat aloud what is read and put a slash or line after that phrase. Then read the whole sentence aloud as a class. Do the first paragraph together as a class, and then do the second one on your own. The first sentence has been marked for you.

The education system / did not adjust easily / to the law. / Leaders argued in court that sports programs were separate from the educational programs. However, the court ruled that school sports also serve educational goals. Some girls and women won court cases against schools that failed to offer the same opportunities. As schools lost those cases, others decided to change their programs.

Before Title IX high schools did not offer many sports programs for girls. Most girls could not participate in sports like soccer, golf, swimming, volleyball or tennis. If they did have basketball or softball teams, their seasons lasted only for a few games. Although boys traveled in buses, parents usually drove the girls in vans. Often girls had to pay for equipment and make their own uniforms.

What's Happening

IN THE USA?

BY LAWRENCE GABLE
© 2014 What's Happening Publications

SUBJECT: SPORTS, ARTS and SELF-EXPRESSION

Title IX Has Brought Changes for Women

1   The late 1960s and early 1970s were a time of change in the U.S. Americans protested to end the war in Vietnam. They also fought for equal rights for minorities and women. In 1972 a law required schools and universities to give equal opportunities to girls and women. Since then that law, Title IX, has caused remarkable changes.

2   In those days women did not have the same opportunities as men. Medical schools and law schools, for example, limited the number of women that they accepted. Title IX affected schools that got money from the U.S. government. It forced them to give girls and women equal rights in all programs, including sports.

3   The education system did not adjust easily to the law. Leaders argued in court that sports programs were separate from the educational programs. However, the court ruled that school sports also serve educational goals. Some girls and women won court cases against schools that failed to offer the same opportunities. As schools lost those cases, others decided to change their programs.

4   Before Title IX high schools did not offer many sports programs for girls. Most girls could not participate in sports like soccer, golf, swimming, volleyball or tennis. If they did have basketball or softball teams, their seasons lasted only for a few games. Although boys traveled in buses, parents usually drove the girls in vans. Often girls had to pay for equipment and make their own uniforms.

5   The number of high school girls who participate in sports has grown tremendously. During the 1972–73 school year 294,015 girls participated sports. That number has risen to more than three million.

6   Participation in college sports has grown too. Women compete against other colleges and play for teams on campus. In 1972–73 fewer than 30,000 college women participated in sports. Now more than six times that many participate.

7   Schools have learned ways to provide "equal athletic opportunity." Men and women must have equal access to fields, gyms and training rooms, for example. Locker rooms must be the same size and quality. Schools must offer awards for all athletes, and cheerleaders and bands must support both men's and women's teams. The percentage of female athletes must match the percentage of females in the student body.

8   Title IX has helped women in education, not just sports. Now more than five times more women go to medical school, and seven times more attend law school. Today women earn more than half of all college degrees. Women work in professions that mostly only men worked in.

9   Before Title IX people felt that women were not interested in professions or athletics. It turns out that women were interested, and just needed the opportunities. Beyond athletic programs in schools, women are enjoying success in professional sports too. At the 2012 Olympic Games the American team had more women than men for the first time ever.

10   At schools there are still problems in women's sports. There are too few coaches and athletic directors at schools who are women. Scholarships still go primarily only to White athletes. However, Americans can celebrate what Title IX has done. Opportunities exist, and women and girls are participating and succeeding.

QUICK READ/DRAW AND WRITE

Directions: First Reading—As you do your first reading of the article, your teacher will time you for one minute. When time is called, write the number of the paragraph where you stopped. **Paragraph #** _____

In the box below, draw a picture summarizing what you read.

Second Reading—As you do your second reading of the article, your teacher will time you for one minute. When time is called, write the number of the paragraph where you stopped. **Paragraph #** _____

Directions: Now continue reading the rest of the article. Below, write five important words that will help you remember the information from the article.

_____   _____   _____   _____   _____

CLOSE READING ANNOTATION

<u>Third Reading</u>—As you reread each paragraph in the article closely, answer the questions by annotating the text. Each numbered question corresponds to a paragraph in the article where the answer can be found. Write your brief answers in the space below each question.

1. What were some of the changes taking place in the United States during the 1960s and 1970s?

_____

2. What were some of the opportunities denied to women?

_____

3. Why did the education system have trouble adjusting to Title IX?

_____

4. How were opportunities to play sports different for girls and boys?

_____

5. How did this law affect high school sports?

_____

6. What has happened with women's participation in college sports?

_____

7. What is the meaning of "equal athletic opportunity"?

_____

8. What has been the effect on educational opportunities for women?

_____

9. How did the 2012 Olympics reflect the results of Title IX?

_____

10. What are some problems that still exist in spite of Title IX?

_____

GRAMMAR GAMES

Directions: Reread the two paragraphs below. Words have been left out from the sentences. Think about the information from the article you have read and fill in words that make sense. The part of speech of each missing word is provided.

Before Title IX high schools did not offer many sports

_____ for girls. Most girls could not _____ in sports like
(1. plural noun)   (2. verb)

soccer, golf, swimming, volleyball _____ tennis. If _____
(3. conjunction)   (4. pronoun)

did have basketball or softball teams, their _____ lasted only for
(5. plural noun)

a few games. Although _____ traveled in buses, parents usually
(6. plural noun)

drove the girls _____ vans. Often girls had to pay for equipment
(7. preposition)

and _____ their own uniforms.
(8. verb)

The _____ of high school girls who participate in sports
(9. noun)

has grown _____. During the 1972–73 school year 294,015
(10. adverb)

_____ in sports. That _____ has grown to more than
(11. verb)   (12. noun)

three million.

Participation in college sports has grown _____. Women
(13. adverb)

_____ aganst each other and play for _____ on
(14. verb)   (15. plural noun)

campus.

CLOSE READING STRUCTURE

Directions: Understanding the structure of a text is important for two reasons. First, understanding the structure of a selection can help you remember the main idea and important details. Second, most academic writing you will encounter uses text structures to organize ideas.

1. Writers often include a statement in the **introduction** that catches the reader's attention. Then, the writer tells what the article will be about. On the space provided, copy the last sentence of the introduction of this article.

   _____

   _____

2. On the space below, copy the sentence that best states what the author's **claim, main idea,** or **thesis** is for this article.

   _____

   _____

3. On the space below, copy the sentence that shows where the author introduces the other side's **opinions,** or **opposing claims.**

   _____

   _____

4. Near the end of an article, a writer often restates the claim and summarizes the evidence. This is called the **conclusion.** On the space below, copy the sentence that best shows where the conclusion to the article begins.

   _____

   _____

IS THAT A FACT?

Directions: Read the definitions of a fact and an inference below. Then read the paragraphs that follow. At the bottom of the page, write an F on the blank if the sentence is a fact. Write an I if the sentence is an inference. Use the following definitions:

Fact—a statement that can be proven true from the paragraph

Inference—a guess as to what MIGHT be true, based on what you have read and what you already know about the subject

Title IX has helped women in education, not just sports. Now more than five times more women go to medical school, and seven times more attend law school. Today women earn more than half of all college degrees. Women work in professions that mostly only men worked in.

Before Title IX people felt that women were not interested in professions or athletics. It turns out that women were interested and just needed the opportunities. At the 2012 Olympic Games the American team had more women than men for the first time ever.

_____ **1.** There is a lot more to Title IX than just sports.

_____ **2.** Before Title IX many women did not try to go to medical or law school.

_____ **3.** Today women earn more college degrees than men.

_____ **4.** Women are now encouraged and supported to become athletes.

_____ **5.** Title IX has been a very productive and positive law.

_____ **6.** If Title IX had not been enacted, women would not be able to experience equality in education and sports.

SUMMARIZING ABCs

Directions: Now that you've read the article on Title IX, see how many words you can write about women, equal rights, and sports in the boxes below.

A–C	D–F	G–I
J–L	**M–O**	**P–R**
S–T	**U–V**	**W–Z**

Name _____ Date _____

REACTION GUIDE

Directions: Now that you have read and studied information about "Title IX Has Brought Changes for Women," reread the statements below, which you responded to before reading the article. Then think about how the author might respond to these statements. If you think the author would agree, put a checkmark on the line before the number. If you think the author would disagree, put an X on the line. Then below the statement, copy the words, phrases, or sentences from the article that provide evidence of the views stated by the author. Also note if there is no evidence to support the statement.

_____ **1.** Equal rights for women is a fairly new idea.

Evidence: _____

_____

_____

_____ **2.** A lot of people think that women are not as qualified as men to do certain jobs.

Evidence: _____

_____

_____

_____ **3.** Women and girls are usually not interested in playing sports.

Evidence: _____

_____

_____

SENTENCE TRANSITIONS

An informational essay answers questions and provides information. Writers use transitional phrases to link ideas. Some transitional words and phrases include *to show, to prove, because, to explain, to verify, due to, instead of, furthermore, as a result of,* and *in order to.*

Directions: Complete the following sentences using the phrases given.

Example: Title IX became a national law. Title IX became a national law *as a result of women wanting equal access to sports programs*.

1. Title IX was instituted *in order to*

_____

2. The courts had to rule on school sports *due to*

_____

3. Schools had to give "equal athletic opportunity" *as a result* of

_____

4. In the 2012 Olympics more women participated than men *because of*

_____

5. You only need to cite college graduation statistics *to prove*

_____

PICKING UP PUNCTUATION

Semicolons (;) are used to separate parts of sentences. **Colons (:)** show that a list follows, and are also used in greetings in business letters. Read the rules below to learn how to use them.

Semicolons: Use a semicolon to join the parts of a compound sentence when you don't use *and, but, or,* or *nor*. Remember that a compound sentence has two complete sentences in it. **Example**—Participation in women's sports has grown; women compete against each other in many sports.

You can also use semicolons to separate parts of a list if the things being listed use commas. **Example**—Now there are professional women's sports teams in cities including Los Angeles, California; New York, New York; and Chicago, Illinois.

Colons: Use a colon to introduce a list of things. **Example**—Women are now allowed to compete in these sports: swimming, rowing, golf, and soccer.

Use a colon after the formal greeting in a business letter or a letter of complaint. **Example**—Dear Principal Johnson:

Use a colon between the hours and minutes when showing time. **Example**—1:30 p.m.

Directions: Place the correct semicolons and colons in these sentences.

1. In 1972 a law required universities to give equal opportunities to girls and women it has resulted in remarkable changes.

2. Dear Senator

3. After Title IX the number of women playing on the school's teams were soccer, 25 basketball, 16 softball, 29 and tennis, 15.

4. Because of Title IX, more women now go to these kinds of schools law, medical, and engineering.

5. It's 730 in the morning.

ANALYZING A PROMPT

Directions: Read the writing prompt in the box below. Then follow the directions to learn how to analyze and answer it.

> You are a vice principal in charge of a school sports program. A group of parents is circulating a petition saying that the school should not implement Title IX. They argue that it holds back the male athletes and gives girls an unfair advantage in school overall. Your principal has asked you to prepare a report that points out how Title IX has helped advance not only girls, but boys as well. Explain the benefits of Title IX and describe how this law has been productive for all people. Use information from the article to help make your point.

1. A writing prompt begins with some background information known as the **set up.** Underline the sentences that set up this assignment.

2. Use the following **R.A.F.T.** technique to finish analyzing the prompt.

Role: What are you supposed to be to answer it? A student? A politician?

Write what you are here: _____

Audience: To whom are you writing? A friend? A particular group?

Write who it is here: _____

Format: Check to see what type of writing you are doing. Is it an essay, a letter, a speech, a story, a description, an editorial, or a report?

Write what it is here: _____

Task: Another sentence in the prompt will tell you what you must do, or your "task." Question words like **why, how,** or **what** may tell the task.

If the question word is **why,** you will *give the reasons* that something is done.

If the question word is **how,** you will *explain the way* that something is done.

If the question word is **what,** you will *identify the thing* that is done.

Below, copy the sentence or question that describes your task.

_____

_____

_____

WHAT'S YOUR POINT?

When writing an essay it is important to have a strong **claim**. A claim, or **thesis statement,** states the main point the writer wants to get across. Once the thesis is introduced, the body of the essay should support that thesis with key points that provide evidence.

The information presented in the article "Title IX Has Brought Changes for Women" explains the progress that has been made for women's equality in sports and in education. In particular, it shows that the increased success of women in college and professional sports is a sign of the law's success.

Directions: Which of these sentences provides the best **claim** for an essay on this topic? Circle the letter of your choice.

a. Women are as qualified as men when it comes to sports.

b. The implementation of Title IX has been met with many challenges.

c. Title IX is a law that provides women with equal opportunities to those of men, and it has allowed women to be successful in many areas including education and sports.

In the space below, explain what is weak or wrong about the other two sentences.

1. _____

_____

_____

2. _____

_____

_____

ASSESSMENT

1. Support the claim that schools and universities treated women and men unequally before Title IX. Look back through the article. Then on the space below, cite three pieces of evidence from the article to support this claim.

a. _____

_____

b. _____

_____

c. _____

_____

2. Circle the letters of the two conclusions below that are best supported by evidence from the article.

a. Before Title IX women participated in as many sports as men.

b. Title IX has helped women in other areas besides sports.

c. Everyone thought Title IX was a fair thing for women and men.

d. Title IX was the biggest change to happen in the 1960s and 1970s.

e. Title IX survived because sports are seen as part of an educational program.

3. Circle the letter of the paragraph that indicates that some schools changed their programs because they did not want to challenge Title IX in court.

a. paragraph 1

b. paragraph 2

c. paragraph 3

d. paragraph 4

Unit 4: Sports, Arts, and Self-Expression

4. What evidence does the author include to support the idea that Title IX has not solved all the problems of inequality between men and women? Below, cite two pieces of evidence from the article.

a. _____

_____

b. _____

_____

5. A student has made a plan for a research report. Read the plan and the directions that follow.

Research Report Plan

Topic: women's inequality in America

Audience: high school students

Research Question: In what areas do women in America still have

opportunities unequal to those of men?

The student needs to find a credible, or trustworthy, source with relevant, or recent, information. Circle the letter of the source below that would **most likely** have credible and recent information.

a. www.womenrule.com—This site highlights the history of women who have overcome hardships throughout history—women who have become leaders, scientists, and business executives.

b. www.whathappenedtotitleix.com—Title IX made a big difference in making Americans aware that women deserved equal treatment in sports and education. But this nation still struggles with inequality between the sexes in many professions.

c. www.womenandsports.com—The role and participation of women in sports have grown tremendously since the 1970s. This site shows how women today are becoming major players in our favorite sports.

Name _____ Date _____

ANTICIPATION GUIDE

Directions: Before you read the article "Museum Looks for Art's Rightful Owner," read the statements below. If you agree with a statement, put a checkmark on the line next to it. If you disagree, put an X on the line.

_____ **1.** People who dig up old artwork should be able to keep it.

_____ **2.** It's okay to buy art that was stolen hundreds of years ago.

_____ **3.** Very rare art should remain in the country where it was created.

Once you have responded to the statements above, write in the section below why you agree or disagree with each statement.

1. _____

_____

2. _____

_____

3. _____

In the box below, draw a picture of what you think this article is about.

PREDICTING ABCs

Directions: The article you are going to read is about returning stolen art. See how many boxes you can fill in below with words relating to this topic. For example, put the word *painting* in the P–R box. Put at least one word in every box, and then try to write a word for every letter.

A–C	D–F	G–I

J–L	M–O	P–R

S–T	U–V	W–Z

TIME MY READ #1

Directions: With a partner, see how many words you can read correctly in 45 seconds. As you read, your partner will put an X through any word read incorrectly on his or her copy. When you are finished, trade your books or papers, and let your partner read while you keep score. Count the total number of words you read correctly. Write this score at the bottom of your page.

restore display protect provenance conquer prohibit Nazi looter	8
excavate allies civilization illegal threaten exchange preserve heritage	16
complicated museum archeological insist recognize protest expand claim	24
restore display protect provenance conquer prohibit Nazi looter	32
excavate allies civilization illegal threaten exchange preserve heritage	40
complicated museum archeological insist recognize protest expand claim	48
restore display protect provenance conquer prohibit Nazi looter	56
excavate allies civilization illegal threaten exchange preserve heritage	64
complicated museum archeological insist recognize protest expand claim	72
restore display protect provenance conquer prohibit Nazi looter	80

Number of words read correctly _____

ECHO READING

Directions: When you read, you should make breaks, and sometimes pauses, between groups of words. As your teacher reads each phrase, repeat aloud what is read and put a slash or line after that phrase. Then read the whole sentence aloud as a class. Do the first paragraph together as a class, and then do the second one on your own. The first sentence has been marked for you.

Italy made agreements / in 2006 / with several American museums. / The Metropolitan Museum of Art in New York and Boston's Museum of Fine Arts returned some art. In exchange Italy promised to loan other pieces in the future. Italy also wanted 52 pieces back from the Getty. At first the museum agreed to return 26 items. They included statues, figurines and pottery.

The Getty wanted to keep two especially important pieces. "Aphrodite" is a limestone statue from the fifth century B.C. Italy claimed that this statue was excavated illegally. In 2007 the museum agreed to return it in 2010. The "Getty Bronze" is a life-sized statue of an athlete. Before the museum bought it, Italian courts had said that it did not belong to Italy. However, in 2010 an Italian court demanded the statue's return.

What's Happening
IN CALIFORNIA ?

BY LAWRENCE GABLE
© 2014 What's Happening Publications

SUBJECT: SPORTS, ARTS and SELF-EXPRESSION

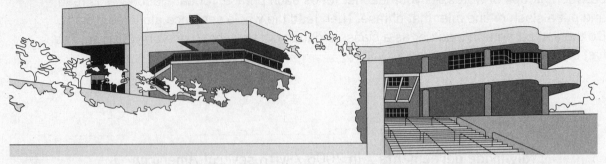

Museum Looks for Art's Rightful Owner

1   Running an art museum is complicated. It involves finding, buying, displaying, protecting and restoring art. It also involves recognizing provenance, the rightful ownership of works of art. The J. Paul Getty Museum in Los Angeles has had problems with that in recent years. Italy wants the museum to return some pieces.

2   Proving provenance is important for several reasons. Before a museum pays millions for a piece, it wants proof that it is not fake. It also does not want to buy art that has been stolen.

3   Wars are a source of stolen art. In World War II, for example, the Nazi government in Germany stole art from Jews and nations it conquered. Then the victorious Allies stole a million pieces from Germany. Sixty years later pieces are still being returned to their rightful owners.

4   The United Nations prohibits the trade of stolen art. In 1970 it defined art as "cultural property." Now 191 countries prohibit and prevent the illegal trade and ownership of art. Art experts believe that it helps. In the Iraq War, for example, looters stole 15,000 objects from the Iraq Museum in 2003. Several countries, including the U.S., returned 4,000 pieces in the years immediately after that.

5   It is hard to prove the provenance of ancient art. Many museums have pieces from ancient Egyptian, Greek, and Roman civilizations. In fact, thieves still excavate pieces from tombs and archaeological sites. Museums try to be careful. Even so, countries like Italy protest and want pieces back.

6   Italy made agreements in 2006 with several American museums. The Metropolitan Museum of Art in New York and Boston's Museum of Fine Arts returned some art. In exchange Italy promised to loan other pieces in the future. Italy also wanted 52 pieces back from the Getty. At first the museum agreed to return 26 items. They included statues, figurines and pottery.

7   The Getty wanted to keep two especially important pieces. "Aphrodite" is a limestone statue from the fifth century B.C. Italy claimed that this statue was excavated illegally. In 2007 the museum agreed to return it in 2010. The "Getty Bronze" is a life-sized statue of an athlete. Before the museum bought it, Italian courts had said that it did not belong to Italy. However, in 2010 an Italian court demanded that statue's return.

8   The Getty Museum will continue to talk with Italy about this piece. It uses art to expand the cultural knowledge of visitors. It also tries to preserve the heritage of cultures that made the art. Like other great museums, it must decide whether that also means returning even more pieces to where they came from.

GET A CONTEXT CLUE

Directions: Below are sentences from "Museum Looks for Art's Rightful Owner." First, read the sentence. Then, look back in the article and reread the paragraph in which the sentence is found. Circle the best answer to each question.

"It also involves recognizing *provenance*, the rightful ownership of works of art."

1. The word *provenance* means

    A. who sells art
    B. the history of ownership
    C. who steals art
    D. who can buy art

"The United Nations *prohibits* the trade of stolen art."

2. The term *prohibits* means

    A. likes
    B. doesn't allow
    C. allows
    D. helps

"In fact, thieves still *excavate* pieces from tombs and archaeological sites."

3. The word *excavate* means

    A. buy
    B. find
    C. dig up
    D. clean

"In *exchange* Italy promised to loan other pieces in the future."

4. The term *exchange* means

    A. trust
    B. trade
    C. regret
    D. time

"Italy claimed this statue was excavated *illegally*."

5. The word *illegally* means

    A. in a quick way
    B. in a smooth manner
    C. with ownership rights respected
    D. not in accordance with the law

"It also tries to *preserve* the heritage of cultures that made the art."

6. The word *preserve* means

    A. to keep safe
    B. to sell
    C. to destroy
    D. to buy

WORD MAP

Directions: Follow the directions to map the word in the box below.

illegal

List two more words that mean the same.

List two more examples of an illegal action.

List two more words that mean the opposite.

unlawful

murder

legal

Draw a picture below to help you remember the meaning.

Write a definition IN YOUR OWN WORDS.

LOOK WHO'S TALKING

Directions: Below are sentences that relate to "Museum Looks for Art's Rightful Owner." Look back in the article and reread the paragraph in which you find the reference. Circle the best answer to each question.

1. **In the last sentence of paragraph 2, the word *it* refers to**

   A. the art
   B. the museum
   C. Italy
   D. Los Angeles

2. **In the fourth sentence of paragraph 4, the pronoun *it* refers to**

   A. the art objects
   B. the prohibition of trade
   C. the selling of the art
   D. the victorious Allies

3. **In the first sentence of paragraph 5, the word *it* refers to**

   A. proving who owns the art
   B. excavating the tombs
   C. museums being careful
   D. protesting from Italy

4. **In the last sentence of paragraph 6, the word *they* refers to**

   A. the 26 items
   B. who stole the pieces
   C. the people of Italy
   D. the Getty Museum

5. **In paragraph 7, in the second-to-last sentence, the word *it* refers to**

   A. the Getty Museum
   B. the excavation
   C. the "Getty Bronze"
   D. the loaning of pieces in the future

6. **In the first sentence in paragraph 8, *this* refers to**

   A. the "Getty Bronze"
   B. the country of Italy
   C. the other great museums
   D. "Aphrodite"

HOW'S IT ORGANIZED?

This article is organized as a problem that needs solving.

Directions: Answer these questions in the spaces at the bottom.

1. Why is provenance a problem for museums?

2. Who has this problem?

3. What has been a major cause of this problem?

4. What has the United Nations said about the problem?

5. Why is Italy involved in this problem?

6. What solutions have been tried?

7. What results have come from these solutions?

8. What problems still need to be solved?

Answers:

1.	
2.	
3.	
4.	
5.	
6.	
7.	
8.	

*On a separate sheet of paper write a summary of what your notes say about the problems with stolen works of art.

IS THAT A FACT?

Directions: Read the definitions of a fact and an inference below. Then read the paragraph that follows. At the bottom of the page, write an F on the blank if the sentence is a fact. Write an I if the sentence is an inference. Use the following definitions:

Fact—a statement that can be proven true from the paragraph.

Inference—a guess as to what MIGHT be true, based on what you have read and what you already know about the subject.

The Getty will continue to talk with Italy about this piece. It uses art to expand the cultural knowledge of visitors. It also tries to preserve the heritage of cultures that made the art. Like other great museums, it must decide whether that also means returning even more pieces to where they came from.

_____ **1.** Museums try to expand their visitors' cultural knowledge through art.

_____ **2.** The Getty is concerned about Italy's wishes.

_____ **3.** The Getty Museum may have to return other pieces to other countries.

_____ **4.** The Getty would like to keep any pieces that it thinks aren't stolen.

_____ **5.** Preserving a country's heritage and culture is important.

MAKE A SPACE

Directions: Below are sentences that are missing punctuation and capitalization. First draw slash marks (/) between the words. Then rewrite each sentence in the space below it by filling in the missing punctuation and capitalization.

Example:

runninganartmuseumiscomplicated

Running an art museum is complicated.

1. theunitednationsprohibitsthetradeofstolenart

_____

_____

2. themuseuminsiststhatitneverknowinglyboughtstolenpieces

_____

_____

3. warsareasourceofstolenart

_____

_____

4. infactthievesstillexcavatepiecesfromtombsandarchaeologicalsites

_____

_____

_____

TIME MY READ #2

Directions: With a partner, see how many words you can read correctly in 45 seconds. As you read, your partner will put an X through any word read incorrectly on his or her copy. When you are finished, trade your books or papers, and let your partner read while you keep score. Count the total number of words you read correctly. Write this score at the bottom of your page

restore display protect provenance conquer prohibit Nazi looter	8
excavate allies civilization illegal threaten exchange preserve heritage	16
complicated museum archeological insist recognize protest expand claim	24
restore display protect provenance conquer prohibit Nazi looter	32
excavate allies civilization illegal threaten exchange preserve heritage	40
complicated museum archeological insist recognize protest expand claim	48
restore display protect provenance conquer prohibit Nazi looter	56
excavate allies civilization illegal threaten exchange preserve heritage	64
complicated museum archeological insist recognize protest expand claim	72
restore display protect provenance conquer prohibit Nazi looter	80

Number of words read correctly _____

Is the score higher than it was in Time My Read #1? _____

Name _____ Date _____

WORD PARTS

Directions: A **suffix** is added to the end of a base word to change how it's used in a sentence. Look at the sentence below.

It also involves recognizing the rightful **ownership** of works of art.

In the word *ownership, owner* is the base word. The suffix *–ship* means "the state or condition of something." *Ownership* is the state of being the owner of something. Write a definition for each word below. Try not to use the base word in the definition. If you don't know the base word, look it up in a dictionary or ask a partner.

1. friendship—_____

2. membership—_____

3. dictatorship—_____

4. citizenship—_____

5. companionship—_____

6. scholarship—_____

7. championship—_____

8. marksmanship—_____

9. leadership—_____

10. mentorship—_____

Directions: Draw pictures to show the meanings of two of the words.

Unit 4: Sports, Arts, and Self-Expression

SUMMARIZING ABCs

Directions: Now that you've read the article on museums returning stolen art, see how many words you can write about this subject in the boxes below.

A–C	D–F	G–I
J–L	**M–O**	**P–R**
S–T	**U–V**	**W–Z**

SENTENCE SUMMARIES

Directions: Below are four key words or phrases from the article "Museum Looks for Art's Rightful Owner." Your job is to summarize, or restate, what you've learned in this article by using these four words or phrases in two sentences. Then, as a challenge, try to use all four words or phrases in one sentence to summarize the article.

Key Words or Phrases

J. Paul Getty Museum   Italy

stolen art   United Nations

Sentence Summaries:

1. _____

_____

2. _____

_____

Challenge Summary (all four words or phrases in one sentence!):

1. _____

_____

REACTION GUIDE

Directions: Now that you have read and studied information about "Museum Looks for Art's Rightful Owner," reread the statements below, which you responded to before reading the article. Then think about how the author might respond to these statements. If you think the author would agree, put a checkmark on the line before the number. If you think the author would disagree, put an X on the line. Then below the statement, copy the words, phrases, or sentences from the article that provide evidence of the views stated by the author. Also note if there is no evidence to support the statement.

_____ **1.** People who dig up old artwork should be able to keep it.

Evidence: _____

_____

_____

_____ **2.** It's okay to buy art that was stolen hundreds of years ago.

Evidence: _____

_____

_____

_____ **3.** Very rare art should remain in the country where it was created.

Evidence: _____

_____

_____

TAKE A STAND

Directions: People often have differing feelings or opinions about an issue. When they discuss or argue their opposing views, they are taking part in a debate. A good persuasive argument is based on a claim that is supported by

Facts—statements that can be proven true

Statistics—numerical data gotten through research

Examples—instances that support an opinion

You and a partner are going to debate two of your other classmates. The topic you are going to debate is the following:

Very rare art should stay in the country where it was created.

Decide with the other pair who will agree and who will disagree with this statement. Then answer these questions in order to win your debate.

1. What are your two strongest points to persuade the other side? (You can do Internet research to include facts, statistics, and examples.)

   A. _____

   B. _____

2. What might the other side say to argue against point A?

   _____

   _____

3. What might the other side say to argue against point B?

   _____

   _____

4. What will you say to prove the other side's arguments are wrong?

   _____

   _____

   _____

ASSESSMENT

Comprehension: Answer the questions about the following passage.

Running an art museum is complicated. It involves recognizing provenance, the rightful ownership of works of art. Proving provenance is important for several reasons. Before a museum pays millions of dollars for a piece, it wants proof that it is not a fake. It also does not want to buy art that has been stolen. Wars are a source of stolen art. In World War II, for example, the Nazi government in Germany stole art from the Jews and nations it conquered. Then the victorious Allies stole millions of pieces from Germany. Sixty years later, pieces are still being returned to their rightful owners.

1. How would you define the word *provenance*?

_____

_____

2. Why do you think countries steal art during wars?

_____

_____

3. What was the author's purpose for writing this article?

_____

_____

Fluency: The words in the two sentences below are all connected. The sentences are also missing punctuation and capitalization. Draw slash marks (/) between the words. Then rewrite sentence by filling in the punctuation and capitalization.

1. atfirstthemuseumagreedtoreturntwentysixstolenpieces

_____

2. inexchangeitalyhaspromisedtostartloaningotherpiecesinthefuture

_____

_____

Fluency: Read the three sentences below. Imagine where you would pause within each sentence as you read it aloud. Draw a slash (/) mark between the phrases where you would pause. The first slash is done.

3. Many museums / have pieces from ancient civilizations.

4. Before the museum bought it, Italian courts had said that it did not belong to Italy.

5. In fact, thieves still excavate pieces from tombs and archaeological sites.

Vocabulary: Based on what you have learned in this lesson, match the following words with their definitions. Write the letter of the definition on the blank in front of the word it defines.

1. _____ excavate   **A.** to keep safe

2. _____ dictatorship   **B.** being part of a group

3. _____ illegal   **C.** to trade

4. _____ provenance   **D.** skill in shooting a gun

5. _____ mentorship   **E.** unlawful

6. _____ exchange   **F.** to dig something out of the ground

7. _____ marksmanship   **G.** the history of ownership

8. _____ prohibit   **H.** being a teacher of someone

9. _____ preserve   **I.** to not allow

10. _____ membership   **J.** a government ruled by one person

Name _____ Date _____

ANTICIPATION GUIDE

Directions: Before you read the article "Once Upon a Time There Were Two Brothers . . . ," read the statements below. If you agree with a statement, put a check on the line next to it. If you disagree, put an X on the line.

_____ **1.** Fairy tales are a part of every country's culture.

_____ **2.** Children should read fairy tales because the evil characters always get punished.

_____ **3.** Typically, children's stories, such as fairy tales, teach important lessons.

Once you have read and responded to the statements above, write in the section below why you agree or disagree with each statement.

1. _____

_____

2. _____

_____

3. _____

_____

In the box below, draw a picture of what you think this article is about.

WORDSTORM

Directions: It's good to know more than just the dictionary definition of a word. Completing a wordstorm lets you write down information to help you understand what a word means, how it's related to other words, and how to use it in different ways.

What is the compound word?

fairy tale

Here is the sentence from the text in which the compound word is used:

"For two hundred years Grimms' Fairy Tales have captured the

imaginations of children around the world."

What are some other words or phrases that mean the same thing?

_____

What are three things you know about fairy tales?

1. _____ 2. _____ 3. _____

Name three people other than teachers who would likely use this word.

1. _____ 2. _____ 3. _____

Draw a picture below that reminds you of the compound word *fairy tale*.

LANGUAGE MINI-LESSON

Remember that a **sentence** is a group of words that states a complete thought. The **subject** of a sentence is all the words that tell who or what did the action. Subjects usually come at the beginning of a sentence. The subject is underlined in the following sentence: <u>The Brothers Grimm</u> published stories in Germany.

Sometimes the subject does not come before the verb. In **inverted sentences,** the subject comes after the verb.

Questions: In most questions, the subject comes after the verb or between the parts of the verb phrase.

Do you think <u>the tales</u> are scary?

Why were <u>these brothers</u> writing the stories?

Sentences Beginning with Here or There: In some sentences starting with *here* or *there,* the subject comes after the verb.

Example: Here comes <u>the scariest part of the story</u>.

There goes <u>Snow White</u>.

Other Inverted Sentences: There are other reasons why a sentence might be inverted. Sometimes it is for effect, sometimes it is when indicating who is speaking, and sometimes it is when a sentence starts with an adverb.

Example: Into the woods ran <u>Snow White</u>.

Example: "I must find her," said <u>the Prince</u>.

Example: Never was <u>a love</u> more true.

Commands: In a command, the subject is not included in the sentence at all, but it is usually *you.*

Read this folk tale. (The meaning is "<u>you</u> read this folk tale.")

Directions: Write the subject of each sentence on the blanks that follow.

1. Why did the Brothers Grimm love folk tales? _____

2. Please sit and listen to their stories. _____

3. There are many castles along the "Fairy Tale Road." _____

4. From the small villages came people telling stories. _____

5. Here in this library are books of Grimm's Fairy Tales. _____

ECHO READING

Directions: When you read, you should make breaks, and sometimes pauses, between groups of words. As your teacher reads each phrase, repeat aloud what was read and put a slash or line after that phrase. Then read the whole sentence aloud as a class. Do the first paragraph together as a class, and then do the second on your own. The first sentence has been marked for you.

The Brothers Grimm / became fascinated / with stories from the past / about common people. / They felt that such stories had educational value because they reflected the most basic values of a culture. As a result, the Grimms began collecting oral and written folk tales. Many of them were hundreds of years old. Since their tales came from different regions and lands, often they ended up with multiple versions of the same tale. In that case they chose one version over the others because they felt it expressed more about a culture.

Their first volume included 86 tales, and the second volume in 1815 held another 70. The popularity of their collection of tales surprised them. The Brothers Grimm had expected the tales to be interesting to scholars, not children. As their collection became popular, the Grimms began to edit their tales.

What's Happening

IN THE WORLD?

BY LAWRENCE GABLE
© 2014 *What's Happening Publications*

SUBJECT: *SPORTS, ARTS and SELF-EXPRESSION*

Once Upon a Time There Were Two Brothers ...

1 In 1812 two brothers in Germany, Jacob and Wilhelm Grimm, gave the world a great gift. They published stories that they had collected from Germany and other lands. The book was called "Children's and Household Tales." The first volume appeared on December 20, 1812. In 2013 Germany honored the Brothers Grimm all year long.

2 The brothers were born in 1785 and 1786. As university students they studied old written works to learn about cultures. They published articles and books on German literature from the Middle Ages.

3 The Brothers Grimm liked stories from the past about common people. They felt that such stories taught about the most basic values of a culture. As a result, the Grimms began collecting oral and written folk tales. Many of them were hundreds of years old. Their tales came from different regions and lands, so often they ended up with multiple versions of the same tale.

4 Their first volume included 86 tales, and the second volume in 1815 held another 70. The popularity of their tales surprised them. The Brothers Grimm had expected the tales to be interesting to scholars, not children. As their collection became popular, the Grimms began to edit their tales.

5 Over the years they published seven different editions of the tales. Those first tales are unlike those in the final edition from 1857. Most of the originals are shorter because they have little description. Their emphasis is on action and solving a conflict. The Brothers Grimm added details, but removed violent or sexy scenes that appealed only to adults.

6 Even after editing, the tales included some violence. For example, Snow White's envious stepmother dies when she has to dance in red-hot iron shoes at the wedding. At the end of "Cinderella" doves peck the stepsisters' eyes out.

7 Scholars have studied the fairy tales' appeal. They feel that children find security in seeing a world that punishes evil people. In addition, children appreciate that common people who are kind achieve happiness.

8 In Germany there is a "Fairy Tale Road." It goes from the Grimms' hometown of Hanau north to Bremen. Along the 370-mile route are fifty towns and cities related to the fairy tales. Visitors can see statues of characters, walk through forests and visit castles. In 2013 a number of places held exhibits, festivals, parades and puppet shows. In Bremen a statue honors the four clever animals that were the Bremen Town Musicians.

9 Jacob and Wilhelm Grimm did more than publish those famous fairy tales. They also collected folk music, and published collections of Irish and Scandinavian folk tales. They inspired other European scholars to collect tales too. In 1838 they also began writing a German dictionary. Sixteen years later they published the first few volumes. Twentieth century scholars finished the dictionary in 1961.

10 Germany celebrated the Brothers Grimm for good reason. Except for the Bible, their tales are the best-selling book in the German language. Beyond that, their stories appear in 160 languages and dialects. Those two scholars produced something far greater than they ever expected. For 200 years Grimms' Fairy Tales have captured the imaginations of children around the world.

QUICK READ/DRAW AND WRITE

Directions: <u>First Reading</u>—As you do your first reading of the article, your teacher will time you for one minute. When time is called, write the number of the paragraph where you stopped. **Paragraph # _____**

In the box below, draw a picture summarizing what you read.

<u>Second Reading</u>—As you do your second reading of the article, your teacher will time you for one minute. When time is called, write the number of the paragraph where you stopped. **Paragraph # _____**

Directions: Now continue reading the rest of the article. Below, write five important words that will help you remember the information from the article.

_____ _____ _____ _____ _____

CLOSE READING ANNOTATION

Third Reading—As you reread each paragraph in the article closely, answer the questions by annotating the text. Each numbered question corresponds to a paragraph in the article where the answer can be found. Write your brief answers in the space below each question.

1. What was the gift that the Brothers Grimm left to the world?

_____

2. Why did the brothers study old written works?

_____

3. Why did the brothers become interested in stories about common people?

_____

4. How did people react to their stories?

_____

5. Why do you think the brothers started changing some of the stories?

_____

6./7. What do scholars think about the brothers' stories?

_____

8. How does Germany recognize the contributions of the brothers?

_____

9. What are some of the other achievements of the brothers?

_____

10. What has been the impact of the Brothers Grimm on the world?

_____

GRAMMAR GAMES

Directions: Reread the three paragraphs below. Words have been left out from the sentences. Think about the information from the article you have read and fill in words that make sense. The part of speech of each missing word is provided.

In 1812 two _____ in Germany, Jacob and Wilhelm Grimm,
      (1. plural noun)

gave the world a great gift. They published stories _____ had
      (2. pronoun)

collected from Germany and _____ lands. The _____
      (3. adjective)   (4. noun)

was called "Children's and Household Tales." The first volume

_____ on December 1812. In 2013 Germany honored the
   (5. verb)

Brothers _____ all year long.
      (6. proper noun)

The brothers were born in 1785 _____ 1786. As
      (7. conjunction)

university students they _____ old written works to learn
      (8. verb)

about cultures. _____ published articles on German literature
      (9. pronoun)

from the Middle Ages.

The Brothers Grimm liked stories from the past _____
      (10. preposition)

common people. They felt that such stories _____ the most
      (11. verb)

basic values of a culture. As a result, the Grimms _____
      (12. verb)

collecting oral and _____ folk tales.
      (13. adjective)

HOW'S IT ORGANIZED?

This article is organized as an informational text—a main idea is presented and then supported with specific details.

Directions: Answer these questions in the spaces below.

1. Who are the Brothers Grimm?

2. Where did their stories come from?

3. How many stories did they first publish?

4. How many editions did they end up publishing?

5. Why do the stories appeal to children?

6. What were some of the other publications of the brothers?

Answers:

1.	
2.	
3.	
4.	
5.	
6.	

The main idea of a selection reflects what the paragraph or sentences are about. Put an X on the space next to the sentence that best states the main idea.

_____ **1.** The stories of the Brothers Grimm have appealed to many children.

_____ **2.** Fairy tales are stories to which all children can relate.

_____ **3.** The Brothers Grimm have produced works of literature that have captivated people all over the world.

Explain why your choice best states the main or central idea.

_____

_____

IS THAT A FACT?

Directions: Read the definitions of a fact and an inference below. Then read the paragraphs that follow. At the bottom of the page, write an F on the blank if the sentence is a fact. Write an I if the sentence is an inference. Use the following definitions:

Fact—a statement that can be proven true from the paragraph

Inference—a guess as to what MIGHT be true, based on what you have read and what you already know about the subject

---

In 1812 two brothers in Germany, Jacob and Wilhelm Grimm, gave the world a great gift. They published stories that they had collected from Germany and other lands. The book was called "Children's and Household Tales." The first volume appeared on December 20, 1812. In 2013 Germany honored the Brothers Grimm all year long.

The Brothers Grimm liked stories from the past about common people. They felt that such stories taught about the most basic values of a culture. As a result, the Grimms began collecting oral and written folk tales. Many of them were hundreds of years old. Their tales came from different regions and lands, so often they ended up with multiple versions of the same tale.

_____ **1.** There is a lot of interest in children's fairy tales.

_____ **2.** Many of the stories were made up before 1812.

_____ **3.** The stories were often about common people.

_____ **4.** Many of the stories were told from generation to generation.

_____ **5.** Many of the stories that the brothers used were not from Germany.

_____ **6.** Sometimes the oldest stories are people's favorite because they have been around for such a long time.

TIC-TAC-TOE SUMMARIZING

When you **summarize** in writing, you present all the key points the author is trying to make.

Directions: Write four sentences to summarize the article about the Brothers Grimm. To help you, there are nine words or phrases in the Tic-Tac-Toe graphic organizer below. To write a sentence, you must use three words or phrases in a row. The row can be horizontal (—), vertical (I), or diagonal (/).

Germany	folk tales	scholars
literature	children	regions
collections	evil	imagination

1. _____

   _____

2. _____

   _____

3. _____

   _____

4. _____

   _____

REACTION GUIDE

Directions: Now that you have read and studied information about "Once Upon A Time There Were Two Brothers . . . ," reread the statements below, which you responded to before reading the article. Then think about how the author might respond to these statements. If you think the author would agree, put a checkmark on the line before the number. If you think the author would disagree, put an X on the line. Then below the statement, copy the words, phrases, or sentences from the article that provide evidence of the views stated by the author. Also note if there is no evidence to support the statement.

_____ **1.** Fairy tales are a part of every country's culture.

Evidence: _____

_____

_____

_____ **2.** Children should read fairy tales because the evil characters always get punished.

Evidence: _____

_____

_____

_____ **3.** Typically, children's stories, such as fairy tales, teach important lessons.

Evidence: _____

_____

_____

Name _____ Date _____

TAKE A STAND

Directions: People often have differing feelings or opinions about an issue. When they discuss or argue their opposing views, they are taking part in a debate. A good persuasive argument is based on a claim that is supported by

Facts—statements that can be proven true

Statistics—numerical data gotten through research

Examples—instances that support an opinion

You and a partner are going to debate two of your other classmates. The topic you are going to debate is the following:

Children should read fairy tales because they teach good morals.

Decide with the other pair who will agree and who will disagree with this statement. Then answer these questions in order to win your debate.

1. What are your two strongest points to persuade the other side? (You can do Internet research to include facts, statistics, and examples.)

   A. _____

   B. _____

2. What might the other side say to argue against point A?

   _____

   _____

3. What might the other side say to argue against point B?

   _____

   _____

4. What will you say to prove the other side's arguments are wrong?

   _____

   _____

   _____

WHAT'S THE COMBINATION?

Writing is more interesting when the writer joins, or combines, short sentences. Follow the directions below to learn different ways to combine two sentences.

What to do: You can join two sentences using the words *and, but, or, so, because,* or *nor,* which are called **conjunctions.** When the subject, or person or thing doing the action, is the same for both sentences, you can use it once instead of twice in the combined sentence. When the verb, or action being done, is the same, you can sometimes use that only once. Sometimes you can use other repeated words only once, too. In the example below, *mother* is the subject of both sentences and *loves* is the verb.

Example: My *mother* **loves** to cook. My *mother* **loves** to play softball. My *mother* **loves** to cook **and** play softball.

Directions: Combine these sentences using the method above. Use the word or words in parentheses to join the sentences. See how many repeated words you can use just once in each new sentence.

1. The Brothers Grimm liked to study. They also liked to write stories. (and)

_____

2. The brothers wrote stories. The brothers did not write stories for children. (but)

_____

3. The brothers' stories became very popular. The stories were published in many editions. (so)

_____

4. Their stories do not draw criticism. Their stories do not frighten children. (or)

_____

5. People all over the world can read the stories. They can visit Germany to see where the brothers lived. (and)

_____

6. The brothers published famous fairy tales. They also inspired many other scholars. More and more people are now reading their stories. (and) (so)

_____

ANALYZING A PROMPT

Directions: Read the writing prompt in the box below. Then follow the directions to learn how to analyze and answer it.

> You are a librarian, and a group of parents has requested that you remove Grimm's Fairy Tales from the shelves because they are too violent. You have been asked to prepare an essay that tells of the history and significance of the Grimms' stories. The essay is going to be published because many parents may not attend the meeting that is scheduled at the library. Using the article, explain the historical significance of the stories and tell how these stories are important for children to read.

1. A writing prompt begins with some background information known as the **set up.** Underline the sentences that set up this assignment.

2. Use the following **R.A.F.T.** technique to finish analyzing the prompt.

Role: What are you supposed to be to answer it? A student? A politician?

Write what you are here: _____

Audience: To whom are you writing? A friend? A particular group?

Write who it is here: _____

Format: Check to see what type of writing you are doing. Is it an essay, a letter, a speech, a story, a description, an editorial, or a report?

Write what it is here: _____

Task: Another sentence in the prompt will tell you what you must do, or your "task." Question words like **why, how,** or **what** may tell the task.

If the question word is **why,** you will *give the reasons* that something is done.

If the question word is **how,** you will *explain the way* that something is done.

If the question word is **what,** you will *identify the thing* that is done.

Below, copy the sentence or question that describes your task.

_____

_____

ANALYZING INFORMATIONAL TEXT

1. Informational articles are written to provide data or descriptions that explain something. Below name three groups that might be interested in reading this article besides students and teachers.

   a. _____ b. _____ c. _____

2. What main point is the author making in this article?

   _____

   _____

3. Give two of the most important facts you learned in this article.

   a. _____

   b. _____

4. **Domain-specific vocabulary** consists of words used in a specific subject, such as math, social studies, or science. Reread the article and list six domain-specific words used with this subject. After you select the words, write their definitions on the lines provided

   a. _____ : _____

   b. _____ : _____

   c. _____ : _____

   d. _____ : _____

   e. _____ : _____

   f. _____ : _____

ASSESSMENT

1. The author claims that the Brothers Grimm changed the content of their tales over the years. Cite three pieces of evidence from the article to support this claim.

a. _____

_____

b. _____

_____

c. _____

_____

2. One can infer that the country of Germany is proud of the Brothers Grimm. Circle the letters of the two paragraphs that show Germany's pride.

a. paragraph 1

b. paragraph 3

c. paragraph 5

d. paragraph 8

3. Circle the letter of the sentence that best describes how paragraph 3 explains what was most important to the Brothers Grimm

a. Paragraph 3 explains that the Brothers Grimm collected both oral and written tales.

b. Paragraph 3 explains that many of the tales were hundreds of years old.

c. Paragraph 3 explains that many tales came from different lands but were similar in some way.

d. Paragraph 3 explains that the Brothers Grimm chose stories of the common people because these taught the most basic values of a culture.

4. The author states that the Brothers Grimm were scholars with many accomplishments besides fairy tales. Cite three pieces of evidence from the article to support this claim.

a. _____

_____

b. _____

_____

c. _____

_____

5. A student is writing a newspaper article about the Brothers Grimm. Read the paragraph from the student's draft and complete the task that follows.

Some people collect stamps, some collect baseball cards or coins, but the Brothers Grimm are known world-wide for collecting stories. Born in 1785 and 1786, the brothers began to study old written works at university. They didn't study maps or charts though. After graduating, the brothers traveled to many lands collecting tales. Obviously travel was hard back then. They discovered that tales from different places often told a similar version of the same story. The first volume of tales included 86 tales!

Below, copy the two sentences that should be removed from this paragraph because they do not provide important information about the underlined sentence.

a. _____

_____

_____

b. _____

_____

_____

Unit 4: Sports, Arts, and Self-Expression

Name _____ Date _____

ANTICIPATION GUIDE

Directions: Before you read the article "Court Gives Saggy Pants a Lift," read the statements below. If you agree with a statement, put a checkmark on the line next to it. If you disagree, put an X on the line.

_____ **1.** Certain groups have the right to tell people what to wear.

_____ **2.** Laws banning fashion are against our freedom of expression.

_____ **3.** A city should be able to ban fashion that people find offensive.

Once you have responded to the statements above, write in the section below why you agree or disagree with each statement.

1. _____

_____

2. _____

_____

3. _____

_____

In the box below, draw a picture of what you think this article is about.

PREDICTING ABCs

Directions: The article you are going to read is about dress codes and the law. See how many boxes you can fill in below with words relating to this topic. For example, put the word *pants* in the P–R box. Put at least one word in every box, and then try to write a word for every letter.

A–C	D–F	G–I

J–L	M–O	P–R

S–T	U–V	W–Z

TIME MY READ #1

Directions: With a partner, see how many words you can read correctly in 45 seconds. As you read, your partner will put an X through any word read incorrectly on his or her copy. When you are finished, trade your books or papers, and let your partner read while you keep score. Count the total number of words you read correctly. Write this score at the bottom of your page.

decency fashion opposes ban undergarments fashion defenders exposure	8
indecent exposing charged buttocks disgusting represents freedom expression	16
style defenders disgusting bare charges amendment choices uniforms	24
decency fashion opposes ban undergarments fashion defenders exposure	32
indecent exposing charged buttocks disgusting represents freedom expression	40
style defenders disgusting bare charges amendment choices uniforms	48
decency fashion opposes ban undergarments fashion defenders exposure	56
indecent exposing charged buttocks disgusting represents freedom expression	64
style defenders disgusting bare charges amendment choices uniforms	72
decency fashion opposes ban undergarments fashion defenders exposure	80

Number of words read correctly _____

ECHO READING

Directions: When you read, you should make breaks, and sometimes pauses, between groups of words. As your teacher reads each phrase, repeat aloud what was read and put a slash or line after that phrase. Then read the whole sentence aloud as a class. Do the first paragraph together as a class, and then do the second one on your own. The first sentence has been marked for you.

Many places / also have dress codes. / Some professions require workers to wear uniforms, and some employers limit what employees can wear. Pro basketball players follow a dress code off the court. Schools can restrict what students and teachers wear. In general, dress codes apply to private settings.

A number of places have banned saggy pants. Their laws define how low pants can be. Officials in Augusta, Georgia, considered changing its decency law. It would have made "exposure of the buttocks" illegal, but not exposing boxer shorts. City officials voted not to change the law after all.

Plenty of people argue that laws should stay away from fashion. People have different tastes in what looks good. Some other clothes show a lot of bare skin or undergarments, but they are not indecent.

BY LAWRENCE GABLE
© 2014 What's Happening Publications

SUBJECT: SPORTS, ARTS and SELF-EXPRESSION

Court Gives Saggy Pants a Lift

1 In recent years boys and young men have been wearing their pants low. Often their boxer shorts show. This may be a cool fashion to them, but many towns think it is indecent. Riviera Beach, Florida, made it illegal, but the county's public defender challenged that law a year later.

2 There are decency laws everywhere in the U.S. They protect people from things that are morally offensive. The laws apply to things like public behavior, art, TV, and even personalized license plates.

3 Many places also have dress codes. Some professions require workers to wear uniforms, and some employers limit what employees can wear. Pro basketball players follow a dress code off the court. Schools can restrict what students and teachers wear. In general, dress codes apply to private settings.

4 The attempts by cities to ban saggy pants fall somewhere between dress codes and decency laws. Cities are not trying to create public dress codes. They already have decency laws, but they do not cover boxer shorts. Some people find the fashion disgusting and want to ban it.

5 A number of places have banned saggy pants. Their laws define how low pants can be. Officials in Augusta, Georgia, considered changing its decency law. It would have made "exposure of the buttocks" illegal, but not exposing boxer shorts. City officials voted not to change the law after all.

6 The American Civil Liberties Union (ACLU) opposes laws against saggy pants. The organization has offered to represent individuals in court. It believes that such laws go against the right to freedom of expression. The ACLU also fears that cities could use them unfairly against young Black men and the poor.

7 There is a certain racial origin to the style. Hip-hop artists made sagging pants popular. They may have taken the style from prisons where prisoners do not have belts. For quite a while the style was popular mostly with young Blacks, but now many others also wear saggy pants.

8 In 2008 people in Riviera Beach voted for a law against sagging pants. In the first year the city charged nearly two dozen young men. After a 17-year-old had to spend a night in jail, a judge declared the ban unconstitutional. However, the city kept its law, so the public defender's office went to court.

9 The public defenders wanted the court to drop the charges against some young men. They argued that the U.S. Constitution protects fashion as freedom of expression. One witness, a fashion instructor, told the court that saggy pants have spread into the mainstream. She showed photos of David Beckham and Zac Efron wearing pants low.

10 Plenty of people argue that laws should stay away from fashion. People have different tastes in what looks good. Some other clothes show a lot of bare skin or undergarments, but they are not indecent. People who do not like sagging pants, but do not want laws against them, know that they will go away because fashions change.

11 In April 2008 a judge ruled against Riviera Beach's law. She said that the style may be "tacky or distasteful," but that the Fourteenth Amendment protects such choices. Since then officials in a few other towns have succeeded in passing laws against saggy pants. In Riviera Beach, though, where a court made the decision, pants can still sag.

GET A CONTEXT CLUE

Directions: Below are sentences from "Court Gives Saggy Pants a Lift." First, read the sentence. Then, look back in the article and reread the paragraph in which the sentence is found. Circle the best answer to each question.

"They protect people from things that are morally *offensive*."

1. The word *offensive* means

    A. acceptable
    B. extreme
    C. disagreeable
    D. rarely done

"Schools can *restrict* what students and teachers wear."

2. The word *restrict* means

    A. to shock
    B. to warn
    C. to limit
    D. to question

"The attempts by cities to ban saggy pants fall somewhere between dress codes and *decency* laws."

3. The word *decency* means

    A. what is helpful
    B. what is unusual
    C. what is proper for most
    D. what is likeable

"A number of places have *banned* saggy pants."

4. The word *banned* means

    A. made impossible
    B. sometimes allowed
    C. approved
    D. not allowed

"After a 17-year-old had to spend a night in jail, a judge declared the ban *unconstitutional*."

5. The word *unconstitutional* means

    A. follows the laws
    B. promotes a law or code
    C. turns things around
    D. violates people's rights

"One witness, a fashion instructor, told the court that saggy pants have spread into the *mainstream*."

6. The word *mainstream* means

    A. general population
    B. youthful population
    C. hip-hop population
    D. marginalized population

Name _____ Date _____

WORD MAP

Directions: Follow the directions to map the word in the box below.

> **freedom**

List two more words that mean the same.

right

List two more examples of a freedom.

freedom of speech

List two more words that mean the opposite.

restriction

Draw a picture below to help you remember the meaning.

Write a definition IN YOUR OWN WORDS.

LOOK WHO'S TALKING

Directions: Below are sentences that relate to "Court Gives Saggy Pants a Lift." Look back in the article and reread the paragraph in which you find the sentence. Circle the best answer to each question.

1. **In the opening sentence, the word *their* best refers to**

   A. the county
   B. the public defenders
   C. the boys and young men
   D. the laws

2. **In the third sentence of paragraph 4, the first use of the word *they* refers to**

   A. the cities
   B. the laws
   C. the dress codes
   D. the people

3. **In the fourth sentence of paragraph 5, the word *it* refers to**

   A. the law
   B. the people
   C. the exposure
   D. the city officials

4. **In the last sentence of paragraph 7, the word *others* refers to**

   A. Hip-Hop artists
   B. people
   C. prisoners
   D. young African-Americans

5. **In the second sentence of paragraph 9, the word *they* refers to**

   A. the witnesses
   B. the court
   C. David Beckham and Zac Efron
   D. the public defenders

6. **In the last sentence of paragraph 10, the word *they* refers to**

   A. the fashion
   B. the saggy pants
   C. the people who don't like saggy pants
   D. the laws

HOW'S IT ORGANIZED?

This article is organized as cause and effect, in which one thing happens which causes an effect, or reaction. This reaction often starts another event.

Directions: Answer these questions in the spaces at the bottom.

1. What is the cause of the controversy in this article?

2. What effect does this fashion have on some people?

3. How did Augusta, Georgia, respond to the controversy?

4. How did the ACLU react to Augusta's action?

5. How did Riviera Beach, Florida, respond to the controversy?

6. What event brought the controversy to court in Riviera Beach?

7. What did the judge decide about Riviera Beach's law?

Answers:

1.	
2.	
3.	
4.	
5.	
6.	
7.	

*On a separate sheet of paper write a summary of what your notes say about the issue of saggy pants in Riviera Beach.

IS THAT A FACT?

Directions: Read the definitions of a fact and an inference below. Then read the paragraph that follows. At the bottom of the page, write an F on the blank if the sentence is a fact. Write an I if the sentence is an inference. Use the following definitions:

<u>Fact</u>—a statement that can be proven true from the paragraph

<u>Inference</u>—a guess as to what MIGHT be true, based on information you have read and what you already know about the subject

> The attempts by cities to ban saggy pants fall somewhere between dress codes and decency laws. Cities are not trying to create public dress codes. They already have public decency laws, but they do not cover boxer shorts. Some people find the fashion disgusting and want to ban it. A number of places have banned saggy pants. Their laws define how low pants can be. The American Civil Liberties Union (ACLU) opposes laws against saggy pants.

_____ **1.** Some people feel they have a right to tell people how to dress.

_____ **2.** Some people are disgusted by this fashion.

_____ **3.** The ACLU does not want bans on saggy pants.

_____ **4.** Cities do not all have the same laws about saggy pants.

_____ **5.** The people who offend the public are usually males.

_____ **6.** The ACLU stands up for people's rights.

MAKE A SPACE

Directions: Below are some sentences that are missing punctuation and capitalization. First draw slash marks (/) between the words. Then rewrite each sentence in the space below it, by filling in the missing punctuation and capitalization.

> Example:
>
> there /are / decency / laws /everywhere / in / the / us
>
> There are decency laws everywhere in the U.S.

1. theattemptsbycitiestobansaggypantsfallsomewherebetween dresscodesanddecencylaws

_____

_____

2. hiphopartistsmadesaggingpantspopular

_____

_____

3. plentyofpeoplearguethatthelawshouldstayawayfromfashion

_____

_____

4. thejudgesaidthatthefourteenthamendmentprotectssuchchoices

_____

_____

TIME MY READ #2

Directions: With a partner, see how many words you can read correctly in 45 seconds. As you read, your partner will put an X through any word read incorrectly on his or her copy. When you are finished, trade your books or papers, and let your partner read while you keep score. Count the total number of words you read correctly. Write this score at the bottom of your page.

decency fashion opposes ban undergarments fashion defenders exposure	8
indecent exposing charged buttocks disgusting represents freedom expression	16
style defenders disgusting bare charges amendment choices uniforms	24
decency fashion opposes ban undergarments fashion defenders exposure	32
indecent exposing charged buttocks disgusting represents freedom expression	40
style defenders disgusting bare charges amendment choices uniforms	48
decency fashion opposes ban undergarments fashion defenders exposure	56
indecent exposing charged buttocks disgusting represents freedom expression	64
style defenders disgusting bare charges amendment choices uniforms	72
decency fashion opposes ban undergarments fashion defenders exposure	80

Number of words read correctly _____

Is the score higher than it was in Time My Read #1? _____

WORD PARTS

Directions: A **base word** is a word that can stand alone. A **suffix** is added to the end of a base word to change how it's used in a sentence. The suffix *–ful* means "full of" *(thoughtful)*; "characterized by" *(beautiful)*; or "tending to be" *(harmful)*. Write eight words that end with the suffix *-ful* on the lines below. Share the words with the rest of the class.

1. _____   5. _____

2. _____   6. _____

3. _____   7. _____

4. _____   8. _____

Directions: The suffix *-al* turns an action verb into a noun. In the following sentence, see how the **verb** *remove,* which means "to take away," becomes a **noun.**

The tow truck helped in the *removal* of the wrecked car.

The suffix *–al* also can turn a **noun** into an **adjective** that describes something. For example, the noun *parent* becomes the adjective *parental.* (Sometimes *–al* is part of the base word, so it is not a suffix, as in the words *cereal* or *meal.*)

Write definitions for the nouns and adjectives below. Try not to use the base word in the definition. If you don't know the base word, look it up in a dictionary or ask a partner.

1. **national—** _____

2. **survival—** _____

3. **approval—** _____

4. **cynical—** _____

5. **dismissal—** _____

6. **biblical—** _____

7. **tropical—** _____

8. **critical—** _____

SUMMARIZING ABCs

Directions: Now that you've read the article about dress codes and the law, see how many words you can write about this topic in the boxes below.

A–C	D–F	G–I
J–L	**M–O**	**P–R**
S–T	**U–V**	**W–Z**

Unit 4: Sports, Arts, and Self-Expression

SENTENCE SUMMARIES

Directions: Below are four key words or phrases from the article "Court Gives Saggy Pants a Lift." Your job is to summarize, or restate, what you've learned in this article by using these four words or phrases in two sentences. Then, as a challenge, try to use all four words or phrases in one sentence to summarize the article.

Key Words or Phrases

dress codes   U.S. Constitution

ACLU   indecent

Sentence Summaries:

1. _____

_____

2. _____

_____

Challenge Summary (All four words or phrases in one sentence!):

1. _____

_____

REACTION GUIDE

Directions: Now that you have read and studied information about "Court Gives Saggy Pants a Lift," reread the statements below, which you responded to before reading the article. Then think about how the author might respond to these statements. If you think the author would agree, put a checkmark on the line before the number. If you think the author would disagree, put an X on the line. Then below the statement, copy the words, phrases, or sentences from the article that provide evidence of the views stated by the author. Also note if there is no evidence to support the statement.

_____ **1.** Certain groups have the right to tell people what to wear.

Evidence: _____

_____

_____

_____ **2.** Laws banning fashion are against our freedom of expression.

Evidence: _____

_____

_____

_____ **3.** A city should be able to ban fashion that people find offensive.

Evidence: _____

_____

_____

Name _____ Date _____

TAKE A STAND

Directions: People often have differing feelings or opinions about an issue. When they discuss or argue their opposing views, they are taking part in a debate. A good persuasive argument is based on a claim that is supported by

Facts—statements that can be proven to be true

Statistics—numerical data gotten through research

Examples—instances that support an opinion

You and a partner are going to debate two of your other classmates. The topic you are going to debate is the following:

A city should have the right to ban fashion that is offensive.

Decide with the other pair who will agree and who will disagree with this statement. Then answer these questions in order to win your debate.

1. What are your two strongest points to persuade the other side? (You can do Internet research to include facts, statistics, and examples.)

   A. _____

   B. _____

2. What might the other side say to argue against point A?

_____

_____

3. What might the other side say to argue against point B?

_____

_____

4. What will you say to prove the other side's arguments are wrong?

_____

_____

ASSESSMENT

Comprehension: Answer the questions about the following passage.

Many places also have dress codes. Some professions require workers to wear uniforms, and some employers limit what employees can wear. Pro basketball players follow a dress code off the court. Schools can restrict what students and teachers wear. Cities are not trying to create public dress codes.

A number of places have banned saggy pants. Their laws define how low pants can be. Officials in Augusta, Georgia, considered changing its decency law. It would have made "exposure of the buttocks" illegal, but not exposing boxer shorts. City officials finally voted not to change the law after all.

1. Why are some dress codes allowed while some fashions are banned?

_____

_____

_____

2. What was the author's purpose for writing about Augusta, Georgia?

_____

_____

_____

Fluency: The words in the following two sentences are all connected. The sentences are also missing punctuation and capitalization. Draw slash marks (/) between the words. Then rewrite each sentence by filling in the punctuation and capitalization.

1. **theaclualsomaintainsthatcommunitiescouldtargetyoungblackmenand womenunfairly**

_____

_____

Name _____ Date _____

2. officialsconsideredchangingpublicdecencylawsbutchangedtheirminds

_____

_____

Fluency: Read the three sentences below. Imagine where you would pause within each sentence as you read it aloud. Draw a slash (/) mark between the phrases where you would pause. The first slash is done.

3. Now / the city will consider whether to take its case to another court.

4. In Riviera Beach most of the voters approved the ban.

5. Plenty of people argue that laws should stay away from fashion.

Vocabulary: Based on what you have learned in this lesson, match the following words with their definitions. Write the letter of the definition on the blank in front of the word it defines.

1. _____ beautiful

A. disagreeable

2. _____ offensive

B. finding fault with someone or something

3. _____ dismissal

C. what is proper for most people

4. _____ restrict

D. no longer allowed

5. _____ freedom

E. the act of telling someone to leave

6. _____ mainstream

F. to control or limit

7. _____ critical

G. the general population

8. _____ banned

H. liberty

9. _____ unconstitutional

I. pleasing to look at

10. _____ decency

J. violating people's legal rights

Name _____ Date _____

ANTICIPATION GUIDE

Directions: Before you read the article "Now You See It, Now You Don't!," read the statements below. If you agree with a statement, put a checkmark next to it. If you disagree, put an X on the line.

_____ **1.** The popularity of tattoos is a fairly new phenomenon.

_____ **2.** Tattoos can create many different problems for people.

_____ **3.** A tattoo is a sign of respect.

Once you have read and responded to the statements above, write in the section below why you agree or disagree with each statement.

1. _____

_____

2. _____

_____

3. _____

_____

In the box below, draw a picture of what you think this article is about.

PREDICTING ABCs

Directions: The article you are going to read is about tattoos. See how many boxes you can fill in with words relating to this topic. For example, put the word *ink* in the G–I box. Put at least one word in every box, and then try to write a word for every letter.

A–C	D–F	G–I
J–L	**M–O**	**P–R**
S–T	**U–V**	**W–Z**

LANGUAGE MINI-LESSON

A **sentence** is a group of words that states a complete thought. When a group of words does not state a complete thought, it is called a **fragment**. Sometimes a fragment is missing a subject, sometimes it is missing a verb, and sometimes, it just doesn't make sense on its own. **Example**—"Because he wanted a tattoo." Even though there's a subject, *he,* and a verb, *wanted,* it is not a sentence, because it can't stand on its own—it's incomplete. "Because he wanted a tattoo" explains why something happened, but we don't know what it was that happened. "He went to the tattoo parlor because he wanted a tattoo" is a complete sentence.

Directions: For each number below, put an S in the blank if it's a complete sentence. Put an F in the blank if it's a fragment.

1. _____ Tattoos have represented many different things.

2. _____ For a long time, scientists believed tattooing began in Egypt.

3. _____ After "The Iceman" was discovered.

4. _____ Used to identify slaves.

A **run-on sentence** is two or more sentences written as if they were one sentence. **Example**—"Lasers shoot light into the skin the light breaks the ink into particles."

There are a number of ways to fix a run-on sentence. One way is to break it into separate complete thoughts. You can do this by adding a **period** (.) at the end of one thought and **capitalizing** the first letter of the next word. **Example**—"Lasers shoot light into the skin. The light breaks the ink into particles."

A second way to fix a run-on sentence is to join the parts using a **semicolon** (;). **Example**—"Lasers shoot light into the skin; the light breaks the ink into particles."

A third way to fix a run-on sentence is to join the parts using a conjunction. Common conjunctions are the words **and, but, nor,** and **or.** When using a conjunction to join two sentences, always put a comma at the end of the word before it. **Example**—"Lasers shoot light into the skin, and the light breaks the ink into particles."

Directions: The following sentence is a run-on. Below, rewrite it first by breaking it into two sentences. Then rewrite it again by joining the two thoughts with a conjunction.

Now doctors can remove tattoos people compare the pain to bee stings.

_____

_____

 © Houghton Mifflin Harcourt Publishing Company Unit 4: Sports, Arts, and Self-Expression

ECHO READING

Directions: When you read, you should make breaks, and sometimes pauses, between groups of words. As your teacher reads each phrase, repeat aloud what is read and put a slash or line after that phrase. Then you will read the whole sentence aloud as a class. Do the first paragraph together as a class, and then do the second one on your own. The first sentence has been marked for you.

Tattoos / have represented / different things. / In Peru and Chile women had tattoos related to childbirth. The Greeks and Romans used tattoos to identify slaves, or to show membership in a religion. Some Native American tribes used tattoos to gain power and beauty. Two thousand years ago the Chinese marked criminals with tattoos. Europeans became familiar with tattoos in the late 18th century.

In 1771 the Englishman Captain Cook returned from Tahiti and New Zealand. He told about the islanders' use of tattoos. In fact, the English word "tattoo" comes from the Polynesian word "tatau." Getting a tattoo in Europe then became fashionable. It was expensive, and royal families got them as a sign of their wealth. European and American sailors began getting tattoos in ports around the world. Some tattoos, of anchors, for example, served as symbols of protection from danger on the seas.

What's Happening

IN THE USA?

BY LAWRENCE GABLE
© 2014 *What's Happening Publications*

SUBJECT: *SPORTS, ARTS and SELF-EXPRESSION*

1 People around the world have gotten tattoos for thousands of years. In recent years they have become popular in America too. So has the desire to remove them. This is especially true among people who got them as gang symbols. Now many cities will pay for treatments that remove those tattoos. In 2013 Walla Walla, Washington, joined them with a program called INK OUT.

Now You See It, Now You Don't!

2 For a long time scientists believed that the earliest tattooing was done in Egypt. Several female mummies had them on the tops of their thighs. However, the discovery of "The Iceman" in 1991 changed that belief. He lived in 3200 B.C., and he had fifty tattoos.

3 Tattoos have represented different things. In Peru and Chile women had tattoos related to childbirth. The Greeks and Romans used them to identify slaves, or to show membership in a religion. Some Native American tribes used tattoos to gain power and beauty. Two thousand years ago the Chinese marked criminals with tattoos.

4 Europeans became familiar with tattoos in the late 18th century. In 1771 the Englishman Captain Cook returned from Tahiti and New Zealand. He told about the islanders' use of tattoos. In fact, the English word "tattoo" comes from the Polynesian word "tatau."

5 Getting a tattoo in Europe then became fashionable. It was expensive, and royal families got them as a sign of their wealth. European and American sailors began getting tattoos in ports around the world. Some tattoos, of anchors, for example, served as symbols of protection from danger on the seas.

6 The popularity of tattoos grew in the U.S. too. Even so, for most of the 1900s tattoos remained a symbol for outsiders like motorcyclists, rock musicians and gang members. Now, though, more than 45 million Americans have tattoos.

7 Throughout the years some people have wanted to get rid of their tattoos. The methods always were crude and painful. For example, people used to cut or scrape them off. They also used acid to form a scar over the tattoo. One surgical method put skin grafts over the tattoos. However, now doctors use lasers to remove them. People compare the pain to bee stings or being splattered with hot grease. It usually requires 6–12 treatments and can cost from $250 to $2,500.

8 Lasers shoot light into the skin. The light breaks the ink into particles. The body absorbs them slowly, so the treatments take place weeks apart. Each time the laser penetrates deeper and causes the tattoo to fade. In most cases a light shadow of the tattoo remains on the skin.

9 Tattoo removal programs began in the early 1990s. Like other programs around the U.S., Walla Walla's INK OUT program places certain requirements on participants. Former gang members cannot be older than 21 years old. The free treatments remove only tattoos that show. Participants must have a job or be in school. They also must perform community service.

10 As some people get older they want to cut their connections to a gang. However, their gang tattoos still mark them. Having such a tattoo usually makes getting a new start more difficult. Many large American cities, and now even smaller ones like Walla Walla, are happy to help them by making their visible tattoos invisible.

QUICK READ/DRAW AND WRITE

Directions: First Reading—As you do your first reading of the article, your teacher will time you for one minute. When time is called, write the number of the paragraph where you stopped. **Paragraph # _____**

In the box below, draw a picture summarizing what you read.

Second Reading—As you do your second reading of the article, your teacher will time you for one minute. When time is called, write the number of the paragraph where you stopped. **Paragraph # _____**

Directions: Now continue reading the rest of the article. Below, write five important words that will help you remember the information from the article.

_____ _____ _____ _____ _____

CLOSE READING ANNOTATION

Third Reading—As you reread each paragraph in the article closely, answer the questions by annotating the text. Each numbered question corresponds to a paragraph in the article where the answer can be found. Write your brief answers in the space below each question.

1. What is the author's purpose in writing the first paragraph?

_____

2. Why was the discovery of "The Iceman" so significant?

_____

3. What does the author contrast, or show differences between, in paragraph 3?

_____

4. From where did the word *tattoo* come?

_____

5. Why did mostly royal families get tattoos in Europe?

_____

6. How does the author define outsiders?

_____

7. Why did the author tell the reader about early methods of removing tattoos?

_____

8. What was the author's purpose for writing paragraph 8?

_____

9. Which part of the article does the author refer back to in paragraph 9?

_____

10. How do the last three words in the article make the writing interesting?

_____

GRAMMAR GAMES

Directions: Reread the paragraphs below. Words have been left out from the sentences. Think about the information from the article you have read and fill in words that make sense. The part of speech of each missing word is provided.

Tattoos have represented different things. In Peru

_____ Chile _____ had tattoos related to
(1. conjunction)   (2. collective noun)

childbirth. The Greeks and Romans used _____ to identify
(3. pronoun)

slaves, or to _____ membership in a religion. Some Native
(4. verb)

American tribes _____ tattoos to gain power and beauty. Two
(5. verb)

thousand years ago _____ Chinese marked criminals
(6. article)

_____ tattoos.
(7. preposition)

Europeans _____ familiar with tattoos in the late 18th
(8. verb)

_____ . In 1771 the Englishman Captain Cook returned from
(9. noun)

Tahiti and New Zealand. He told _____ the islanders' use of
(10. preposition)

tattoos. In fact, the English word "tattoo" _____ from the
(11. verb)

Polynesian _____ "tatau." Soon, getting a tattoo
(12. noun)

_____ fashionable.
(13. verb)

CLOSE READING STRUCTURE

Directions: Understanding the structure of a text is important for two reasons. First, understanding the structure of a selection can help you remember the main idea and important details. Second, most academic writing you will encounter uses text structures to organize ideas.

1. Writers often include a statement in the **introduction** that catches the reader's attention. Then, the writer tells what the article will be about. On the space provided, copy the last sentence of the introduction of this article.

_____

_____

2. On the space below, copy the sentence that best states what the author's **claim, main idea,** or **thesis** is for this article.

_____

_____

3. On the space below, copy the sentence that shows where the author introduces the other side's **opinions,** or **opposing claims,** about the popularity of tattoos.

_____

_____

4. Near the end of an article, a writer often restates the claim and summarizes the evidence. This is called the **conclusion.** On the space below, write the sentence that best shows where the conclusion to the article begins.

_____

_____

IS THAT A FACT?

Directions: Read the definitions of a fact and an inference below. Then read the paragraph that follows. At the bottom of the page, write an F on the blank if the sentence is a fact. Write an I if the sentence is an inference. Use the following definitions:

Fact—a statement that can be proven true from the paragraph

Inference—a guess as to what MIGHT be true, based on what you have read and what you already know about the subject

Tattoo removal programs began in the early 1990s. Walla Walla's INK OUT program began in 2013. Like the programs in other cities, it places requirements on participants. Former gang members cannot be older than 21 years old. Participants must have a job or be in school. They also must perform community service. As some people get older they want to cut their connections to a gang. However, their gang tattoos still mark them. Many large American cities are happy to help them by making their visible tattoos invisible.

_____ **1.** Some people are having second thoughts about their tattoos.

_____ **2.** There are some places that are now making tattoo removal available.

_____ **3.** People who are getting tattoos removed have to have a job or be in school.

_____ **4.** Cities use tattoo removal as a way of rehabilitating some people, especially gang members.

_____ **5.** Many cities are very eager to help people remove their tattoos.

_____ **6.** Some people feel that tattoos have a negative impact.

SUMMARIZING ABCs

Directions: Now that you've read the article on tattoos, see how many words you can write about this topic in the boxes below.

A–C	D–F	G–I
J–L	**M–O**	**P–R**
S–T	**U–V**	**W–Z**

REACTION GUIDE

Directions: Now that you have read and studied information about "Now You See It, Now You Don't!," reread the statements below, which you responded to before reading the article. Then think about how the author might respond to these statements. If you think the author would agree, put a checkmark on the line before the number. If you think the author would disagree, put an X on the line. Then below the statement, copy the words, phrases, or sentences from the article that provide evidence of the views stated by the author. Also note if there is no evidence to support the statement.

_____ **1.** The popularity of tattoos is a fairly new phenomenon.

Evidence: _____

_____

_____

_____ **2.** Tattoos can create many different problems for people.

Evidence: _____

_____

_____

_____ **3.** A tattoo is a sign of respect.

Evidence: _____

_____

_____

SENTENCE TRANSITIONS

An informational essay answers questions and provides information. Writers use transitional phrases to link ideas. Some transitional words and phrases include *to show, to prove, because, to explain, to verify, due to, instead of, furthermore, as a result,* and *in order to.*

Directions: Complete the following sentences using the phrases given.

Example: Some cities helped with tattoo removal. Some cities helped with tattoo removal *in order to help people start a new life*.

1. Walla Walla, Washington, started its INK OUT program *in order to*

_____

2. Some people want to remove their tattoos *due to*

_____

3. Tattoos became very popular in Europe *as a result* of

_____

4. Royal families started wearing tattoos *to show*

_____

5. As some people get older, they get their tattoos removed *because*

_____

PICKING UP PUNCTUATION

Parentheses ( ) are used in sentences to set off information that is related or connected in a small way to the rest of the sentence. **Example**—In South America (Peru and Chile especially), women had tattoos related to childbirth.

Dashes (—) are used to show a sudden change of thought from the rest of the sentence. **Example**—In 1771 the Englishman Captain Cook—who joined the merchant navy as a teenager—returned from Tahiti and New Zealand and told about the islanders' use of tattoos.

Hyphens (-) are used in a number of ways. See how they are used below.

1. Use a hyphen to break a word apart when it doesn't fit at the end of a line. Hyphens used this way must be placed in words that have two or more syllables (tattoo), be placed between two of the syllables (tat-too), and leave at least two letters on each line. **Example**—Captain Cook told of the islanders' use of **tat-toos**.

2. Use a hyphen in certain compound words. **Example**—*mother-in-law*

3. Use a hyphen in most spelled-out numbers greater than twenty and less than one hundred. **Example**—*twenty-one* (but thirty, forty, and so on)

4. Use a hyphen in spelled-out fractions unless the denominator already is hyphenated. **Example**—*one-half* and *three-fifths* (but one thirty-second)

Directions: Correctly place parentheses, dashes, and hyphens in the sentences below.

1. The Greeks used tattoos to identify slaves and to show membership in a reli gion.

2. Captain Cook the first European to see Australia was a self confident sailor who also sailed to New Zealand. At least three fourths of the natives had tattoos.

3. Former gang members cannot be older than twenty one to get the free treat ments to remove tattoos.

4. Walla Walla, Washington famous for its sweet onions has a tattoo removal program called INK OUT.

ANALYZING A PROMPT

Directions: Read the writing prompt in the box below. Then follow the directions to learn how to analyze and answer it.

> You have been asked to help create a tattoo removal program for your town. You will create a brochure to explain that tattoos have historical significance but are sometimes abused by gangs and criminals. You need to show how tattoo-removal methods can be effective, and you need to help the community by giving reasons for people to use this program. Use information from the article.

1. A writing prompt begins with some background information known as the **set up.** Underline the sentences that set up this assignment.

2. Use the following **R.A.F.T.** technique to finish analyzing the prompt.

Role: What are you supposed to be to answer it? A student? A politician?

Write what you are here: _____

Audience: To whom are you writing? A friend? A particular group?

Write who it is here: _____

Format: Check to see what type of writing you are doing. Is it an essay, a letter, a speech, a story, a description, an editorial, or a report?

Write what it is here: _____

Task: Another sentence in the prompt will tell you what you must do, or your "task." Question words like **why, how,** or **what** may tell the task.

If the question word is **why,** you will *give the reasons* that something is done.

If the question word is **how,** you will *explain the way* that something is done.

If the question word is **what,** you will *identify the thing* that is done.

Below, copy the sentence or question that describes your task.

_____

_____

WHAT'S YOUR POINT?

When writing an essay it is important to have a strong claim. The **claim,** or **thesis statement,** states the main point the writer wants to get across. Once the thesis is introduced, the body of the essay should support that thesis with key points that provide evidence.

The information presented in the article "Now You See It, Now You Don't!" explains the history of tattoos and notes that some cities are starting tattoo-removal programs. The discussion also includes reasons why people currently are interested in removing their tattoos.

Directions: Which of these sentences provides the best **claim** for an essay on this topic? Circle the letter of your choice.

a. Despite their rich cultural history, tattoos can be problematic for some people these days.

b. Tattoos have a strong tradition in culture and are increasing in popularity.

c. Some cities offer tattoo removal, but it is a long and painful process.

Now in the space below, explain what is weak or wrong about the other two statements.

1. _____

_____

_____

2. _____

_____

_____

ASSESSMENT

1. Circle the letters of the conclusions below that are not supported by evidence from the article.

    a. The earliest tattooing was done in Egypt.

    b. Tattoos represent different things to different people.

    c. The English word "tattoo" comes from the Polynesian word "tatau."

    d. In the old days in Europe, one needed to be wealthy to get a tattoo.

    e. More than 45 million Americans have tattoos.

2. The author has structured this article in two distinct sections. Circle the two letters that best describe the two sections.

    a. One section is about the history of tattoos.

    b. One section is about how tattoos are used.

    c. One section is about gangs and tattoos.

    d. One section is about tattoo removal.

    e. One section is about lasers.

3. The author states that having a gang tattoo "usually makes getting a new start more difficult." Circle the letters of the choices below that you infer might support the author's statement.

    a. Members of other gangs might attack the person.

    b. Cool people don't wear tattoos.

    c. Employers may think the person is a former criminal.

    d. Tattoos are vulgar and rude.

4. What evidence does the author give that tattoos have meant different things to different cultures? Below, cite three pieces of evidence from the article.

a. _____

_____

b. _____

_____

c. _____

_____

5. A student is writing an informative article about tattoo removal for a magazine. Read the paragraph from the student's article and complete the task that follows.

Tattoos can be painful to put on, but in the old days they were even more painful to take off. Some people used to cut away the top layers of skin, often leaving a bad scar. Others used acid with similar results. Another method was to take skin from somewhere else in the body and graft, or sew, it over the tattoo.

Lasers shoot intense beams of light into the skin. The laser breaks up the ink particles, but slowly. Patients often have to go back for six to twelve treatments. The body eventually absorbs the ink, but treatments must be weeks apart and can cost large sums of money.

The writer needs a better transition sentence between the two paragraphs above. Circle the letter of the sentence below that best connects the information in the two underlined sentences above.

a. People wanted something that didn't leave such bad scars.

b. The chance of infection with old methods made them dangerous.

c. These older methods were cheap, but very painful.

d. Today, science has brought us new, less painful ways to remove tattoos.

Quarterly Performance Assessment

The Globetrotters Still Know How to
Play the Game!

BY LAWRENCE GABLE
© *2014 What's Happening Publications*

QUARTERLY ASSESSMENT

THE GLOBETROTTERS STILL KNOW HOW TO PLAY THE GAME!

1 In the 1920s some young Black men in Chicago formed a basketball team. When 24-year-old Abe Saperstein took control of the team, they began playing teams in small towns all around the U.S. Ever since then fans have known this team as the Harlem Globetrotters.

2 The team began traveling as the "New York Globetrotters." Whites in small towns were shocked when Black players arrived, because Blacks were not allowed to play pro basketball then. Adding "Harlem" to the name identified it as a Black team.

3 The Globetrotters played their first game in January 1927. Three hundred fans attended. The team traveled to small towns in Mr. Saperstein's car. Their first game in a major city came in Detroit in 1932.

4 The Globetrotters won most games easily. Then in 1939 they were leading a game 112–5, so they began to clown around. The crowd loved it, so the team started doing it regularly. It developed entertaining routines with fantastic dribbling, passing and trick shots.

5 The players entertained fans, but their goal still was to win games. In fact, in 1940 the Globetrotters won the World Basketball Championship. Then in 1948 and 1949 they beat the best pro team, the Minneapolis Lakers. In the "World Series of Basketball" the Globetrotters played a series of games every year against the best college players. The Globetrotters won every series from 1950 to 1958.

6 The Globetrotters helped the National Basketball Association (NBA) develop. After the Lakers' losses to the Globetrotters, the NBA signed its first Black players in 1950. The Globetrotters also helped attract fans to the young league by playing games before some of the NBA's games.

7 Because the Globetrotters were so good, many small-town teams did not want to play them. So in 1953 Mr. Saperstein convinced a friend to develop a team to oppose the Globetrotters regularly. The Washington Generals became the team's traveling opponents. They lost thousands of games to the Globetrotters.

8 In the 1950s the Globetrotters' fame spread. They made their first tours of other continents. At home they appeared on national television. The team developed four different squads, and each one played every night.

9 Basketball's Hall of Fame has honored the Globetrotters. It has inducted both Mr. Saperstein and the organization itself. Several players are also in the Hall. Marques Haynes was a magnificent dribbler and passer. Meadowlark Lemon played for 24 years and won fans with his charm and incredible hook shot from half court.

10 Unfortunately the team's popularity fell in the 1970s and 1980s. The tremendous growth of the NBA and college basketball took fans away. Also, several TV shows made the Globetrotters into cartoon characters. People had forgotten that the Globetrotters are fine players. In the 1990s they began scheduling tough games against college teams, and fans returned.

11 The Harlem Globetrotters introduced most of the world to basketball. They have played more than 22,000 games in 118 countries. Now they hope to play games every year against the NBA champion, the college champion, and international teams. After entertaining many millions of people for decades, the team still can play serious basketball.

ASSESSMENT

1. Underline the sentences below that support the inference that the team became "clowns" accidentally.

The Globetrotters won most games easily. Then in 1939 they were leading 112-5, so they began to clown around. The crowd loved it, so the team started doing it regularly. It developed entertaining routines with fantastic dribbling, passing and trick shots.

2. Support the claim that the Globetrotters are some of the best basketball players in the world. On the lines below, cite evidence from the article to support this claim.

a. _____

_____

b. _____

_____

_____

c. _____

_____

3. This question has two parts. First, answer **Part A.** Then, answer **Part B.**

Part A: Which of these inferences about the author's point of view is best supported by the text? Circle the letter of the correct choice.

a. The author believes Mr. Saperstein is a hero.

b. The author was disappointed when the team's popularity fell in the 70s and 80s.

c. The author was surprised the Globetrotters helped the NBA develop.

d. The author wanted the team to have better transportation in the early days.

Part B: Which sentence from the text supports your answer to **Part A.**

a. The Globetrotters helped the National Basketball Association (NBA) develop.

b. So in 1953 Mr. Saperstein convinced a friend to develop a team to oppose the Globetrotters regularly.

c. Unfortunately the team's popularity fell in the 1970s and 1980s.

d. The Harlem Globetrotters introduced most of the world to basketball.

4. Which of the following sentences from the article best supports the conclusion that the members of the National Basketball Association believe the Globetrotters had many great players?

    a. The tremendous growth of the NBA and college basketball took fans away.

    b. Basketball's Hall of Fame has honored the Globetrotters.

    c. The Harlem Globetrotters introduced most of the world to basketball.

    d. Several players are also in the Hall.

5. A student is writing a report describing how the Globetrotters grew from a small unknown team to an international sensation. Read the draft of the introduction below and the directions that follow.

       They began on the streets of Chicago—a group of young black men who could play basketball. Well, not just "play" basketball, but really PLAY basketball. When a young man named Abe Saperstein spotted them on the court, he realized that these talented athletes could be famous. He took control of the team and began to travel with the "New York Globetrotters," but things were tough at first.

The student took these notes from reliable sources:

They won almost all of their early games.

They had little money at first and had to travel in Mr. Saperstein's car.

Some white people were not happy to see blacks playing professional basketball.

Crowds loved it when the team clowned around.

It took them five years on the road before they played in a major city.

They played mostly in small towns in the beginning.

Directions: Using information from the student's notes, write one paragraph developing the idea that is presented in the last sentence of the introduction.

_____

_____

_____

